EINSTEIN'S GERMAN WORLD

❖❖❖❖❖❖❖ FRITZ STERN ❖❖❖❖❖❖❖

Einstein's
German World

❖❖

PRINCETON UNIVERSITY PRESS

PRINCETON AND OXFORD

Fifth printing, and first paperback printing, 2001
Paperback ISBN 0-691-07458-5

*The Library of Congress has cataloged the cloth edition of
this book as follows*

Stern, Fritz Richard, 1926–
Einstein's German world / Fritz Stern.
p. cm.
Includes bibliographical references and index.
ISBN 0-691-05939-X (alk. paper)
1. Germany—Intellectual life—History—20th century.
2. Brain drain—Germany—History—20th century.
3. Political persecution—Germany—History—20th century.
4. Technology transfer. 5. Antisemitism—Germany.
6. Einstein, Albert, 1879–1955. 7. Jewish scientists—
Germany—History—20th century. I. Title.
DD239.S74   1999
943.087—DC21   99-20128

This book has been composed in Palatino

Printed on acid-free paper. ∞

www.pup.princeton.edu

Printed in the United States of America

5   7   9   10   8   6

To Elisabeth

◆◆◆◆◆◆◆◆◆◆ CONTENTS ◆◆◆◆◆◆◆◆◆◆

◆◆◆   A NOTE FROM THE AUTHOR   ◆◆◆

EARLIER versions of several chapters in this volume appeared in German in a collection entitled *Verspielte Grösse. Essays zur deutschen Geschichte des 20. Jahrhunderts* (Munich, 1996). In addition, the following essays were originally published elsewhere, in English; with the exception of Chapter 8, they have been substantially revised for the present volume.

Chapter 4. "Walther Rathenau and the Vision of Modernity," in David Wetzel, ed., *From the Berlin Museum to the Berlin Wall: Essays on the Cultural and Political History of Modern Germany* (Westport, Conn., 1996), pp. 87–107.

Chapter 5. "Historians and the Great War: Private Experience and Public Explication," *Yale Review* 82, no. 1 (January 1994), pp. 34–54.

Chapter 7. "Freedom and Its Discontents: The Travails of the New Germany," *Foreign Affairs* 72, no. 4 (September-October 1993), pp. 108–125.

Chapter 8. "The Goldhagen Controversy: One Nation, One People, One Theory?" *Foreign Affairs* 75, no. 6 (November-December 1996), pp. 128–138.

EINSTEIN'S GERMAN WORLD

The small circle of men who earlier were bound
together harmoniously was really unique and in
its human decency something I scarcely encountered again.

Einstein to Max von Laue, 1934,
about their common past in Berlin

You ask about my attitude to Germany. . . . I can
best express it metaphorically: I feel like a
mother who sees that her favorite child has gone
hopelessly astray.

Lise Meitner to a Dutch
physicist friend, October 1945

A country of mass murderers.

Einstein to Max Born, October 12, 1953

❖❖

IT WAS IN April 1979 in West Berlin. Raymond Aron and I were
walking to an exhibit commemorating the centenary of the
births of Einstein, Max von Laue, Otto Hahn, and Lise Meitner.
We were passing bombed-out squares and half-decrepit man-
sions of a once proud capital, our thoughts already at the exhibit, when Aron suddenly stopped at a crossing, turned to me,
and said, "It could have been Germany's Century." Aron,
French scholar and Jew who had studied in Berlin in the early
1930s and had seen German promise turn to nemesis, mused
on what might have been. In the ensuing years I have extended
my studies of German scientists, of German creativity and destruction, which I had already begun then. In preparing this
work on Einstein's German world for publication twenty years

later, I recognize the resonance of the theme that Aron had so casually, so memorably set.

In the history of modern Europe, there has always been a preeminent power—successively Spain, France, Holland, Britain—a nation that combined material strength with cultural greatness. In the three decades before the Great War, Germany was the country in ascendancy, and its physical power, with its strident militaristic ethos, seemed to be balanced by cultural, especially scientific achievement. This was Germany's first chance to achieve European preeminence. The only other country at the time growing with similar dynamic energy was the United States, it too marked by immense material power, embarked on an imperial course, and exemplary in the promotion of scientific-technological innovation. The German theologian and academic statesman Adolf von Harnack was right when he said in 1907: "Geographically America is for us among civilized countries the most distant; intellectually and spiritually, however, the closest and most like us." In the twentieth century these two powers had violent alternations of intimacy and enmity; the American Century began as the German one ended. And for the last half of this century, historians have tried to understand the German question. Increasingly they have sought their answers in what I have always believed is its inescapable context, Europe, a context I now happily realize includes the United States as well. This book is part of that quest.

In the late eighteenth century a cultural renaissance erupted in the German lands; Europeans, in awe of artistic and philosophic achievements, began to speak of Germany as a land of poets and thinkers. Germans themselves referred to that period, roughly 1770–1830, as the Age of Genius, the *Geniezeit*. (For Germans, the word *Genie* has a special ring, denoting creative powers of demonic magnitude.) By the mid-nineteenth century in economic terms, after 1871 and unification in political terms, and by the end of the century in scientific-technological terms—Germany was transformed into a country of doers and innovators, of world-renowned natural scientists still steeped in Germany's humanistic culture. The very names of Einstein, Ehrlich, Planck, and Haber—and the extended and sometimes fractious family of scientists among whom they lived and worked—evoke the greatness of this period, expressed as it was also in German culture more broadly defined, when German writers and artists had the intuition of uneasy modernity. This might be called Germany's second *Geniezeit*, one fraught with danger.

Einstein's German world illustrates the ambiguities of German greatness—even before the Great War began the nation's process of stoppable self-destruction. We see clusters of excellence in the lives of some of its representative individuals; they were imbued with a faith in science that was then still innocent, a faith akin to religion; they were shielded by ties of friendship, supported by a disciplined society, driven by organized ambition, empowered by an unrivaled educational system.* German science and German society were intricately linked—hence the historian may justifiably pay heed to the nonscientific aspects of the scientists' lives.

By the late nineteenth century, Germany had developed an academic-industrial and, later, military complex that was supported and sustained by its authoritarian state, whose leaders combined class-induced political myopia with a confident grasp of the immense utility of science. Fritz Haber, inventor of the process for the fixation of nitrogen from the air, was one of

---

* One of the great mathematicians of the century, Hermann Weyl, who had lived in that European milieu before coming to the United States, said much later, in 1946: "We may well envy the nineteenth century for the feeling of certainty and the pathos with which it praised the sacrosanctity and supreme value of science and the mind's dispassionate quest for truth and light. We are addicted to mathematical research with no less fervor. But for us, alas! its meaning and value are questioned . . . from the practical-social side by the deadly menace of its misuses." Skúli Sigurdsson, "Physics, Life, and Contingency: Born, Schrödinger, and Weyl in Exile," in Mitchell G. Ash and Alfons Söllner, eds., *Forced Migration and Scientific Change: Emigré German-Speaking Scientists and Scholars after 1933* (Washington, D.C., 1996), p. 68.

the first German scientists to forge exceptionally close and profitable ties to German industry. In his and other scientists' lives we see the attractiveness of this new and dynamic Germany, and often an almost unreflective subservience to the state. In the case of Einstein, there was a distaste for Germany's authoritarian militarism, whose most aggressive elements became dominant in the Great War and survived after Germany's defeat, in infinitely more embittered fashion, subverting the brave attempts to build a German democracy on the ruins of the old empire. Einstein's comprehensive yet simplistic hostility to what might be called the official Germany of Kaiser Wilhelm's times, like his experience of nationalist rage in Weimar Germany, had an analogue in the deep anxiety over Germany's political capability expressed by self-conscious patriots such as Walther Rathenau, Max Weber, and the theologian Ernst Troeltsch.

Put too simply, Germany's elites—most especially the materially declining old agrarian-feudal class, many of the rising captains of industry and banking, and the professoriate—saw themselves as guardians of the nation's special character; they thought or imagined that Germany was beset by a ring of external enemies, and more importantly by internal enemies. The mounting tide of Social Democracy seemed to them to threaten their values, their privilege, their property.* Only a nation so internally divided could have welcomed the outbreak of war in 1914 with the extravagant hope that war would unify its

---

* There were many exceptions, of course. Consider one: Robert Bosch, born in 1861, founder of the Bosch concern that still today furnishes almost every automobile with electric or electronic devices, who in 1883–84 was in the United States and wrote his bride back home: "You see, I am a Socialist. . . . Socialism is something Great and Noble, and to understand it completely . . . you need volumes of books that exist but that our government prohibits and hence they are not easily accessible." Bosch may have been the only person to have learned socialism in America; he translated youthful sentiment into mature action; in 1906 he introduced the eight-hour day and paid vacations for his workers—and earned from his fellow industrialists the sobriquet "the red Bosch." Theodor Heuss, *Robert Bosch* (Stuttgart and Tübingen, 1948), pp. 63, 66–67.

people through sacrifice. Instead, the long war—conducted on the German side under ever more radical leadership—bred an atmosphere of suspicion and distrust that, upon Germany's defeat, erupted into both actual and latent civil war. Rathenau's life and his assassination in 1922 exemplify the travails of the postwar Weimar Republic, the impressive efforts made to salvage German promise that finally the horror of National Socialism totally perverted.

Einstein's German world was one in which Christians and Jews (or individuals of Jewish descent) lived and worked together; in the relatively protected realm of science, prejudice against Jews gradually yielded to a recognition of talent and of shared values. (In the Protestant states of Germany, Catholics probably fared worse than Jews—and the conflict between the two Christian religions ran very deep.) German society as a whole was rife with every kind of prejudice—anti-Semitism came in the most diverse guises—from irritation at Jewish success to paranoid fear and fury at the thought of Jewish power threatening German life and virtue. So while German Jews before 1914 prospered in spite of and sometimes even because of these rampant prejudices, they did so at great psychic cost, as the lives of Haber and Rathenau make clear. In no other country were Jews met with so peculiar a mixture of hospitality and hostility, while being so attracted to a country that in many ways treated them—still or forever more?—as second-class citizens. Chaim Weizmann had contempt for what he regarded as ignoble servility and wanted to deliver Jews from it. The full range of Jewish responses to German life before Hitler emerges in these various lives, as does the still terrifying failure of the German elites to resist Hitler's march to total power. That failure was the precondition of Nazi success.

ON earlier occasions I have acknowledged that I find the essay a particularly congenial mode: it allows for a more speculative, a more tentative tone, for a more personal voice. Some of the essays in this book were originally given in the form of lectures; some of them involved extensive study in private and public archives on three continents, a journey of discovery that was a pleasure in itself. My focus is largely biographical; I have tried to find the points where private lives and public realms intersect that illuminate them both. In a life like Planck's we see the collision between the commands of personal integrity and the commands of criminal political power.

The work of historians, their spoken and unspoken premises, have been an abiding interest of mine. We know that history is both a science—or an academic discipline—and an art, that the very openness of the past and the role of contingency within it demand analytical and imaginative judgment, both of which are affected by the historians' engagement with their own times. Hence my concern with the response of major historians to the experience of the Great War: their interpretations influenced the development of the discipline itself and, as always, they helped to mold a people's collective memory; their work is often a political datum. Beyond obeying the austere demands of their professional discipline, historians bear a moral responsibility, and the greater the reach, the heavier the responsibility.

The centrality and, eventually, the terror of German history in our century have made its study and interpretation compelling and infinitely complex. The record of German historians before Hitler—to say nothing of their record under Hitler— was largely dictated by nationalist imperatives and, in the Weimar years, by a studied avoidance of the self-critical inquiries that Germans often call fouling your own nest. Immediately after 1945, there was among German historians a wish to explain National Socialism as having been an aberration, an accident of German history.* Allied publicists—not historians—

---

* A mere example from the very beginning: in May 1945, Siegfried Kaehler, a conservative German historian who had kept his distance from National Socialism, wrote his son about Germany's fate, and about the German past that had been left intact by the defeat of 1918 but sullied and endangered by the "piedpiper" Hitler. "If universities should continue to exist, then our task will

painted a similarly distorted picture in reverse, insisting that
National Socialism was the very culmination of German history, a view that the National Socialists had themselves propa-
gated. What has been achieved in the half-century since has
been extraordinary: a gradual reexamination of German history and the place of National Socialism in it, beginning within
Germany with the work of Karl-Dietrich Bracher in the mid-
1950s and continuing with several generations of truly outstanding German historians, not to mention non-Germans
such as Alan Bullock or Gordon Craig or James Sheehan, who
have contributed so much to an understanding of the German
past. These years have witnessed great historical debates, but
they no longer run along nationalist lines; German history has
been largely integrated into European and international history and freed from narrow ideological entrapments. A recent
exception—Daniel Jonah Goldhagen's *Hitler's Willing Executioners: Ordinary Germans and the Holocaust*—has had the unusual fate of being sharply criticized by historians yet widely
read by a public that seems to welcome simplistic answers to
the most terrifying questions. I have included my own essay
on this historiographical-political phenomenon.

Some of these essays bear a personal note. I caught glimpses
of the world I wrote about, I learned from many conversations,
I read candid letters of the past. Some of the lectures express
my concern for those Germans who have committed themselves to build and preserve a liberal society and a democratic
state, for the colleagues who with such acuity and professional
energy have analyzed German history and have helped to
build an international community of scholars.

In the same personal vein I have written of present-day
events. I was thrilled by the world-historical transformation of

---

be to preserve and protect the record of the true and real Germany against the
calumnies, already begun, by democratic-Jewish propaganda and by Anglo-
Saxon self-righteousness." Siegfried A. Kaehler, *Briefe 1900–1963*, ed. Walter
Bussmann and Günther Grünthal (Boppard am Rhein, 1993), p. 300.

1989 and the self-liberation of Eastern Europe, but I was concerned about the long-term psychological difficulties of uniting the peoples of two German states held apart for so long. I realized that formal unification gave Germany that rarest of opportunities, a second chance: this time to become the preeminent power of Europe in a peaceful fashion. To seize that chance would require rare feats of statesmanship and the recognition of the responsibilities of power. One instance of such statesmanship has been the belated reconciliation between Germany and Poland, to which I devote the final and most personal essay. "Lost Homelands" is an all-too-human experience of our collective past.

It has not been Germany's century—at least not in the sense that Aron meant that it might have been. But German terror, at its most savage in the Holocaust, haunts the moral imagination of all of us. It could not be otherwise. There are also lessons to be learned from the German catastrophe, one of which was intimated in a letter Lise Meitner wrote in 1945: "It is tragic," she remarked, "that even people like Laue and Otto [Hahn] did not understand to what fate their passivity delivered their own country." No country, no society, is shielded from the evils that the passivity of decent citizens can bring about. That is a German lesson of the twentieth century—for all of us.

PART ONE

The Promise of
German Life

◆◇◆◇◆◇◆◇◆◇◆◇◆ 1 ◆◇◆◇◆◇◆◇◆◇◆◇◆

Paul Ehrlich: The Founder of Chemotherapy

◆◆

A natural scientist must be at once a general and
a spy.

Richard Willstätter, 1913

◆◆

In May 1990 I gave the opening lecture at the dedication of the new
Paul Ehrlich Institute in Langen, near Frankfurt am Main. The lecture, a historical-biographical portrait, was followed by a scientific
symposium. Subsequently, my friend Günther Schwerin, Paul Ehrlich's grandson, presented Rockefeller University with the complete
Ehrlich Archive, which he had ingeniously retrieved after the Second World War. To make use of these materials proved irresistible,
and I revised the previously unpublished lecture utilizing these
new and untapped sources. I am indebted to the Rockefeller Archive Center in Tarrytown, New York, for their friendly assistance.

◆◆

I AM A HISTORIAN with but a limited knowledge of the natural
sciences. Still, I have been trying to understand certain aspects
of the history of science in the decades preceding and following the First World War, chancing into this area as a result of
my research on Fritz Haber and Albert Einstein, their circle of
friends, and the political-scientific ambience they worked in. I

was fascinated by these figures, and especially intrigued by their devotion to a science that then still seemed to be innocent, untainted. One could sense the passion that inspired their great accomplishments. What, we may ask, were the prerequisites for their commitment and success? What was the scientific ethos of the era? What factors lay behind that burst of creativity which propelled German scientists to such prodigious and pioneering achievements?

The life of an individual scientist, such as Paul Ehrlich, may help to shed light on the wellsprings of scientific progress. He was both genius and a representative figure. Though he was totally centered on and committed to his research, with little interest in the world about him, that world—and his friends and rivals—helped to shape his life. His biography shows how external factors both impeded and facilitated his creativity. Perhaps there is a certain gap in our understanding of these interrelations: literature in the natural sciences often neglects the human-historical dimension, while historians until recently have paid too little attention to the sociopolitical importance of natural scientists.

I realize that the historical guild may view my fascination with the human side of natural scientists as old-fashioned at best. The great physiologist Hermann von Helmholtz once spoke about the "inner psychological history" of science; even Einstein stressed the "reciprocity between scientific accomplishment and greatness of character." Though one can be intrigued by that "inner" history, one must not lose sight of the close connections in earlier eras between scientists and the intellectual, political, and economic world.

Sheer energy and fortitude, disciplined intuition and stamina, appear to be determinative in the life of the scientist, despite the dangers and disappointments they experience. And in Germany during the early years of the twentieth century, there were geniuses of research. The word "genius" in German has a special overtone, even a tinge of the demonic, a mysterious power and energy; a genius—whether artist or scientist—

is considered to have a special vulnerability, a precariousness, a life of constant risk and often close to troubled turmoil. It was precisely in the same era that Thomas Mann embarked on his lifelong preoccupation with and analysis of the vulnerability of the artist. Artists and great scientists have a certain affinity. Someone observed that although Ehrlich "never created works of art in the strict sense, he had qualities closely akin to those of the artist." There are also many differences: the artist is commonly an isolate, living in a kind of permanent jeopardy; the scientist, by contrast, usually has an institutional home, a cluster of collegiality and even friendship that makes bearable the inevitable frictions and occasional meanspiritedness of colleagues. Ehrlich had his full taste of the good and the bad—the latter perhaps more clearly discernible in the private correspondence.

In writings by and about Ehrlich, certain words recur: "genius," "leader," "warrior-hero." This is also true of Rudolf Virchow, Louis Pasteur, Robert Koch, and many others. It was how they were characterized, and it was the tone of public praise. Theirs was a historical moment in which often heroic individual researchers, putting their very lives at risk, forged a new world. Ehrlich's generation stood on the threshold of what the theologian Adolf Harnack termed in 1905 "science as a large-scale enterprise." And perhaps more than anyone else, Paul Ehrlich proved just how much one individual could accomplish: thanks to his discoveries in the laboratory, clinicians were able to save countless lives. The later historian Felix Gilbert was correct in observing that "in the intellectual life of the modern era, natural scientists became the new heroes."

I believe that Paul Ehrlich, born in 1854, was part of a second Age of Genius in Germany, indeed one of its key representatives. Only recently have we recognized this era for what it was, an era of pioneering discovery and invention when scientific and experimental medicine was making its first huge strides. In Germany the enormous advances made in the chemical industry during the nineteenth century, and the invention

of synthetic dyes, became the foundation for progress in biological and virological research. There was widespread, un-
bounded faith in the perfection of empirical or positivistic science—a conviction that humans could comprehend nature and
control its forces. Rudolf Virchow, physician, research scientist,
and a fierce champion of liberalism against Bismarck, speaking
in 1865 at the fortieth Congress of German Natural Scientists
and Physicians, observed: "For us, science has become a religion." And in 1873: "We too have a creed: faith in the progress
of our knowledge of the truth." Emil Du Bois-Reymond spoke
of "natural science as the world conqueror in our day." Until
the First World War, this was the predominant tone in the
world of science and industry. At the founding convention of
the Kaiser-Wilhelm-Society in January 1911, the renowned
chemist Emil Fischer—in Ehrlich's presence and alluding to his
work—declared that the future did not lie in the conquest of
colonial empires; rather, "chemistry and with it, more generally, all of natural science is the true land of boundless opportunities." And there was solid evidence to back up this faith:
practical knowledge was triumphing in the struggles against
infection, against epidemic diseases, against the scourge of infant mortality.

In public, many scientists averred their trust in the progress
and potential of science, yet in numerous unpublished documents—private letters from Ehrlich, Einstein, Haber, and Willstätter, for example—one can sense their unpretentiousness,
their doubts, their dissatisfaction with their own work. This
was precisely because they were animated by such a powerful
faith in science: the more lofty the aspirations of science as a
collective enterprise, the more understandable the modesty of
the individual researcher. Certainly there were also human
frailties: ambition, jealousy, desire for fame. But Willstätter's
plea to Ehrlich in 1903 was characteristic: "Please lower very
greatly the scientific assessment you so generously accord me.
I find it depressing to be overestimated by a research scien-

tist for whom I have such great admiration. I feel I'm just a beginner."[1]

The advance of natural science also had critics and opponents—Nietzsche, for example, and, in an analogous but different way, Max Weber—who sensed the profound hazards lurking in the unqualified faith in science. There were also groups of people who thought that science endangered their interests, who imagined that positivistic science threatened their monopoly on morals in education and religion. We know that various church and religious leaders opposed the claims of science. Distortions and misunderstandings abounded. Many of the great scientists experienced in themselves a sense of the mystery of the universe; they hoped to serve and aid humanity without destroying its faith in the abiding mystery of the universe.

Paul Ehrlich was born into this world of progress, which he came to enrich with singular success. He was born in 1854 in Strehlen (now a Polish town, Strzelin), near Breslau (Wroclaw), the son of a prosperous Silesian-Jewish family. His scientific interests were awakened by his mother's cousin, the distinguished pathologist Carl Weigert. Already as a medical student he was fascinated by physiological research and recognized the huge potential for physiological experimentation that industrially manufactured dyes made possible. He had a special "love," as Willstätter noted, for the new dyes, especially methylene blue and its potential as a biological reagent. And he had an intuitive grasp of the bond linking chemistry, biology, and medicine. His earliest investigations led him to the concept that governed his future work: "that chemical affinities govern all biological processes." It was "the dawn of that great age in which medicine and chemistry forged their alliance for the benefit of all mankind," as Otto Warburg wrote.

Ehrlich's path as a scientist was not an easy one. He was a loner: though a physician, he was unwilling to enter clinical practice; though a researcher, he was devoid of ambition to teach. There had already been renowned successes in biomedical research, such as Pasteur's developing a vaccine for rabies. Ehrlich worked in the developing field of immunology, convinced that the body's natural immune system could be fortified by chemical means. Finally, it was he who invented chemotherapy, indeed coined the term. But neither his passion for independence nor his work plans fitted the structure of scientific research at the time. Only the support given him by three exceptional personalities gave him the chance to develop his brilliant gifts to the full.

In 1878, the famous internist Theodor Frerichs, for a time Bismarck's personal physician, brought the young Ehrlich to the famed Charité Hospital in Berlin. Frerichs himself was convinced that the exactitude of physics and chemistry should have its analogue in medicine; under his sympathetic aegis, Ehrlich was able to dedicate himself totally to research. Frerichs recognized the young genius, of whom these lines by Theodor Fontane, written at the time, serve as a fitting description:

> Gifts, who is without them?
> Talents—mere toys for children.
> Seriousness makes the man, application the genius.*

For even then, the young Ehrlich was distinguished by seriousness, unswerving commitment, by his impassioned, iron concentration and his sublime forgetfulness regarding all trivialities. In 1882, Robert Koch delivered his lecture "On Tuberculosis," in which he set forth his discovery of the rod-shaped tubercle bacilli responsible for what he insisted was the infec-

---

> *   Gaben, wer hätte sie nicht?
>   Talente—Spielzeug für Kinder.
>   Erst der Ernst macht den Mann, erst der Fleiss das Genie.

Theodor Fontane, "Unter ein Bildnis Adolf Menzels," *Gedichte* (Stuttgart und Berlin, 1908), p. 325.

tious disease of tuberculosis. Ehrlich later wrote: "Everyone in attendance was deeply moved, and for me that evening has remained etched in my mind as my greatest scientific event." Soon thereafter Ehrlich developed an improved method of staining tubercle bacilli—and he and Koch became friends.

In fact, Frerichs and Koch became models for Ehrlich, and at the same time important promoters of his work. When Koch, only eleven years Ehrlich's senior, died in 1910, Ehrlich wrote a long obituary that reveals a good deal about his own life; the unconscious autobiographical elements of such eulogies should be listened to. He spoke of the "epoch-making work of the young doctor from Wollstein, Robert Koch," who demonstrated the "specificity of bacterial strains and their sole responsibility in the genesis of infectious diseases." Then he went on to the external circumstances that had helped Koch:

> Unknown and far removed from centers of scientific research . . . he was deeply engrossed in problems which the foremost scientists had struggled in vain to solve. By astute and unflagging application, he was able to provide answers so authoritative as to earn him the admiration and unqualified recognition of his contemporaries. And perhaps it was propitious that his genius and energy were given free rein to pursue his trailblazing ideas, undisturbed and unimpeded—a genius and an energy that in so exceptional a way combined to form his personality.

Was this not an apt description of Ehrlich himself?
He went on:

> It seems only natural that upon such a man—champion of science, bold and victorious leader in the battle against the deadliest common epidemics, universally acclaimed cultural celebrity—the highest honors were bestowed. . . . All of us who knew him will always admire his masterful genius as a researcher, his superior intellect, his inexhaustible capacity for work, his prodigious energy, and, last but

not least, his heroic courage. That courage enabled him to
defy the greatest dangers. Through it he became the great
figure he was for us all and will remain for future generations: a defender of the common welfare, a victorious
commander and leader in the fight against its fiercest foes.

Commemorating the memory of a paragon, Ehrlich did not
realize the extent to which he himself had come to emulate his
model, but posterity is well aware of it.

Ehrlich sounded a military note, jarring perhaps today, but
normal in Wilhelmine Germany and in the developing field of
bacteriology; Koch himself had often invoked similar metaphors, especially in his successful struggle to put bacteriologi-
cal research and knowledge at the service of German public
health, improving sanitary conditions in overcrowded cities. It
was also an era when the "chief" was deemed almighty, the
embodiment of scientific authority, surrounded in clinic and
laboratory by a retinue of subalterns. Since Ehrlich's career
was also shaped by strife, his use of these military metaphors
seems all the more understandable.

In March 1885, Frerichs died suddenly; his successor did not
properly appreciate Ehrlich's worth and had him transferred
to clinical duty—this at the cost of his scientific work. That
marked the beginning of an unhappy period at the Charité for
Ehrlich and his wife, Hedwig Pinkus, whom he had wed a
short time before. Her love and understanding, not to mention
her private wealth, were to prove enduring sources of solace
and comfort for him.*

---

* Ehrlich's love letters to his nineteen-year-old fiancée overflow with affection and candor; their style well expresses his personality, even as they seem
characteristic of the prevailing notions of the special decency and nobility inherent in womankind. He thanks her for having rekindled his "enthusiasm for the
Good and Beautiful," but "it's such a shame that life's ordinary demands and
impediments are so importune that I can scarcely find the time . . . to hint to you
in a few words what I feel." Ehrlich to Pinkus, July 28 and February 2, 1883, Paul
Ehrlich Collection. Ehrlich practiced his own parsimonious orthography: he
defied German convention by not capitalizing nouns and was indifferent to the
rules of punctuation. Rockefeller Archive Center, Pocantino Hills, N.Y.

In 1890, Koch announced that he had successfully created tuberculin, the sterile liquid containing substances extracted
from the tubercle bacillus, which could be used in the diagno-
sis and cure of tuberculosis. This internationally acclaimed success led in Germany to the establishment in 1892 of a state Institute for Infectious Diseases, which was deemed a necessity
in the globally competitive world of medicine. (The fact that in
the same year, Bismarck's banker Gerson von Bleichröder, acting anonymously, made a million marks available for a hospital where patients would be treated in accordance with Koch's
methods, has not been noted, not even in a standard biography
of Koch.) In 1892, Koch brought Ehrlich, whom he held in high
esteem, to the institute as "research associate." The institute
was intended to deal with all infectious diseases, not just tuberculosis, particularly after tuberculin proved a failure in
therapy.

Ehrlich now began to work with Emil von Behring at the
Koch institute. The Koch institute in general and Behring and
Ehrlich in particular benefited from the growing eagerness of
the German chemical industry, Farbwerke Hoechst especially,
to support academic research that would produce practical
and profitable results—in this instance involving the production of immunizing serum. Behring and Ehrlich were markedly
different in personality: Behring rather authoritarian and con-
tentious, Ehrlich vulnerable and yet stubborn, reticent and
even reclusive. Together they concentrated their work on fighting diphtheria: at the time, some 45,000 children in Germany
alone contracted the disease every year, and half of these died
agonizing deaths. Behring discovered an antitoxin, but it was
Ehrlich who learned how to develop the serum in live horses
by slowly increased injections and then to standardize the
required dosage for humans. With the help of August Lau-
benheimer, research director of the chemical company Farb-
werke-Hoechst, that plant was commissioned to produce the
substance: "Every vial of diphtheria serum from Farbwerke-
Hoechst bears the label: manufactured according to Behring-

Ehrlich."[2] Behring and Ehrlich had come to an agreement in 1892 regulating the distribution of profits between them, and their joint labors liberated humankind from a horrible scourge. Their initially successful cooperation alternated with bitter disputes. Ehrlich was convinced that Behring had taken advantage of him financially, while denigrating his superior scientific achievement.

At this point in his career, Ehrlich needed help, and he found it in the person of Friedrich Althoff, a department head in the Prussian Ministry of Education from 1882 to 1907; he was the commanding figure in Prussia's academic life. He was controversial in his time and remains so today: his achievements were great, his methods questionable. His ambition was to make Prussia's universities and research centers the best in the world, even against the will of opinionated professors with their insistence on autonomy, and in the teeth of prevailing religious biases. Althoff knew that in the battle against infectious diseases, Ehrlich was one of the most brilliant scientists anywhere—and, ultimately, one of the most successful. Soon a genuine friendship developed between the two, a bond that brought professional benefits to both men.

Althoff recognized that Ehrlich was unhappy with his subordinate position in Koch's institute, so in 1896 he set up a new state Institute for Serum Research and Serum Testing in Steglitz, a suburb of Berlin, and named Ehrlich its director. But that, too, was to prove only a temporary solution. Althoff succeeded in convincing the mayor of Frankfurt am Main, Franz Adickes, that his city's fame would be enhanced by establishing a Royal Institute for Experimental Therapy there, headed by Ehrlich and jointly financed by the city and the Prussian state, with contributions from industry and private donors—a further example of the emergence of an industrial-scientific-state complex that gave German science its all-important social setting. Ehrlich moved to Frankfurt, where the institute was inaugurated in 1899.

In 1906, a dream long cherished by Althoff and Ehrlich finally came true: the widow of the Jewish banker Georg Speyer
donated an additional building to Ehrlich for his biomedical research and experimental chemotherapy, and the Speyer
Foundation provided generous funding for his work. The
Georg-Speyer House, as it was called, was interdisciplinary
from the outset and had close ties with industry. Ehrlich was
working with modest, even primitive facilities and equipment,
but the institute grew, and even though operations were always kept on a tight budget, new tasks were taken on, new
staff appointed. Scarce funds restricted research, and Althoff,
knowing how fierce the foreign competition was and adept at
raising private money, complained to Ehrlich, "It is truly lamentable that we in Germany don't also have wealthy people
who can provide for our institutes along the lines of the lar-
gesse given the Pasteur Institute [in Paris]. . . . Why can't the
tycoons in Frankfurt like B. Metzler . . . etc., donate millions for
your institute!"[3]

It was in Frankfurt that Ehrlich made his great theoretical
and practical discoveries. Here he conducted his celebrated
research on immunity, here he proved that antibody formation could be stimulated, and therefore that substances protecting against infection could be produced in strengths that
made their use in medical treatment possible. In 1906 Ehrlich defined his hopes dramatically; he thought that "in the
chemist's retort" substances would be created that would "be
able to exert their full action exclusively on the parasite harbored within the organism and would represent . . . magic
bullets which seek their target of their own accord." Ehrlich's
English friend and colleague, the Nobel laureate Sir Henry
Dale, noted in 1950 that "Ehrlich's imaginative genius" led him
to develop his side-chain theory of the formation of anti-
bodies, which is still today the basis of chemotherapy. He
searched for "substances which, by virtue of their chemical
structure and combining properties, would directly attach

themselves to, and be able thus to kill or weaken, the infecting organisms, but would leave the tissues of the infected patient unharmed."

Ehrlich's private letters attest to his close bonds of friendship with Althoff and report on his vexing difficulties. Althoff was his friend, benefactor, and go-between, but the main trouble-maker was Behring, another protégé of Althoff's. As early as 1900, Althoff had to assure Ehrlich, "We shall never launch any campaigns against you. . . . In your mutual interest, the con-stant feuding [with Behring] must not be allowed to become a permanent fixture."[4] Money was one problem here, as well as Behring's limited regard for Ehrlich's merits. Six years later, Ehrlich complained that Behring had been unfair to him over the diphtheria serum, and was now making new demands that would gravely injure the work of Ehrlich's institute: "A feeling of deep bitterness still wells up in me when I recall that time— not because of the material losses I suffered and have forgot-ten, but because of the enormous ruthlessness with which von Behring began the game and played it out. It was only thanks to my help that he could mount the saddle and his first act was to kick the man who had aided him, and whose assistance, however uncongenial, was indispensable."

But any further harm to his institute Ehrlich found intoler-able: "Without being immodest, I think I can say that the Insti-tute has everywhere won full recognition and even emulation in the development of modern research on immunity—and that not only as an Institute for testing new products—but that also my work and that of my associates have contributed im-portantly to the advance of modern science."[5]

Ehrlich had wanted to dedicate his most important work to Althoff, who, understandably gratified, accepted the honor: "I have been deeply moved by your intention to dedicate the publication of your path-breaking studies on side-chain theory to me. I feel in no way deserving of such a great honor, but since in the past I have endured so many and in part truly un-deserved attacks, I shall now gratefully accept this honor, equally undeserved, bestowed on me by such an outstanding friend."[6]

And when in 1907 Althoff for reasons of health resigned from his post, Ehrlich wrote him an official letter, the text of which so pleased Althoff that he copied it out and distributed it to friends:

> You have done more to further the advance of science in all fields than anyone else, and I believe we have you to thank above all others for the fact that we are still today in the leading position. May the future keep this primacy from slipping from us. I myself owe you both my entire career and the chance I had to bring my ideas to practical fruition. Shunted about as an assistant, forced into impossible conditions, totally ignored by the university, I thought myself quite useless. I never received a call to even the most minor position and was regarded as a person without a field—i.e., as totally useless. If you, with your strong hand and brilliant initiative, had not come to my aid and, in your untiring zeal and benevolent friendship, had not arranged a place where I might work, I would have been left to wither away entirely.[7]

This generous appraisal was typical of Ehrlich, though somewhat unfair to Frerichs and the others who had earlier supported him.

Althoff died in 1908—shortly before his protégé was awarded the Nobel Prize (shared jointly with Élie Metchnikoff) for his work on immunology. Ehrlich had earned earlier distinctions, and others followed: honorary doctorates from Oxford and elsewhere, medals and honors, an honorary professorship and an imperial appointment to the rank of Privy Councillor (with the address Your Excellency, a rare high honor). Ehrlich was a founding member of the executive board of the Kaiser-Wilhelm-Society. He was nominated for a second Nobel after inventing Salvarsan, but his early death prevented his receiving this very rare double distinction.

All this recognition and success came with repeated strife and animosity. For example, Ehrlich had to defend himself against attacks by the Swedish scientist Svante Arrhenius, for whom a Nobel Institute for Physical Chemistry had been founded in 1905. Commenting in a letter to his old friend and colleague Albert Neisser on this feud, Ehrlich noted, "Physical chemists comprise one of the best-organized cliques anywhere in the world, acting in unison to push each other forward."[8]

Ehrlich's ties were international, his fame widespread throughout the scientific community. In medicine, there already emerged something like "globalization," albeit dominated by the West. In 1904, he lectured in the United States, later in England and across Europe; his often improvised talks, as he himself described them, gained him close friends in the Anglo-American world, some of whom induced John D. Rockefeller to donate $10,000 for the support of Ehrlich's institute. He cultivated contacts with colleagues everywhere: he asked for snake venom from Africa, studied tropical diseases such as sleeping sickness, maintained close ties with Japanese and, of course, with European scientists. The major (and for a time last) international medical congress in London in 1913 feted Ehrlich as the most eminent research scientist in the world.

In 1911, Ehrlich gave a paper on Salvarsan at the Congress of Natural Scientists in Karlsruhe, the gathering, as we will see, where Fritz Haber and Albert Einstein first met; a year later, he delivered the principal lecture, "Modern Initiatives in Therapy," at Haber's Kaiser-Wilhelm-Institute. Ehrlich, Haber, and Einstein: two generations of German-Jewish scientists who intellectually and materially enriched their country and enhanced its worldwide prestige. A triumvirate of diverse personalities, all three outstanding representatives of the second Age of Genius.

Ehrlich's institute—the equal and rival of the Institut Pasteur and the Rockefeller Institute—investigated the etiology of and possible therapy for various diseases and was among the first to undertake cancer research. But Ehrlich's greatest triumph—after years of experimentation—was his discovery of Salvarsan, the "magic bullet" also known as 606—605 earlier solutions having proved ineffectual. The trade name alluded to one of its ingredients, arsenic, which he, together with his Japanese colleague Sahachiro Hata, had developed as a chemotherapeutic agent against the syphilis spirochete. It made possible the most effective treatment to date for syphilis, which at the turn of the century was claiming more and more victims; its third stage—paresis—ended in wretched and painful death. The great dramas of the time, such as Ibsen's, alluded to the tragedy of syphilis, even if decorum dictated that its name be unmentioned. Only a few decades earlier, the famous English doctor Samuel Solly had praised syphilis as God's retribution for sinners, admonishing people to live a moral life (not unlike the situation today, where the battle against AIDS is waged with extremely limited funding and against similar moralizing). Through Ehrlich's work, humanity was largely freed from this scourge—a fact that the sanctimonious hypocrites of the day greeted critically.

Ehrlich himself had other worries. At the 1910 Congress of Internists in Wiesbaden, he had distributed 65,000 units of Salvarsan gratis to colleagues and was extraordinarily meticulous in following up on the results. A "Salvarsan war" erupted: countless complaints alleged adverse side effects or unsuccessful treatment. "But the most unpleasant thing," he wrote in 1910, "is that there is a marked contrast between my own personality, which is anything but bold, and my scientific conviction that the disease ought to be vanquished by one mighty, possibly hazardous, blow, rather than to apply a mild but ineffective therapy, leaving the patients to their fate."

Ehrlich's enemies gleefully made his setbacks known, and his wife noted in her diary: "Paul is in very low spirits. . . . He says a Brazilian told him that Professor Finger [in] Vienna had two cases of deafness in his clinic as a result of 606, considered the drug poisonous and would campaign against it."[9] There was even a legal suit involving Salvarsan therapy, and Ehrlich had to appear in court. But Ehrlich himself unceasingly tracked the results of his cure, concerned about the effectiveness of Salvarsan, worried about improper applications of it. He knew that "the step from the laboratory to the patient's bedside . . . is extraordinarily arduous and fraught with danger." Correctly sensing enemies lurking in the field, in early 1911 he wrote to his friend Simon Flexner at the Rockefeller Institute: "The past year was a very hard one for me and I really feel how nervously exhausted I am. I must also say that I could have become old and have died without having had any notion of the meanness of mankind, which I now have had to experience." Constant conflicts exacerbated the burden of a furious work schedule. But Salvarsan proved a success: Ehrlich cured countless sufferers from what had once been all too often a fatal affliction. His labors, however, did grave harm to his own health.

In 1914, on the occasion of his sixtieth birthday, Ehrlich's unique standing was internationally celebrated. A comprehensive commemorative volume offered a "description of his scientific contributions." Despite his motto, "Work hard, publish little," he had some 212 publications to his name by then, the first having appeared when he was only twenty-three. His colleagues admired him not just for his successful results, but for the masterly methods he employed in achieving them, which in turn expressed his unfailing sense for science's proper tasks and potential: "We are not masters of nature, but its pupils." The guiding principle at his institute was "a unified direction in research, while allowing the individual the greatest possible scope for independent work." To another American friend, Samuel Meltzer, he wrote, "I was always particularly proud of the art of 'marching off' [Die Kunst des Abmarsches]"—by which he meant his ability to leave a field that had become barren. And it is true that he lost no time with matters that gave him no pleasure, leaving it to others to reap the harvest of many of his ingenious ideas. Most scientists praised his exemplary ethical attitude, and the enormous care he took in intro-

ducing new medicines. Ever self-critical, he resented the unfair, denigrating criticisms of some colleagues.

In the volume honoring Ehrlich's sixtieth birthday, Richard
Willstätter wrote: "Before our eyes the images of the great
thinkers and artists of the past rise up . . . when we admire the
universality of Paul Ehrlich's work, and recognize how versa-
tile was his work as a chemist and how deeply, the breadth
notwithstanding, he penetrated into the problems of organic
chemistry. . . . As a chemist, Ehrlich is the pupil of no other
master; he is not borne along, or even influenced, by any tide
of his time; by his intuition and the power of his personality,
vast new fields are being opened up for us." A genius origi-
nated the field of modern chemotherapy—a field of incomparable medical importance for our century.*

Renowned for his passion for work and his scintillating
spontaneous monologues about scientific questions, Ehrlich
was also a loving husband and the happy father of two daughters, whose weddings he lived to see. Unlike Haber or Einstein,
his family life was tranquil and happy. Prodigiously well-read
in science (though not in literature), Ehrlich developed what he
dubbed the technique of "diagonal reading," rapidly scanning
a page from top left to bottom right, pausing only for what was
important to him. He was always pressed for time. His wife
commented: "Paul can only work at the very last moment."[10]
Like Haber, he relaxed by reading detective novels. Arthur
Conan Doyle's portrait hung on the wall of his study, and the

---

* Perhaps Ehrlich could be described as one of those rare individuals who
was both hedgehog and fox: he had one great idea—that all biological processes
are chemical in nature—and he tirelessly pursued many therapeutic means to
provide immunity to or cure for various diseases. Yet another American friend
of Ehrlich's, Dr. Christian A. Herter, in a celebrated Columbia lecture in 1909,
said: "The imagination of a Darwin or Pasteur, for example, is as high and pro-
ductive a form of imagination as that of Dante, or Goethe, or even Shakespear
[sic] if we regard the human uses which result from the exercise of imaginative
powers and mean by human uses not merely meat and drink, clothes and shel-
ter, but also the satisfaction of mental and spiritual needs." Columbia University
Quarterly, 1909–1910, p. 19.

author sent him some of his books as presents. Perhaps he had a kind of elective affinity with Sherlock Holmes: his motto, "We have to learn how to take aim," also applied to Holmes's practiced knack for discovery. Both unearthed deadly secrets.

Ehrlich had no regard for his own health. He lived for his work, and from our perspective he seemed unwise: it was said that his absolute staples were mineral water and an all-day diet of the strongest cigars. He tended to view vacations and regular meals as disagreeable interruptions that he tolerated out of love for his family. In the winter of 1914–15, he collapsed from exhaustion and in August 1915 succumbed to a second stroke. By then, science had lost its innocence in the Great War, and Ehrlich's world lay in ruins.

Emil von Behring spoke at his open grave, lauding Ehrlich as a *"magister mundi"* in medical science, his personality an *"anima candida"*: "In our harsh era of a ruthless struggle for existence, you [*Du*] always remained so pure and untainted in your disposition, so tender in your sentiments, that any who knew you had to sense sharp pangs of conscience if ever they dared to treat you harshly." Were these belated pangs of Behring's own conscience, a graveside confession? Nonetheless, the friend-foe had understood him.

Ehrlich scarcely had time for or interest in politics, yet we know of two somewhat contrary instances when he was a participant in historical events. In 1913, Chaim Weizmann visited Ehrlich in his laboratory and persuaded him to join the project of establishing a Jewish university in Jerusalem; Weizmann regarded Ehrlich's support as uniquely important. After a trip to Paris in February 1914, Ehrlich reported his impressions of the possible French assistance that would come for the planned university, to be financed by Edmond de Rothschild. Weizmann hoped that Ehrlich would work out a plan for a research institute at the university in Jerusalem, a project to be presented to Baron Rothschild for additional support. The outbreak of war put a quick end to the projected venture, but it is clear that Ehrlich, unlike most German Jews, wanted to champion the "Jewish-national" cause. His report on a conversation with the physician and scientist Georges Widal provides insight into his own views: "Widal is rather indifferent when it comes to [Jewish] national questions. . . . One factor, partially affecting his case, is that although he is Jewish, he has never had any adverse personal experiences because of this and has enjoyed a brilliant career right from the start. Of course, he is a very outstanding and capable individual."[11]

But in consonance with the great majority of Jews in Germany, Ehrlich was also quite able to support the "German-national" side in the war. He too signed the ill-conceived Manifesto of the 93 in October 1914—undoubtedly much to the chagrin of his many friends and admirers in the Allied countries. The Ehrlich Archives offer no clue as to who might have solicited his signature, but, as we shall see in the next chapters, other great scientists, Planck, Haber, and Willstätter for example, signed as well.*

Paul Ehrlich was a Jew and remained so all his life, yet at the same time, his identity as a German was for him an absolute given. And it was as a German that he was celebrated abroad. In Germany, he suffered the disappointments that were the common lot there of all Jews. I doubt that any of the great Jewish scientists could escape the virtually unquestioned bias of the day; neither baptism nor outstanding achievement could shake society's fundamental outlook. Ehrlich triumphed after he had encountered hindrances and hostility; he was troubled by the far worse obstacles faced by fellow Jews who lacked genius. In his own case, and this was symptomatic of the times, the slights were mitigated by the personal engagement of colleagues and superiors who gave him both practical and moral

---

* For details about the manifesto, see Chapter 3, "Together and Apart," in this volume. There is a certain irony that one of the best-known German pacifists, Friedrich Wilhelm Foerster, wrote Ehrlich's long-time secretary, thanking her for her reminiscences of Ehrlich: "Yes, he is the kind of German as God had willed him." Foerster to Martha Marquardt, Paris, September 17, 1929, Paul Ehrlich Collection.

support—Frerichs, Koch, Althoff, and others. At its higher levels, Germany was distinguished by harmonious creativity. Yet prejudice—and I intentionally avoid the term anti-Semitism, due to its racist and populist overtones—was practically universal.

This *ressentiment* of Jews had a certain seductive force for Germans, and it may have also brought them some advantage, permitting them a sense of moral superiority while categorizing certain specific traits—ruthless ambition, dogged self-assertion, a desire for power and money—as typically Jewish. That prejudice expressed a sense of one's own uprightness. At the same time, it masked a double anxiety: fear of possible contamination by those very traits that one maligned or might already be infected with; anxiety that Jews, by these very same qualities, might effectively challenge the position and intellectual patrimony of their Christian colleagues.

So German Jews encountered both animosity and friendship. The obstacles that prejudice put in their way often had a contrary effect: anti-Semitism served as the sting that spurred Jews on to overachievement, to maintain their own in often subliminal competition. The biographies of Ehrlich and his colleagues suggest that the widespread antipathy to Jews in a society marked by a high degree of assimilation proved an unintended impetus for success. Thus Wilhelmine society derived several benefits from its legacy of prejudice: Christians could enjoy the psychic satisfaction of moral superiority and society at large could benefit from the fortuitously enhanced capacity and austere dedication of Jewish scientists. Ehrlich's and Haber's achievements were an immeasurable boon to Imperial Germany, to German industry, to Germany's international prestige. Shulamit Volkov has investigated this pattern of Jewish success in medicine and the natural sciences: the talented young Jewish researcher was initially often placed at a disadvantage and appointed to less demanding posts; he was frequently passed over and condemned to the limbo of a nontenured lectureship (Privatdozent) for longer than others; yet this allowed him time to pursue his own research and develop as a specialist.[12] Ehrlich was spared having to witness the destruction of this unique bond of Christian-Jewish cooperation, or to suffer the abominations of later years.*

This newly established Paul Ehrlich Institute is living proof of historic change. Ehrlich had once commented that if he had to, he could work in a barn, and the institute named for him today is a far cry from a barn. But change also brings new hazards. Today the value of the natural sciences is generally allowed, as are their enormous costs, but science has lost its former innocence, and the technology it helped to create, in all its ambiguity about human life, is a source of concern. The person in the white coat is no longer quite the god he or she once was—true still in my childhood; they too have been demythologized. They too are measured by the degree to which they act responsibly. Increasingly, current science has become "big science," and is dominated less by individual geniuses or giants like Koch, Ehrlich, or, more recently, perhaps, Robert Oppenheimer.

The name of Paul Ehrlich recalls an illustrious era and remains an admonition, a specific summons to moral and civic

---

* His family was not spared. His daughter Stephanie, married to a great industrialist Ernst Schwerin, presided over a splendid salon in Breslau, which the writer Gerhart Hauptmann much liked to attend—until 1933. In 1937, Ernst Schwerin was warned of his impending arrest and emigrated with his family to the United States. In 1938 he was deprived of his German citizenship and dispossessed—a term that had a fateful double meaning for German Jews. Paul Ehrlich's widow emigrated only after the *Kristallnacht* pogrom of November 1938.

My mother's family was related to Ernst Schwerin's family. I vividly remember the close friendship in Breslau and in the United States between my parents and Stephanie Schwerin. (I studied at the same gymnasium in Breslau that Paul Ehrlich attended—at a time when he had become an "unperson," and I can still recall addressing his widow as "Your Excellency" in her American exile.) When I spoke at Stephanie Schwerin's funeral in New York in 1966, I said that she exuded not only great benevolence but a quiet, grave authority; she was a true representative of the German *Bürgertum*.

In 1989 the Bundesbank issued a new 200 deutschmark bill with Paul Ehrlich's portrait and a microscope on it—a curious form of restitution.

responsibility. The German catastrophe in part made possible by German science enfeebled its scientific community. German scientists committed terrible atrocities or kept silent in the face of crimes that violated all human decency. German science and the nation as a whole have been offered something grand and rare in human history and life: a second chance, an open door to a new beginning in a new Europe. I wish the Paul Ehrlich Institute every success in realizing this opportunity and this promise. To conclude with a variation on a favorite phrase of Ehrlich, I wish it "the four essentials—money, patience, skill, and luck."

Max Planck and the Trials
of His Times

◈◈

Germany's leading scientific societies commemorated the fiftieth anniversary of Max Planck's death on October 4, 1997, in a general ceremony. A German physicist assessed his great scientific contributions, and I was asked to speak about his place in German life.

◈◈

MAX PLANCK had a commanding presence on the stage of German history. He was universally admired as a scientist-citizen of the world and as a patriot, yet he was sorely tried and tested as both in his own country. In its ascendancy, he furthered Germany; in its decline, he tried to salvage what could be salvaged. He helped to shape the history of his country and he came to suffer from its deformations; through the prism of his life, that history can be better understood. He acquired a moral authority that in good times raised him to the first servant of science and in evil times plunged him into terrible quandaries.

In our times and in my discipline, it has become rare to speak of individual greatness. Of course the concept has been much abused, like so many others. But not to recognize true stature in a person is a terrible loss, a needless relinquishing of a historical reality. In his work and character, his sense of decency and commitment to practical reason, his unassuming dignity, Max Planck embodied greatness. His joyous capacity for admiration reminds one of Jacob Burckhardt's words: "The power of veneration within us is as essential as the object to be venerated."[1]

Max Planck was born in Kiel in 1858 into a stable world, at least stable in retrospect, midway between the failed revolution of 1848 and the successful unification of 1871; he died eighty-nine years later amidst the ruins of his devastated country. He was heir to honored family traditions: his paternal great-grandfather and his grandfather were widely learned theologians, his father taught law, and his mother came from a family of East Prussian pastors. Theology and civil law were the very pillars of bourgeois life then. It was an age when life had a widely accepted, predictable character: there was little discord between family and society; the precepts of decorum and culture were known and generally observed. This was the case, anyway, for a distinct and privileged stratum: an upper class that enjoyed social and material security, aspired to the harmonious development of the personality, and cultivated knowledge of the classics and the arts, though some even then displayed their learning like ornamental jewelry. There was as yet no cacophony of banal influences. Planck's lifework was dedicated to the advancement of science and in accordance with the humanistic tradition he was raised in; he sought to preserve its unity and to present its philosophical foundations clearly. Much in his life he regarded as self-evident: the attachment to family and fatherland, the sense of duty, and the passion for work.

The fatherland was taken for granted; identification with one's native land particularly in the nineteenth century was conditioned by historical and psychological factors, reinforced by the dramatic historic events, by the impact of Napoleon's conquest or Bismarck's unification of Germany. For Planck, loyalty to the state and patriotic pride were unquestioned values that were part of the family patrimony: Lutheran trust in state authority whose supreme task was to administer justice, to serve as the guarantor of morality and security.

Planck acquired his humanistic education at Munich's Maximilian Gymnasium. A mathematics teacher encouraged his mathematical abilities, but such were his gifts that he did not have the convenience of possessing but one overriding talent. He had remarkable musical gifts and great enthusiasm for music, yet in realistic modesty he decided to relegate music to a life-enhancing avocation. His daily piano playing brought harmony and balance to his life; music also afforded social contacts that his reserve and distance might otherwise have thwarted. It offered chances for companionship, as did the later trios he played with Einstein and his son Erwin. Planck was also an ardent mountain climber well into old age. For him, as for many fellow physicists and other mere mortals, walking in the Alps was joy—joy in the delights of solitude, in nature's sublimity, in the concentrated exertion and accomplishments.*

As a quite young man, Planck chose to study physics, even though he could well imagine himself in classical philology or history. He completed his *Habilitation* in Munich when only twenty-two, but discouragements ensued: Ludwig Boltzmann did not read his thesis and, moreover, theoretical physics had only two professorships in Germany at the time. The field was a neglected speciality and the presumption was that it had been plowed to completion with everything important having already been accomplished. Planck marked time for five long years, during which he had his first encounters with academic envy and professorial squabbles. Thanks to the intervention of Friedrich Althoff, the enlightened despot of Prussian academe, Planck was offered an appointment in Kiel. This gave him the

---

* Another great physicist, Victor Weisskopf, wrote of his own life of physics, music, and mountaineering: "The joy of insight is a sense of involvement and awe, the elated state of mind that you achieve when you have grasped some essential point; it is akin to what you feel on top of a mountain after a hard climb or when you hear a great work of music." Victor Weisskopf, *The Joy of Insight: Passions of a Physicist* (New York, 1991), epigraph.

material independence that allowed him to marry and establish a family. Five years later, in 1889, he was appointed associate professor in Berlin, and then began his astonishing rise.

And the astonishing rise in German life. This was the start of the Wilhelmine age, when the contradictions in the country became ever greater. The economy was flourishing, science and technology were new thriving harbingers of modernity, as was a new openness in the arts and humanities. Simultaneously appeared the young Wilhelm the Second, the insecure kaiser with his love of pomp, power, and militant bravura (*Schneidigkeit*). He embodied the country's contradictions: convinced that he ruled by divine right, he was simultaneously beguiled by modern technology. After Röntgen's great discovery of the X-ray, the kaiser sent him a telegram: "I praise God for granting our German Fatherland this new triumph of science."[2] God, fatherland, and science: the whole legitimating dogma in one sentence.

The initial years were arduous for Planck: Berlin was a tempting but trying stage. The world-famous university was in a state of explosive growth, and both teaching and research were demanding. Science, or *Wissenschaft*, and education then enjoyed a cachet that is scarcely conceivable today; and in Germany, perhaps even more than elsewhere, culture in the broadest sense became a secular equivalent of the sacred, and as such a revered possession of the educated middle classes. Natural sciences became ever more important, ever more expensive and had to fight for their place in academic life. In Wilhelmine Germany, state and society recognized pure science as a *sine qua non* for national prestige, economic advancement, and military power, while the scientists themselves knew that science and scholarship were international, both competitively or collaboratively. In short, ascendant Germany, a nation of disciplined diligence, provided a favorable milieu for science, but, as always, the personal element was decisive. Extraordinary individuals—passionate in their dedication to research, infused with a common ethos, often shielding themselves from the worst disappointments with themselves or others by their friendships—compose the diverse cohort who shaped Germany's second Age of Genius in the decades before 1914. Max Planck personified this second Age.

In Berlin , metropole of power and scholarship, Planck became one of the principal pillars of scientific and intellectual life. He was a university professor—though famously reticent in taking on too many students—and an active member of the German Physical Society and the Prussian Academy of Science. He scarcely missed a meeting of those groups, and soon assumed important functions and offices in them. The members of the academy were drawn from all academic disciplines, and interdisciplinary work was a matter of course, devoid of jargon. The Physical Society began its "Planck era" in 1905, the very moment that Arnold Sommerfeld characterized as the dawn of the "golden age of German physics."[3] Planck also shared editorial control over the leading physics journal. His prodigious activity was a major asset for Berlin, but put a great burden on him as a research scientist and as the head of a family. Many years ago I found in the Munich archive a letter written in 1899 by Planck to Sommerfeld, also a theoretical physicist, in which he declined the invitation to collaborate on an encyclopedia of mathematics: "I have learned from experience over a number of years that a professor in Berlin must, upon proper reflection, use the time left to him after all the endless faculty meetings, exams and reports . . . to further himself and his research; he must, therefore, limit synthesizing presentations to the classroom."[4] "Upon proper reflection," Planck shaped his own life into a harmonious work of art—even in the face of private calamities.

Some of those "endless faculty meetings" involved Planck's brief brush with imperial intolerance. In 1895, the Prussian ministry demanded that a disciplinary procedure be initiated against Leo Arons, a Jewish lecturer in physics, for his involvement in Social Democratic Party activity. Planck, along with the liberal historian Theodor Mommsen and the arch-conservative historian Heinrich von Treitschke, served on a special faculty committee that examined and rejected this request. In this instance, the autonomy of the university and academic freedom were successfully defended.

"Science as a large-scale enterprise," as Adolf von Harnack termed it in 1905, when discoveries were being made fast and furiously, was most demanding, both physically and psychologically. In his moving tributes to colleagues, Planck always emphasized human and personal dimensions, and, as often happens, these encomia contained unconsciously autobiographical elements. Thus about Helmholtz he wrote: "I also came to know his human side and I learned to esteem the man as highly as I always had esteemed the scientist. For in his entire personality, his incorruptible judgment, his unpretentious manner, he embodied the dignity and probity of his science. Added to this was a kindheartedness that touched me deeply. ... A word of acknowledgment or even praise from his lips could delight me more than any external success."[5] Einstein, Max von Laue, Lise Meitner and many of his colleagues regarded Planck himself in the same way.

Planck's own life made him aware of the close kinship between science and art: scientific ideas, he said, originate in "delicate psychological processes within the scientist's mind and world of thought, largely on the level of the unconscious. ... These are divine mysteries."[6] The mystery intrinsic in all creativity often imposes a special vulnerability or fragility on creative persons. This was the epoch when Thomas Mann was portraying the artist's vulnerability, when, as Planck knew, the lives of Boltzmann, Paul Drude, and later Paul Ehrenfest ended in suicide. The Swiss physicist Res Jost correctly noted that "in general, it is difficult for people to imagine the psychological wounds and scars that attend the rise of an acclaimed scientist."[7] Grief and tragedy were Planck's grim companions; notwithstanding, or perhaps for that very reason, he was deeply solicitous about others in his unobtrusive readiness to help.

Within the scientific community, heated debate raged about the nature of scientific knowledge. Planck himself had seen how every advance in knowledge "is accompanied by disconcerting transitional experiences."[8] He thought it part of his responsibility to communicate to a larger public his ideas about the ethos of science and the limits of scientific knowledge. In 1913 he wrote: "The noblest of science's moral qualities and also its most characteristic is without a doubt truthfulness: that fidelity to truth which, through an awareness of personal responsibility, leads to inner freedom. It deserves to be held in far higher regard in our current public and private life."[9] Planck personified this ethos.* But he knew that the answer to the "most important, relentlessly recurrent question in life— how must I act?" cannot derive from science or from laws of causality but must spring from the individual's "moral outlook . . . character . . . and worldview."[10] This demand for personal truthfulness, effort, and commitment fused ascetic austerity and passionate dedication. I see Planck's ethos as an anticipation of Max Weber's superbly demanding "Science as Vocation," a Weberian vow *avant la lettre*. To put it more bluntly: Planck knew that into the temple of science (to use a phrase of Einstein) had crept many mediocrities, eager for the prestige of office, not the seriousness of work. A huge difference, after all, exists between science as a vocation and science as a career.

Planck's paramount philosophical concern was to discover an image of the physical universe, a topic that I can only mention in passing here. In his inaugural address as university rector in 1913, he stated that all scientific work must begin with a hypothesis: "In physics also, the precept holds that there is no

* For more than fifty years Robert K. Merton has analyzed "the ethos of science" in its sociological context. A whole literature has sprung up commenting on his work. My concern is primarily biographical and historical and hence I must limit myself to reminding the reader of Merton's pioneering work. See the collection *The Sociology of Science: Theoretical and Empirical Investigations*, ed. Norman W. Storer (Chicago, 1973).

salvation without faith, at least faith in a certain reality outside us."[11] In a major address in 1929, he said that reason tells us "that each individual, that all human beings, together with our material world, indeed our entire planet, constitute but a negligible nullity within the great, inscrutably sublime expanse of nature, whose laws do not follow whatever emerges in the tiny human brain but existed long before life began and will persist long after the last physicist has vanished from the face of the earth."[12]

In his "Scientific Autobiography"—and the limitation to strictly scientific matters was typical of his reticence—he wrote, "The quest for the absolute seems to me the most exquisite scientific task."[13] As Einstein put it, speaking of Planck, "The longing to behold that prestabilized harmony is the wellspring of the inexhaustible stamina and patience with which Planck dedicated himself to the general problems of science."[14] This search for the absolute, predicated on an assumption of Nature's order, remained science's primary mission. Human knowledge of the laws of nature would deepen, but the quest would be unending. I am reminded here of a stanza from Rilke's *Stundenbuch*, written around the turn of the century:

> I believe in all things heretofore unuttered.
> My most reverent sentiments—these I wish to set free.
> What none have yet dared to desire,
> Will one day spring forth within me.*

The quest for the absolute and religious awe were closely related. Planck was deeply religious, though unattached to any church. In his worldview, nature's absolute order (*Gesetzmässigkeit*) and man's free will coexisted; people were thus not freed from responsibility even in a world permeated by science: "Science and religion . . . need each other. . . . Truthful-

---

* Ich glaube an alles noch nie Gesagte.
Ich will meine frommsten Gefühle befreien.
Was noch keiner zu wollen wagte,
Wird mir einmal unwillkürlich sein.

ness [is the imperative] in the unceasing advance toward an ever more precise knowledge of the natural and spiritual world around us, reverence in contemplating what is forever unfathomable, the divine mystery in one's own breast."[15] Even in the last months of his life, after the catastrophes of war, he continued to lecture on "religion and natural science."* His faith grew in the shadow of terror; his literary gifts remained unimpaired. To read Planck is a singular pleasure: the style of thought and expression, the sober tone of restrained passion testify to his affinity for the classics, for Goethe. His ideas may have lost some relevance in a new age attuned more to biology than physics, but his language remains a model for all scientists of whatever discipline to emulate.

Planck's scientific ethos also determined his assessment of people. In his eyes, intellect and decency were decisive. In judging people, he never thought of applying racial or religious criteria. Although skeptical of admitting female students to the university, he appointed Lise Meitner as his assistant in 1912, an acknowledgment of her creative gifts.

He also thought it was natural to maintain steady contact with colleagues abroad, and membership in foreign academies pleased him. The United States was very much part of the world of global science. In 1909 Planck lectured at Columbia University, making "propaganda for the principle of relativity." A short time before, Paul Ehrlich had also been a guest at Columbia; indeed, many other German scientists visited that other great nation in dynamic growth. Young Americans were flocking to Germany; Harnack was probably correct when he observed shortly before the First World War that

* I. I. Rabi, born forty years after Planck and a fellow Nobel laureate in physics, expressed similar sentiments: "When I discovered physics, I realized it transcended religion. It was the higher truth. It filled me with awe, put me in touch with a sense of original causes. Physics brought me closer to God. . . . Whenever one of my students came to me with a scientific project, I asked only one question, 'Will it bring you nearer to God?' They always understood what I meant." John S. Rigden, *Rabi: Scientist and Citizen* (New York, 1987), p. 73.

"geographically America is for us among civilized countries the most distant; intellectually and spiritually, however, the closest and most like us."[16] Would that appraisal be equally true at the end of the century as it was at the beginning?

Planck could shape his life in the early decades assuming a certain continuity in the political-historical world. The unspoken assumptions of life remained essentially unchallenged. Reluctant revolutionary in science, as a citizen he was loyal to state and monarch, conservative in his fundamental outlook. I doubt that Planck brooded much about politics then. He probably thought himself unpolitical, above the partisan fray, as so many professors did in that era. But that a nonpolitical stance has political consequences—this was overlooked at the time. Planck would not have understood the observation of Gustav Radbruch, the great jurist of the Weimar period, that "nonpartisanship" was the "existential lie" of the authoritarian state.[17] His mission was science, bound to the state in reciprocal gain and steady tension.

Planck's world, familiar and stable, was shattered by the outbreak of the Great War. At first patriotism prescribed political certitude, but doubts, fears, and new responsibilities soon arose. Now he, too, had to confront politics. His voice was heard in public, and in the bustle of committees political disputes became unavoidable.

An accidental circumstance forced Planck instantly to express his political commitment. On August 3, 1914, he was the scheduled speaker at the traditional founders' day festivities at the university, and he began his scientific lecture with a reference to the momentous events of the day: "We do not know what tomorrow will bring. We sense only that almost at once something great and terrifying faces our people, that our homes and lives will be at stake, and the honor, perhaps the survival, of the fatherland. But we can also see and feel in the frightful gravity of the situation that all the moral and physical powers of the country are being fused into a single whole, bursting to heaven in a flame of sacred rage."[18]

Planck's was an early, spontaneous expression of the spirit of 1914, the ardor born of the war's first hours, infused with a pathos that is understandable given that moment; for Planck, it was an unmediated outburst of heart and mind. This pathos was to mark his public speeches throughout the war, while his doubts and sorrow were privately expressed.

August 1914: this effusion of feeling, of sublime communality and joyous readiness for sacrifice, was a prelude to political drama. Especially the academics, especially the upper classes, those who earlier thought of themselves as non- or apolitical, now felt they must assume political-patriotic leadership, and many of them fell prey to rabid chauvinism, as did intellectuals in the Allied nations, and weighty voices were raised in strident unreason. All at once, it became clear that politics would shape and dominate individual lives. But the war with its strict censorship and prevailing chauvinism was a poor introduction to political education.

The great German scientists, who only days and weeks before were extolled around the world, heard the harsh accusations made against Germany and decided to respond in its defense. The result was the Manifesto of the 93, which denied German responsibility for the outbreak of the war, defended the breach of Belgium's neutrality, dismissed as fabrications the alleged atrocities committed by German troops, and proclaimed the identity of German militarism with German culture. The manifesto was signed by Planck and Harnack, Fritz Haber and Paul Ehrlich, and other leading figures. The effect abroad was disastrous. For years to come, the manifesto remained a moral pawn in the hands of the enemy.[19]

Planck experienced the war's horrible fury—and slowly a kind of chasm developed between his public and private life. His speeches retained their harsh tone, but his true aim was to moderate the hatred on all sides. Thus he remained in close contact with one of the great physicists of prewar Europe, Hendrick Antoon Lorentz in Leiden, and tried to reassure him that the Manifesto of the 93—which he and Harnack had signed but read only after its publication—did not quite mean what it said, that final judgments about responsibility would have to await another day. Within the Prussian Academy, he succeeded in preventing the expulsion of members from Allied countries.

Despite the emperor's proclamation that all domestic conflicts must cease (*Burgfrieden*), strife erupted—four years of war polarized and radicalized the nation. The first cause for conflict was the question of war aims: how should the carnage end? In July 1915, when a petition of Pan-German annexationists accumulated almost 1,400 signatures, including many academics, Hans Delbrück launched a counterinitiative, pleading for a negotiated peace: among its 141 signatories were Planck, Harnack, Ernst Troeltsch, and Friedrich Meinecke. Planck belonged to the camp of the "moderates" during the war, true patriots who hoped for a reasonable peace after a German victory.

Planck himself suffered unspeakable personal loss and sorrow: his son Karl, somewhat estranged from his father before the war because of seeming indecisiveness, died of combat wounds incurred near Verdun; his youngest son, Erwin, was taken prisoner by the French. The deaths of his beloved twin daughters, both of whom died in childbirth (in 1917 and 1919), was an unfathomable tragedy.

The sixty-year-old Planck experienced the convulsions of Germany's defeat and revolution, the shattering of everything he had taken politically for granted. At the end of October 1918, he wrote to Einstein of his sense of "piety [toward the crown] and unswerving loyalty to the state to which I belong and of which I am proud, particularly now, in this moment of misfortune."[20] Pride in a time of growth, but love of country in its hour of misfortune—these are familiar sentiments for many of us, I am sure. Just after the revolution, when the Prussian Academy was threatened from within and without, Planck beseeched his colleagues to continue their work: "When the enemy has stripped the fatherland of sword and shield, when we are besieged within by severe crises and perhaps even more trying times loom," then science must be defended, a task for which the academy "is summoned to the front line."[21] Precisely in that "wretched time," as Planck termed it privately, German science was of course a vital necessity; yet it was also crucial for Planck himself. Its safeguarding and support became the principal goal of his prodigious energies. Scientific life, after all, was inseparable from his personal life, the link to friends and colleagues. In calamity Planck rose to his true great stature as the first servant of German science.

How did he view the Weimar Republic? Planck was a staunch monarchist, whose elitist ways were scarcely compatible with the turmoil of popular democracy. After the November Revolution—a misnomer really, since it had left so much intact—those who belonged to the old order felt intellectually and culturally dispossessed. The new regime was well disposed to science, but what of the new culture? A world that could acclaim Georg Grosz and his bitter sarcastic drawings was no longer Planck's world, and the Weimar Republic wasn't either.

Planck probably thought the Republic an unfortunate, temporary embodiment of the eternal German state; he was at best a reluctant "prudential republican" (*Vernunftsrepublikaner*) as many of his friends were. He found himself beset on many fronts and hoped, as he wrote to Sommerfeld in December 1919, to "replace the 'absurdity' of world events ... with 'incomprehensibility.'"[22] (It was a Planckian play on words, I think, alluding to a book by Theodor Lessing then just published and much acclaimed, entitled *History as Rendering the Incomprehensible Comprehensible*.) Yet the world was not really so incomprehensible. He lacked the will that Delbrück, Troeltsch, and many others mustered to revise his earlier views. He could not recognize that in its political irrationality, the old Wilhelmine order had been a disaster; that Germany's leaders bore a certain limited guilt for the outbreak of the war and a heavy burden of guilt for its prolongation and the subsequent defeat—guilt now being foisted on the unfortunate heirs of the old regime. Political insight or truthfulness demanded an overcoming of self.

Nonetheless, Planck was a unique support for his country. His stand and stature were acknowledged internationally; it was largely due to him that Berlin remained the golden hub of the natural sciences. It was he who was instrumental in keeping Einstein in Berlin, and to him that Einstein sent a postcard from Leiden on October 22, 1919, noting that Lorentz "thinks of you always; he repeatedly emphasizes how willingly you complied during the war with his wishes regarding Belgian citizens." Einstein then went on to report the simple news of a world-historical event: that the previous evening, Eddington's letter had been read aloud at the scientific colloquium: "It states that the precise measurement of the plates yielded the exact theoretical value of light refraction. It was providential grace that I could live to witness this."[23] This providential grace must have delighted Planck, because it provided empirical proof for the theory of relativity and confirmed Planck's unswerving support for Einstein's work. Moreover, Einstein now became a veritable national asset, the man best able to help restore the reputation of German science in hostile foreign countries.

When Haber and Friedrich Schmitt-Ott decided in 1920 to set up the Emergency Organization of German Science with a view to securing aid from government and industry, they asked for support from Harnack and Planck. In the world of science, Planck was a key figure, a prospective source of counsel and good judgment. Mounting recognition imposed ever greater burdens—one need think only of Planck's huge international correspondence, executed in his delicate, precise hand.

The early postwar years were especially hard. Planck's memorial address for Heinrich Rubens in 1923 struck a personal note: "Undoubtedly, he suffered unspeakably from the constant spiritual anxieties and disappointments, especially after the conclusion of the so-called peace." Praising Rubens's active collaboration in the London celebrations for the 250th anniversary of the Royal Society in 1912, he added: "That time of an international community of mutual trust lies behind us now, like a beautiful dream, long since vanished and gone."[24]

But neither was there peace within Germany or within the ranks of German science. Political antagonisms exacerbated the rivalries and intrigues that sadly beset academic life in the best of times. In 1920, Planck witnessed the virulent anti-Semitic hate campaign unleashed against Einstein—and he protested publicly. Einstein, warned privately, cancelled his scheduled address at celebrations in 1922 marking the hundredth anniversary of the Society of German Natural Scientists and Physicians. Planck wrote to Laue: "So this trash has actually managed to obstruct a German scientific gathering of historical importance . . . a gang of murderers who, under cover of darkness, furtively pursue their activities unimpeded."[25] "Gang of murderers" was a reference to the murder of Walther Rathenau in June of that year. Planck asked Laue to take Einstein's place, which Laue agreed to do, and Planck thanked him, noting that his appearance instead of Einstein's "has advantages. Namely, it serves to demonstrate that the theory of relativity is not exclusively Jewish, and it takes the wind out of the sails of anyone still wont to think that the entire principle of relativity is nothing but an artful personal advertisement for Mr. Einstein."[26] A year later, Einstein was warned again that his life was in immediate danger; he went to Leiden, and Planck feared he would leave Germany for good: "I am beside myself in anger and rage at those dastardly thugs [*infame Dunkelmänner*] who dared to drive, who succeeded in driving, you from your home, from your place of work."[27] Einstein returned.

That place of work was threatened on many sides, politically and materially. And the intellectual climate was poisoned, too, with a new and ever more pervasive irrationalism that worried many observers. In 1922 came voices of warning from very different quarters: Harnack, for example, declared, "Once again an international romantic wave is sweeping over our fatherland, indeed over the entire cultural landscape of Europe. . . . Instead of 'science,' the call is for 'life,' instead of 'reason' 'intuition,' and a worldview replete with mysterious forces and soul-enhancing elements is supposed to compensate the spirit for the purported collapse of all rational knowledge."[28] Thomas Mann, who during the war had succumbed to the German romantic temptations, now warned against this anti-Western animus and declared his allegiance to the new republic. Planck was concerned about the false prophets of unscientific thinking and their "iridescent froth."[29]

Irrationalism and resentments dampened Planck's hopes for renewed ties between German and Allied scientists. At issue was an end to the Allied boycott of German scientists, who themselves, however, were truculent in refusing any gesture of reconciliation. An intellectual armistice was long in coming. The restoration of international cooperation, for Planck a self-evident necessity, turned out to be slow and laborious.

Planck's responsibilities became ever greater. After Harnack's death in 1930, he succeeded him as chancellor of the Orden Pour le Mérite and as president of the Kaiser Wilhelm Society. It had symbolic significance, this shift in the Orden Pour le Mérite from theologian to scientist, though both men had a philosophic cast of mind. Planck was only seven years Harnack's junior, but was less marked by the Wilhelmine aura than Harnack, who, on the other hand, had been considerably more attached than Planck to the Weimar Republic. But Planck also possessed what Rudolf Vierhaus had praised in Harnack: "the integrity and sovereignty of his personality."[30]

Planck accepted his new leadership functions out of a sense of duty, and, given his immense capacity for work, he acquitted himself faultlessly of all his tasks. He kept his place as master of Berlin physicists, and it was he who persuaded Erwin Schrödinger to come to Berlin as his successor at the university. His colleagues' faith in his character and human wisdom sustained Planck's preeminent place. Lise Meitner's appraisal, from 1958, expressed the common view: "In the forty years I knew Planck and during which he gradually extended trust and friendship to me, I always noted with admiration that he never acted, or refrained from acting, for motives of possible personal gain or harm."[31] Meitner sensed his natural selflessness, which gave him his rare moral authority. He was a gift for German science—which had yet to face its greatest challenge.

History's next blow was the most disastrous: President Hindenburg's appointment of Hitler as Reich chancellor—at first in a cabinet in which the Nazis were a numerical minority. Reactionary politicians had persuaded Hindenburg to give Hitler a position of formal, but limited power; the Nazis' seizure of power, however, came with appalling speed. For millions of Germans, Hitler was a long-awaited redeemer who would deliver them from humiliation and disorder. Among the elites, many believed in Franz von Papen's grand delusion: that Hitler, leader of Germany's largest political party, was now effectively a captive of the conservative camp. These illusions were deeply rooted in Germany's national soil, favored by the Great Depression, massive unemployment, and bloody uncertainties.

Initially, Hitler's triumph was both a challenge and temptation. Here was an extraordinarily deft restaging of August 1914, a celebration of national unity, a great uprising, but this time the enemy was at home, not abroad. Once again politics became political drama, so overwhelming in its power of persuasion that most Germans failed to recognize that they had been robbed of their civil rights and rendered politically impotent. To be sure, Auschwitz was unimaginable, but the character of National Socialism should have been clear, given rhetoric and action. In the fall of 1932, Hitler had publicly identified himself with five stormtroopers who had murdered a Communist in front of his mother in the Upper Silesian town of Potempa. Immediately after the seizure of power, political enemies were dragged to SA cellars and tortured, and in March the press reported the opening of the notorious concentration camp in Dachau—all of this attesting to the regime's inhumanity. Yet even then, people still hoped, fantasized, that these were only temporary horrors, even "understandable" exceptions. A longtime senator of the Max Planck Society, Adolf Grimme, a former Prussian culture minister who endured three years in a Nazi prison, later commented about 1933: "People became victims of their own sense of decency."[32] People could not fathom, did not want to fathom, the brutal indecency of the regime. Yet a proviso is in order: those who did not themselves experience that time of national orgy and terror should be reticent in their judgment—and bear in mind the historical context.

In the spring of 1933, Planck was on a visit to Sicily, in an Italy whose fascist government was much admired by foreigners. I do not know his initial reactions to the new regime: he may have been taken aback, dismayed, but nonetheless impressed. Hitler, after all, was promising to restore German power and to forge a true people's community, proposing a seemingly conservative national agenda. Was that not bound to appeal? Was not the semblance of legitimacy reassuring? The unloved Weimar Republic had after all failed. Planck would have been denying his very self had he allowed himself to question his faith in the state. The state as a criminal agent was an impossible idea for him.

Those probably were his thoughts in a distant land. Within weeks he was rudely confronted with the consequences of National Socialism as it affected people close to him. In January 1933, Albert Einstein was in California; he viewed the new regime as the triumph of the brutal elements in Germany; he called for a worldwide protest against Hitler and refused to return to a country of intolerance and persecution. He told the Prussian Academy he was resigning from it even before Planck asked him to; then came a sorry sequel in which Planck warned his colleagues in the academy that the formal expulsion of Einstein, as the government wished, would "present me with the most distressing conflict of conscience."[33] The academy postponed a decision, but Planck was not spared such conflicts; under National Socialism, a conflict of conscience was the minimal demand made on human decency.

In April 1933, the Law on the Restoration of the Professional Civil Service—that cynical euphemism—ordered the dismissal from the civil service of non-Aryans and persons deemed politically suspect (with the exception of war veterans). "Non-Aryan" made racial descent, not religion, the determining criterion. Fritz Haber, Planck's close associate, a fervent patriot, and director of the Kaiser-Wilhelm-Institute for Physical Chemistry, could have stayed at his post as a war veteran, though a non-Aryan, but he would have had to dismiss his Jewish colleagues. In despair, he preferred to resign, as did James Franck; a few others also chose this honorable option. Planck, one of the very few of Haber's colleagues who was concerned about his predicament, wrote to him in August 1933 that he could not imagine Haber's innermost feelings: "Because the mere attempt to do so makes my heart rebel. In this profound dejection, my sole solace is that we live in a time of catastrophe such as attends every revolution, and that we must endure much of what happens as a phenomenon of nature, without agonizing over whether things could have turned out differently."[34] But this was no phenomenon of nature; whatever else it was, it constituted the wretched failure of the German elites.

At about the same time, Otto Hahn tried to persuade Planck to join a protest against the dismissal of Jewish colleagues: he already had the support of several associates. Planck's reply: "If today thirty professors stand up and protest . . . then tomorrow 150 will come to declare their solidarity with Hitler because they want the [vacated] positions."[35] Perhaps that second figure was an unintentionally generous miscalculation on Planck's part: the number would probably have been greater. A few individuals did protest publicly, yet the general silence in the Third Reich as a whole was deafening. Hahn's initiative would have had considerable moral value and perhaps some practical utility as well: in the spring of 1933 Hitler's regime was still subject to intimidation.

Planck wanted to salvage what was salvageable. Dismayed by the voluntary departure of his successor Erwin Schrödinger, he tried to make clear to other colleagues that they had to stay on. "Continue the work" was the motto, and continuity in both the good and bad sense was the hallmark of German science in the Third Reich. What some practiced on a small scale, Planck did on a large one: ever greater accommodation in public life, unshakeable decency in private life. Age and tradition must also be taken into account: at seventy-five, a man may tend to be more a Pétainist, more an old-style defender of the fatherland than a Gaullist, new-style, revolutionary defender of the fatherland. Planck was devoted to German science, accustomed all his life to accept the authority of the state. To utter "Heil Hitler" was doubtless not easy for him, nor raising his arm in the Nazi salute, but he likely believed that what he called a phenomenon of nature (we might also term it a force of history) required it of him. These feelings led Planck, as president of the Kaiser-Wilhelm-Society, to seek a meeting with Hitler (his report on it has been recently and critically reappraised).[36] Planck wanted to shield Haber and other "valuable" Jews, but had to settle for hoping that the regime would be generous with the Kaiser-Wilhelm-Society in other spheres.*

Only once did Planck risk a public expression of his private decency. At Max von Laue's urging, he decided to organize a memorial for Fritz Haber a year after his death in exile in January 1934. The government and Nazi Party wanted to prevent

---

* On June 10, 1933, Arnold Berliner, the much-admired Jewish editor of *Die Naturwissenschaften*, organ of the Kaiser-Wilhelm-Society, wrote to his friend Wichard von Moellendorff, who had left Germany for Switzerland. He noted how much of value had been destroyed: "And we don't need any more science or art either. The only thing that has remained is what Planck saved of the Kaiser-Wilhelm-Society and one should not underestimate that." Nine years later, on the very eve of deportation, Berliner committed suicide; Max von Laue was the last to see him. Bundesarchiv Koblenz, Nachlass Moellendorff.

such a public ceremony and in any case forbade civil servants from attending. Planck, hoping to persuade the Nazi minister of education, Bernhard Rust, to reconsider his position, reminded him that the Kaiser-Wilhelm-Society had often enough "shown in word and deed its positive attitude toward the state today and its fealty to the Führer and his government." Signed with a "Heil Hitler," the letter received no substantive response.[37] But Planck stuck to his resolve, and the memorial was held with great dignity at Harnack House. The hall was filled, many wives attending in place of their husbands, who had been forbidden or afraid to attend. Otto Hahn gave the principal address and also read a text by the chemist Karl Friedrich Bonhoeffer, Haber's faithful student, who as an academic civil servant was barred from participating. At the end of the stirring ceremony, Planck declared, "Haber kept faith with us; we shall keep faith with him."[38] In that catastrophic time, it took courage to stage this event against the regime's opposition. Sixty-two years later, I should like to express my gratitude: Fritz Haber was my godfather and my parents' avuncular friend.

During the early years of the Hitler regime, Planck tried to defend the interests of pure science, and to that end he had no option but to negotiate with the government. Sometimes he managed to prevail; often the party ideologues carried the day. Thus, his name was sometimes used as a cover for irresponsible decisions—as was Bethmann Hollweg's in the First World War and that of many Germans who held positions of responsibility in totalitarian states. Planck made his compromises, gaining little and surrendering much. But the stance of reluctant accomodation defies facile judgment.

Planck did his duty as he conceived it. He despised much that the new regime did but was probably impressed by some aspects of the new order, by some of its successes. His philosophical lectures often contained indirect criticism; he kept his faith in truthfulness—even in the empire of lies. In August 1934, after Hindenburg's death, he and Laue refused to sign a manifesto drafted by Johannes Stark in support of a plebiscite endorsing the merger of the office of chancellor and president, with Hitler as supreme leader. In the end—and for various reasons—other Nobel laureates also declined to participate, though Laue noted that some notable figures—Furtwängler and Sauerbruch among them—had signed such an appeal. Planck's activities were circumscribed: the Orden Pour le Mérite was de facto suspended; in 1937, he was encouraged to resign from his post as president of the Kaiser-Wilhelm-Society. He submitted to the expulsion of Jews and non-Aryans from various posts and memberships. At some point the government allowed the mention of relativity theory, but Planck refrained from mentioning Einstein's name publicly. (Laue, meanwhile, let Einstein know that he was teaching relativity theory in his seminars, always ironically assuring his students that it had originally been written in Hebrew.)[39] Planck was at times vilified as a "white Jew," yet he had to participate in official ceremonies surrounded by Nazi banners and uniforms; on his eightieth birthday, Hitler sent him congratulations.

Planck regretted the injustice perpetrated against individual Jews; he tried to help where he could. I believe he remained silent about the ever more radical persecution of Jews, about the Nuremberg Laws or the abominations of *Kristallnacht*, about everything that the jurist Ernst-Wolfgang Böckenförde has recently characterized as Germany's civic betrayal of the Jews.[40] But we know that any criticism of the regime's racial policies was dangerous.

When Planck's house in the Grunewald sector of Berlin was destroyed in a bombing raid in 1944, his correspondence was consumed in the flames. In the archives I discovered a letter from Planck to Sommerfeld written in November 1940, when many Germans were still elated over their country's victories on the Western front. These are "sadly grave" times for us, he wrote, adding with a curious mixture of anti-regime defeatism, couched in the repugnant phraseology of the regime, "I, for one, see in current developments basically only a senseless self-decapitation [*Selbstzerfleischung*] of the Aryan-Germanic race. Only the gods know how this will end."[41] In June 1943, Planck met with Lise Meitner in Stockholm and told her, "Terrible things will befall us; we have done terrible things."[42] Many years later, Laue, who had not made any compromises with the regime—and by virtue of formal retirement did not have to—wrote to Meitner: "We all knew that injustice prevailed, *but we did not want to see it*. We deceived ourselves and should not then be surprised that we must pay for it."[43] To my mind, "we did not want to see" can serve as the hallmark of our short century.

Planck came to experience the "terrible things" he alluded to in 1943, personally and mercilessly. His son Erwin, a loyal acolyte of Chancellor Schleicher, had resigned as state secretary in the Reich Chancellery after January 1933; he was in China when the Nazis killed Schleicher and his wife during the Blood Purge of June 1934. He furnished some of the members of the Wednesday Society in 1940 with blueprints for a new constitutional state—the precondition of which was Hitler's removal. Erwin Planck was on close terms with the descendants of Adolf von Harnack and Hans Delbrück, who belonged to groups that sought to rid Germany of Hitler. He probably was in accord with their outlook, but was not privy to any specific plot against Hitler. Given the exceptionally close relations between father and son, we may assume a congruence in their basic ideas, their profound repugnance of the mounting crimes of the regime, their fear of the retribution that would be visited upon Germany. I do not know whether either of them was deluded by the nation's early military victories.

On July 23, 1944—three days after the failure of the plot to kill Hitler—Erwin Planck was arrested; in October, he was sentenced to death by Roland Freisler's People's Court on the basis of his friendship with some of the resisters. Planck tried desperately to save his son's life; he believed that various indirect connections he had with Himmler would make it possible to have the death sentence commuted to a prison term, and various people encouraged him in his hopes. All the more cruel, then, was the indirect news that his son had been executed on January 23, 1945. To Sommerfeld, he wrote: "I have thus been robbed of my closest and dearest friend. My pain cannot be expressed in words."[44] There was no recovery from that loss. Planck had lost two sons in this century's German delirium.

In the history of Europe, Max Planck appears as a German phenomenon: in his rectitude, his achievements, his sacrifices, his moments of political uncertainty. He was a German patriot, but convinced of the absolute necessity of international cooperation. In 1946 he was the only German invited by the Royal Society to the celebration of the three hundredth anniversary of Isaac Newton's birth. He helped in the reestablishment of the Kaiser-Wilhelm-Society, now renamed for him, and his name today is an internationally recognized mark of scientific integrity and research. Memories of the man may have faded—we are the last generation with personal recollection of his times. Perhaps what has also faded is the awareness that human decency, loyalty, and fidelity to truth can be threatened and ravaged by forces of history. As we remember Max Planck's greatness and tragedy today, his son Erwin should also be included in our thoughts. Their lives remain our legacy—and admonition.

Together and Apart: Fritz Haber and Albert Einstein

❖❖

An invitation to speak at the Einstein Centenary in Jerusalem in 1979 first prompted me to write about Einstein's ambivalent relations with Germany. A few years later, in 1983, I was asked to speak at the sixtieth anniversary of the founding of what is now called the Fritz-Haber-Institute-for-Physical-Chemistry in Berlin. Both of those lectures have been previously published.

In 1978, Helen Dukas, who as Einstein's aide over the last twenty-seven years of his life was marvelously knowledgeable about his papers, gave me a file of the Haber-Einstein correspondence and much else from the Einstein Archives, then principally housed and fondly cared for at the Institute for Advanced Study in Princeton. John Stachel extended her help and gave me further access to the Einstein Archives and counsel in using them. I then envisioned a joint study of Haber and Einstein, two friends and near contemporaries, both of whom were important presences in Germany in the decades before Hitler. I collected new archival material in the United States, Europe, and Israel, benefiting as well from my membership on the executive committee of the *Collected Papers of Albert Einstein*—one of the great publishing ventures of our time. The close connections between my parents and Haber, who was my godfather, provided further incentive and access to privately held papers and to personal recollections.

I also accepted invitations to give lectures on Paul Ehrlich, Max Planck, and Chaim Weizmann—scientists and public figures—whose lives were intertwined with those of Haber and Einstein. But the self-liberation of Eastern Europe in 1989 made me wish to turn to other tasks. The present essay, a much shorter version of which was written for a German history of the Kaiser-Wilhelm and Max-Planck-Societies, embodies my archival research over many years, supplemented by selective reading in the vast literature on German science that has appeared in the last decade.

◆◆

> I take pleasure in everything that surpasses my abilities and I rejoice when I can admire.
> *Fritz Haber to Richard Willstätter, ca. 1908*

> The foolish faith in authority [*Autoritätsdusel*] is the worst enemy of truth.
> *Albert Einstein, 1901*

◆◆

IN MARCH 1929, on the occasion of Einstein's fiftieth birthday, Fritz Haber wrote to him:

> Of all the great things I have experienced in the world, the substance of your life and achievement touches me most deeply. In a few centuries the common man will know our time as the period of the World War, but the educated man will connect the first quarter of the century with your name. . . . As for the others, all that will remain will be whatever connection there was between us and the great happenings of our time and in your biography. . . . It won't remain unnoticed that I was your partner for more or less acerbic comments about the business of the [Prussian] Academy with more or less bad coffee that followed the meetings. Thus I serve my own future fame and continued presence in history when for your fiftieth birthday I beg you fondly to take care of yourself so that you will remain healthy and so that I will be able to continue to

mock [people] and have coffee with you and indulge in quiet vanity because I can count myself as belonging to the circle which in a closer and more intimate sense lives with you.[1]

Haber's letter was no mere birthday extravaganza: it defined Einstein's place in Berlin, in the world, and in Haber's heart. By 1929, it had been a decade since the world had begun to acclaim Einstein as the second Newton, as the genius who had revolutionized man's conception of the universe. Most scientists were awed by him, a large part of the public was admiringly mystified by him, a fringe group detested him. Haber, eleven years his senior, a fellow Nobel laureate, was a preeminent chemist known in the scientific world as a talented and indefatigable organizer and promoter of science. He was one of the earliest and most successful scientists to forge a tie between research and industry. The physical chemist Karl Friedrich Bonhoeffer, brother of the martyred theologian Dietrich Bonhoeffer and once Haber's student, wrote of him: "Free of all academic narrowness, he cherished in his work the close reciprocal relationship of technology and pure science. In this way he developed into a scientific personality whose intellectual concern was always devoted to preserving the ties between scientific progress and practical life."[2]

Haber and Einstein first met at a major scientific congress in Karlsruhe in 1911 at which Haber was giving the principal lecture. Haber was about to leave Karlsruhe, where he had led a world-famous laboratory and had discovered the means of fixing nitrogen from the air, a discovery made practicable by the Haber-Bosch process. At the time Einstein was professor of theoretical physics at the German University of Prague; in the scientific world, his papers of 1905 and the special theory of relativity had already marked him as a genius. Soon, in that same year of 1911, Haber came to Berlin to head the Kaiser-Wilhelm-Institute for Physical Chemistry and Electrochemistry, newly financed by Leopold Koppel, a well-known banker of Jewish descent; Einstein came three years later, wooed to

Berlin by Max Planck and Walther Nernst. Haber had used every means to promote Einstein's appointment; in January 1913 he had written to a colleague in the Prussian Ministry of Education that it would be an immense advantage for theoretical chemistry in Berlin to have Einstein there, whom he had already sounded out: "It is a very rare coincidence that not only is such a man available, but his age (34) and personal circumstances favor transplantation, and that his character and his other traits make me very confident of a beneficial relationship."[3]

A famous group photograph taken in 1920 in Haber's institute on the occasion of James Franck's departure for Göttingen shows Franck, Lise Meitner, and Otto Hahn sitting, others standing, and Einstein and Haber perched on the two arms of the couch. The two men *were* in a dominant and unique position: at a time of German greatness, even preeminence, in world science, Einstein exemplified the genius of theoretical conception, Haber that of immediate and practical achievement. Einstein was a solitary master, Haber an impresario of collective greatness. They both gratefully acknowledged the community of scientists they belonged to, the sustaining milieu in which their work flourished.

Haber and Einstein were not only giants of science and intensely private men, but important public figures in the intellectual-social life of twentieth-century Germany: Haber in the service of his country and of science, Einstein in the service of often unpopular political-humanitarian causes. I have found traces of their private and public selves in their correspondence, largely unpublished, in letters that Haber and Einstein wrote to each other, that Haber wrote to his best friend, Richard Willstätter, and that Einstein wrote to Max von Laue. Of course, these letters deal mostly with scientific questions, but they touch other themes as well, for the two men were drawn into politics and public issues by character and by force of events. The Great War and, almost two decades later, Hitler forced them to recognize what Napoleon had said in Erfurt much earlier: Politics is Fate. Their often elegant commentaries are an invaluable source for the history of the times and for the biographies of some of its greatest representatives. Perhaps historian-humanists have undervalued the testimony of their "harder" colleagues, and perhaps historians of science are beginning to clarify the nonscientific dimensions of scientific work.[4]

The letters also express a rare and enviable gift for friendship and candor. Haber, Einstein, Laue, and Willstätter confided in each other, acknowledged to each other their discoveries and their discouragements, their perceptions and their fears. There is no optimum mixture of solitude and friendship that fosters creativity, but I believe these men (and it was very much a man's world) sustained each other in work and through friendship. They had many moments of bleak self-doubt but rarely, perhaps never, any doubt about the value of their common enterprise or the humane quality of their particular group. Until Hitler tore it all asunder, theirs was a tight community of scientists, proud of their achievements and grateful for their collegial life.

In focusing on the private and the public but nonscientific Haber and Einstein here, I am of course omitting an analysis of what was central for them, their work, their reverence for scientific inquiry; but it was inseparable from their inner lives. They knew about the complexity of their own selves and the depths from which their creativity sprang. Thus Haber, who quite often had to apologize for some angry outburst, once wrote to Willstätter: "Oh, dear Richard! Have I so gravely erred that you are still angry! Your approval of me makes me very proud, but your affection means much more to me. Because essentially the psychic is incomparably more important to me than the intellectual and my psyche has simply attached itself to you excessively."[5]

Haber and Einstein formed close collegial relations at once; they esteemed one another. Einstein early on considered Haber an "outstanding physical chemist," and then, in the years

64

CHAPTER 3

1912–14, at a time of great turmoil for him, Haber became his most important confidant and discreet helper. Close personal relations ensued.

Einstein was not blind to his friend's weaknesses, however. In December 1913, he wrote to the woman who was his lover and a few years later was to become his second wife:

Haber's picture unfortunately is to be seen everywhere. It pains me every time I think of it. Unfortunately, I have to accept that this otherwise so splendid man has succumbed to personal vanity and not even of the most tasteful kind. This defect is in fact generally and unfortunately a Berlin kind. When these people are together with French or English people, what a difference! How raw and primitive they are. Vanity without authentic self-esteem. Civilization (nicely brushed teeth, elegant ties, dapper snout [geschniegelter Schnauz], perfect suit) but no personal culture (raw in speech, movement, voice, feeling).

Einstein reversed the then-popular formulation that culture was a German treasure, while others had mere civilization—and of course his own appearance became famous for its quiet protest against German civilization.[6] In appearance, Privy Councillor Haber and self-styled gypsy Einstein were opposites, but less so in spirit. And opposites attract. They complement each other.

In the spring of 1914 Einstein's wife, Mileva Einstein-Marić, and their two sons came to Berlin and for a while they lived with Fritz and Clara Haber, as Mileva had done before. Meanwhile Einstein was a guest at Haber's institute, their rooms close by. Haber knew that Einstein's marriage, long troubled, was near its end; and yet Einstein hesitated and, perhaps impetuously, drew up a memorandum of conditions under which he would stay with Mileva: this astonishing document required her complete subjugation to his monumental will. Mileva told Haber she would accept the conditions, and Einstein wrote to her that she would have to understand that his "sole" reason for thinking of staying with her was his attachment to the boys, that "a friendly relation" with her was out of the question; it would be "a business relation." He would behave correctly "as I would vis-à-vis a strange woman."[7]

This brutal conduct may have been designed to force Mileva to seek a final break, for Einstein wanted to be free for his work and for his new love. By July it came to a separation, and Haber drew up the agreement by which Einstein would pay Mileva 5,600 marks for annual support.* On July 29, Mileva and the boys left Berlin; Einstein said goodbye to them at the railroad station, weeping at the loss of the boys with Haber at his side. "Without him I wouldn't have been able to do it," he later said; distraught, he spent the evening with his friend.[8] Three days later, the Great War broke out.

Einstein—more robust physically and less worldly than Haber—had found a paternal friend who was ready to help, an adviser in practical matters. Haber had been one of the first to know of Einstein's love for his cousin Elsa (who after her divorce had dropped her married name, Löwenthal, in favor of her maiden name, Einstein). On the day after Mileva's departure, Einstein wrote to Elsa that Haber thought she was the right kind of wife for him, since he also thought Einstein was not "a hard non-human [*harter Unmensch*], rather he loves me as he did before."[9]

The greatest discretion was required to avoid a "scandal" in Berlin. Einstein instructed Haber to inform Planck and a few

---

* It may be useful to set that sum in a comparative context. By 1913, an average worker's wage was roughly 1,450 marks, a high civil servant's approximately 7,000 marks, and the highest government officials received between 10,000 and 25,000 marks. This rough scale applied to a period of currency stability—it was sharply different in times of inflation in the 1920s. The settlement also gave Mileva the total stipend of a Nobel Prize that Einstein was expected to be awarded in the future. He proved an excellent investment. For salary scales, see Hans-Ulrich Wehler, *Deutsche Gesellschaftsgeschichte*, volume 3 (Munich, 1995), pp. 606, 1029–1034.

others of his separation. Einstein wanted to keep his relations with Elsa a secret and reconsidered his earlier decision to marry her. He wanted to avoid another entanglement, another imprisonment, as he called it in a letter to his friend Heinrich Zangger in 1915. He also feared that his sons would object to his remarrying. He resented the pressures of Elsa's parents; they sprang from conventional bourgeois considerations.[10] Finally Einstein yielded.

The divorce proceedings began in Zurich in mid-1918, with Einstein acknowledging that he had told his wife of his adulterous affair. A divorce decree was finally granted in February 1919, and in June Einstein married his cousin. Almost precisely a year earlier, he had told Elsa's twenty-year-old daughter, Ilse, that he was in love with her, too, but he left the decision whether to marry the mother-mistress or the daughter (with whom, he said, he desired to have a child) to the two women. Or so Ilse described her dilemma to an older friend.[11] Haber— in such matters far more conventional than Einstein—would not have known of this appalling episode, but for more than a decade Haber was still the mediator between Einstein and Mileva, who lived in sorrowful circumstances in Zurich.

Haber also experienced anguish and failure in his two marriages. Perhaps these similar fates deepened their bond. Haber was one means for Einstein to protect the childlike apartness which, as Erik Erikson once remarked, was his special characteristic.[12] Haber's capacity for friendship was legendary; in 1915 Einstein wrote to a Swiss friend, "At a time like this one realizes that the only thing in the world which is truly worth aspiring to is the friendship of excellent and free persons" who are immune to all manner of calumnies.[13] Haber may have taken special pleasure in holding the hand of the volatile, melancholy, high-spirited Einstein. They shared a marvelous talent for gaiety, for laughter, for ironic contemplation of their world, even if Haber occasionally indulged in pathos and Einstein in irreverent, often mordant wit. No wonder that Schiller

was Haber's favorite author, Heine Einstein's. Their friendship, which ended only with Haber's death, was time and
again invoked in their correspondence. (The familiar "Du" was
missing—perhaps on account of the difference in their ages
and their antithetical styles of life.)

They shared much: both cherished the scientific ethos, even
if their ambitions and professional paths diverged; both were
autodidacts; both had known early, daunting failures. They
both had a sense of their calling and an austere view of their
profession. They would have understood Freud's assessment
in 1910: "Science betokens the most complete renunciation of
the pleasure-principle of which our minds are capable."[14] The
psychic compensations are incalculable. In 1913, Einstein confessed to Elsa, while complaining about his wife and mother:
"No wonder that under these conditions my love for science
flourishes, for it lifts me out of my vale of tears to quiet
spheres, impersonal and without rebuke and complaint."[15]
This emphasis on sacrifice was an expression of the prevailing
notion that suffering was the precondition for creativity. For
Haber and Einstein, the very nobility of science demanded sacrifice and exacted renunciation. In both cases, personal commitment and a steady pattern of overwork took a toll on their
health—and also served as an excuse for their egotistical exploitation of others. The wives of many famous scientists may
have enjoyed acclaim in public but in private had to endure
their husbands' absence and indifference.

Haber and Einstein saw in science the great transcendental
experience; they were awed by nature's inexplicable mysteries.
Einstein opened a speech at Planck's sixtieth birthday in April
1918, saying: "It is a many-mansioned building, this temple of
science." If one of God's angels were to cast out the merely
ambitious and merely practical from this temple, there would
remain "somewhat peculiar, reserved, lonely fellows . . . who
despite these common characteristics would resemble each
other less than do those who were expelled from the crowd."

What led the true followers to the temple? Einstein cited Schopenhauer, saying that one of the strongest motives leading to art and science was "a flight . . . from everyday life with its painful rawness and desolate emptiness, away from the chains of one's own ever-changing desires." Planck's "inexhaustible endurance and patience . . . which makes possible such achievements, resembles the state of a religious person or a lover: the daily striving does not spring from a precept or a program, but from an immediate need."[16]

Haber and Einstein had a sense of science as a call to a special priesthood in a faith only recently established. Both men belonged to a generation whose roots were in the old humanistic culture but who stood at the frontiers of knowledge, where it was exhilarating and exacting to belong to "this band of brothers." The giants were few in number and still sovereignly broad in knowledge. Of course there was conflict and ignominy as well: often enough they encountered rivalry and meanspirited colleagues. Above all, they came to realize that they could not escape the "painful rawness" of everyday life and Germany's tradition-laden anti-Semitism.

They were both born to Jewish parents in a German world in which many Jews flourished, in which Jews experienced their own ascendancy—their own quickened path of modernity—and where, despite and because of their own spiritual and social mobility, they encountered a bewildering range of responses, from reticent hospitality to all manner of anti-Semitic hostility. From the start the two men had different views about the meaning of their Jewishness, about the ways in which their Jewish origins should find expression in their private and public lives. Their differences suggest something of the vast diversity of German Jewry; their friendship suggests something of the solidarity that still prevailed.[17]

By the late nineteenth century, an ever increasing number of Jews, especially well-to-do Jews, found a spiritual home in German culture, in German philosophy, literature, and music. With many German Protestants they shared a *Kulturreligion*, a special veneration of past greatness, of *Bildung*—that hallowed blend of classical learning and humanist cultivation—acquired individually and institutionally, genuinely or by academic certification alone, and it was often *Bildung* with a Christian-ethical tone. In this, they had more in common with secular German *Bürger* than with Orthodox or East European Jews, whose very presence often embarrassed them. But with fellow Jews they shared recollections of a more or less common past and intermittent reminders of the prejudices against them and of remaining disabilities. In Prussia, where most German Jewry lived and where they were excluded from positions of the greatest distinction—from the officer corps and the higher ranks of the civil service, for example—they were disproportionately strong and successful in the free professions, in law, medicine, and science. How were they to grasp that they were prosperous pariahs?

Even secular and successful Jews were deeply divided regarding the prospects that their new legal emancipation would lead to genuine equality. For a small but growing minority, the pull of German culture and their wish for full assimilation in it were so great, and the residual Judaism so feeble, that conversion to Protestantism, a kind of *Vernunftreligion*, seemed a natural step.[18] In the beginning of the nineteenth century, some of the earliest converts thought that Christianity was a higher or better religion than Judaism.[19] Adult conversions, infant baptisms, and mixed marriages became slightly more common among urban Jews in the early years of this century, particularly during the 1920s. The fact that adult conversion or baptism at birth brought with it civic advantages (somewhat easier access to positions in the civil service, which, of course in Germany included all academic posts) spurred some and deterred others, among them men and women of equal or even greater closeness to a Christian faith than those who did convert.

Haber and Einstein chose differing paths, in consonance with their respective backgrounds, characters, and ambitions.

Haber's course was probably closer in spirit to what many upper-class German Jews felt than Einstein's; Einstein's unusual course confirmed his apartness.

HABER's life began in ordered comfort and private grief. His father, Siegfried, a prosperous dye and paint manufacturer in Breslau, was an esteemed city councillor, a *Stadtrat*, a presence in the city's corporate and civic life. Haber's mother died within weeks of his birth in 1868, and nine years later, his father married a much younger woman. In his widowhood, he treated young Fritz with Spartan severity, assuming, as was the German wisdom of the day, that denial or silence would dull the pain of his orphaned state. The son may have been a constant reminder of his own loss, perhaps even imagined as the cause of it. In time three daughters were born to the second Mrs. Haber, and Fritz was very much the older solicitous brother. He was close to his stepmother and stepsisters; the father lavished love on the young wife and three daughters, but the son's independence alarmed him. Haber's vulnerability, his streak of melancholy, the physical fragility and psychic anxiety, was probably related to his motherless childhood. We know little about it, though we do know that in many ways he disappointed his father, who was fully reconciled to him only after his worldwide renown.[20]

Breslau had a large and respected Jewish community. The university, for example, had many Jews on its much-esteemed medical faculty , and in some circles Jewish-Christian collegiality and friendship prevailed. In the decades before 1914, prosperous or professionally successful Jews could face the future with some confidence. For many Jews from the East, like Siegfried Haber's forefathers, Breslau was the true entrance to German life, to German culture and business, the starting point for a great social leap. Like their Christian neighbors, Silesian Jews tended to be Prussian super-patriots, remembering that Frederick the Great had wrested Silesia from Austria in 1740. Siegfried Haber—his very name a gesture of assimilation—

named his son after "der alte Fritz," and added a biblical middle name, Jacob. Following German custom, Fritz never used his middle name, except on a few official documents—an omission of accidental symbolism.

The young Fritz was born three years before Germany's unification; his childhood coincided with Prussia's fervent exaltation of German arms and German unity. An early photograph shows him as a four-year-old with a toy gun in his hand presenting arms, as it were. The picture was prophetic: Haber had a bent for discipline and rank; in later life he was to have especially close ties to the army. One of his favorite authors was Thomas Carlyle, the apostle of hero-worship, and one of the qualities he most admired and consciously came to seek was leadership.

Paternal ambition and prevailing custom shaped Fritz's early schooling. At the age of ten, he was enrolled in the most prestigious of Breslau's five gymnasia, which provided a superb drill in classical and literary studies, as was the ideal of all gymnasia at the time. Jewish students were disproportionately represented in the gymnasia—highly disproportionate to their numerical presence in the population, less so if wealth is the criterion. A gymnasium, of course, offered more than an exacting general education; it conferred privileges and was also the high road to social status. A boy who attended gymnasium for five years could fulfill his military service in one privileged year instead of the two or three years imposed on lesser mortals; a student who completed the full nine years and passed the final examination, the *Abitur*, could automatically enter any German university. So the gymnasium was the gateway to the German *Bildungsbürgertum*, with its broad humanistic learning, its privileges and pretensions. The gymnasium had a special appeal for Jewish parents: it satisfied their wish for education and social recognition.

Fritz was a good but not an outstanding student; in school he acquired a broad literary culture that enriched his whole life and found reflection in his lifelong delight in versification;

poetic efforts were highly esteemed in the *Bildungsbürgertum*. Haber's father was wary of the boy's exuberance and occasional high-spiritedness—whether expressed in poetry or in scientific experiments that sometimes ended in mishap and accident.* Fritz's habit of inventing extravagant fairy tales for his stepsisters—indicative of a rich fantasy life—did not help.

As a seventeen-year-old, Fritz passed his *Abitur*, following which and much against his own inclination he took a job in a Hamburg business. But he quit after a few months, returned briefly to Breslau, and in the fall of 1886 enrolled in the University of Berlin to study physics and chemistry; he received his doctorate there—after several years in Heidelberg as well—in 1891. In between he did his one-year service with the army, in a regiment of field artillery stationed in Breslau, which also gave him a chance to attend lectures in philosophy and to participate in the Akademisch-Literarischer Verein (ALV), a largely Jewish fraternity substitute where he found congenial partners in cultured conversation.**

* Years later, Haber told my father that he had participated in the usual *rite de passage* of students on the final night of examinations: they caroused all night with bouts of heavy drinking. He returned home, late, but on his own; the next morning he missed the early family breakfast. The angry father took his three daughters to Fritz's room, pointed to the sleeping stepbrother and admonished all: "Look well, that is how the life of a drunkard begins." Rudolf A. Stern, "Fritz Haber: Personal Recollections," *Leo Baeck Yearbook* 8 (1963), p. 72.

** In 1924 Haber delivered the principal speech for the fiftieth anniversary of the fraternity. He recalled the halcyon years before the war, the unreflected patriotism of the time that "was without political content. What did we care about the struggles of political parties, their alien agitation about economic interests and social questions." One lived in a satiated Reich, "strong in all eternity," safe against any enemy. "And didn't we live in that Reich with all the sense of ordered freedom, with all the carefreeness of a youth educated in modesty, sure in its prospects of an adequate life provided one applied oneself? Wealth was no goal and money no value for which it was worth living, and social questions were far removed from us: because we knew nothing about the worker and we were naively *bürgerlich* to the very depths of our being." Only later, in Wilhelmine Germany, was patriotism mobilized "to master inner difficulties that had arisen from new social questions." A retrospective apologia for the ideals of the unpolitical German—by someone who believed in the old values and excelled in adapting to the new technological-capitalist world. *Aus Leben und Beruf* (Berlin, 1927), p. 29.

Haber's teachers, including Hermann von Helmholtz and Robert Bunsen, were famous, but as lecturers uninspiring. A semester spent at the ETH, the renowned Federal Institute for Technology in Zurich, was not much better, and his own work for the doctorate—then and now a much less exacting requirement in Germany than in the United States—also seemed short of brilliance.

After his doctorate and military service, another commercial interlude followed, including an unhappy stint in his father's business. Siegfried wanted him to carry on the family tradition, perhaps needing the reassurance that comes from a son following in the footsteps of the father. But Fritz had his own bent—science—and his own avocation—literature.* He wanted an academic career, which—in the end—was to be marked by intense practicality, by paradigmatic closeness to industry, business, and politics.

But Haber discovered for himself that there was nothing easy about an academic career. In his magnificent "Science as Vocation," Max Weber in 1918 was to warn against its hazards: "If he is a Jew, of course one says *lasciate ogni speranza* [abandon all hope]. But one must ask every other man: Do you in all conscience believe that you can stand mediocrity after mediocrity, year after year, climb behind you, without becoming embittered and without coming to grief?"[21] To begin with, one needed a professor who would agree to sponsor the *Habilitation*, an original work of research, which brought with it the right to give university lectures. Repeatedly Haber encountered indifference and rejection, including from the eminent chemist Wilhelm Ostwald.

In 1892, as a twenty-four-year-old, Haber was baptized in the Evangelical Church of St. Michael in Jena—to the dismay of

---

* Years later, in Haber's appreciation of the chemist Justus von Liebig, an autobiographical note, conscious or unconscious, crept in: "There is hardly anything more impressive than the passionate will of an outstanding young person who directs his life toward an idealistic, idiosyncratic goal." "Gedächtnisrede auf Justus von Liebig," *Zeitschrift für angewandte Chemie* 41, no. 33 (August 18, 1928), p. 892.

his father. Conversion, a relatively rare step even for assimilated Jews, was in some ways a tacit recognition of what I have called "the silent secularization" that had come to characterize German Protestantism and Judaism alike. Many of the German Protestant bourgeoisie retained but a faint religious commitment; in their liberal Christianity, a synthesis of a new *Kulturreligion* and the ethical imperatives of the New Testament, the church was simply a place for baptism, perhaps for confirmation, for marriage, and for burial. The faith of some Jews was similarly attenuated: they had abandoned Jewish dietary laws, they put their faith in modernity and reason, and they went to temple, if at all, only on the High Holidays. Having distanced oneself from the Jewish heritage, one was a step closer to conversion, which would mark one's association with the historic fundament of European civilization and one's final bond with Germanness, with the German nation. Germans who had propounded Jewish emancipation had more or less tacitly assumed that this emancipation would bring many Jews to the church; it was a kind of unspoken bargain.[22]

Conversion usually involved a mixture of belief and opportunism; in each instance the balance may have been different. I have found no evidence that Haber's conversion marked a great spiritual or intellectual moment. He knew that conversion brought with it practical rewards in the form of greater social acceptance, but it also reinforced the ambiguities and ambivalences that marked the life of German Jews. Converted Jews faced the skepticism of some of their new co-religionists and the likely scorn of some of their old ones.* Haber certainly exemplified another truth: like other converts, he retained his consciousness of the Jews' historic apartness, his ever-present sorrowful pride at their collective suffering and achievement. Most of his friends were Jews or of Jewish descent.

* Christians had many grounds for skepticism. In Shakespeare's *The Merchant of Venice* (act 3, scene 5), the newly converted Jessica repeated to her Christian husband what had been said to her: "You are no good member of the commonwealth, for in converting Jews to Christians, you raise the price of pork."

Haber's conversion sharpened the conflict with his father, who, practical man though he was, had not taken this step; his own brother had. Nor had Haber's best friend in later years, Willstätter, raised in similar circumstances; indeed, he felt very differently about conversion. Willstätter had been deeply moved by the New Testament, he wrote, but "conversion to Christianity was never an option for me" because—and here he quoted Walther Rathenau's words—"a spiritual measure must lose its purity if it leads to material advantages." Like Rathenau, like many other Jews, he rejected conversion as a form of opportunistic capitulation; again like Rathenau, he deeply disliked Germany's ostentatiously rich Jews. "A genuine equality of Jews," he wrote after Hitler's accession to power, "has never been achieved in Germany." I doubt that Haber ever talked with either Willstätter or Einstein about his conversion. It seems to have been a subject shrouded in silence.[23]

An ambitious twenty-four-year-old bent on an academic career must have known the practical advantages in conversion. (Jews had access to the lower academic ranks, but hardly any to the professorial level. Christians of Jewish origin—and the origin was hardly ever forgotten—had a somewhat easier time. The same applied to other positions.) Haber may have been encouraged by a proselytizing Protestant theologian, as his second wife suggests in her utterly unreliable memoirs.[24] But his decision was also consonant with his intense patriotism—which, however, was free of the appalling chauvinism of his time. In addition there was his ambition.

Haber's conversion came after a long stretch of professional frustrations, and these did not cease for some time. For years he cast about, trying to find *métier* and mentor. He had begun by studying the then-dominant field of organic chemistry, but gradually he turned to the newer and less populated field of physical and especially electrical chemistry. At every step he encountered failures and rebuffs. Much later, Willstätter commented that despite Haber's great gifts and rare combination of energy and patience, "his early failure was complete and of long duration."[25]

He paid a price for his restless ambition. He was easily wounded; he had little experience of inner calm. His impatience, his sense of drama, and his yearning for achievement deepened his dissatisfaction. That sense of drama allowed him—especially in moments of exuberance—to tell stories of mixed fact and fantasy, often with a beguiling self-deprecation.*

In 1898, Haber delivered a lecture at the German Electrochemical Society—the forerunner of the Bunsen society—which by its intensity and breadth impressed some and exasperated others; it was anything but an ordinary debut before one's peers. The meeting was chaired by the renowned Friedrich Wilhelm Ostwald, who twenty-four years later recalled the dazzling performance in which, he said, Haber had moved with the speed of an express train, leaving auditors accustomed to a more leisurely pace behind. Ostwald forgot his own annoyance at the brashness of the twenty-nine-year-old. Later that year Haber was made an associate professor at the Karlsruhe Polytechnikum or Technical Institute.[26]

In 1900 Karlsruhe created its first chair in physical chemistry, and a student of Ostwald, Max LeBlanc, was appointed—much to Haber's chagrin. LeBlanc was a mere three years older than Haber, and by this time Haber had already created for himself a reputation inside and outside Germany for his teaching; his laboratory was attracting more and more foreign students. LeBlanc's appointment may have been due to lingering

---

* The best-known of these stories—pure fantasy, of course—has been recounted over and over again: how during an Alpine hike Haber, desperately thirsty, finally came upon a village fountain with good cold water, and thrust his head into the basin at the very moment that an ox did the same; when both emerged, they had exchanged heads. Thereafter, Haber added, his academic career became much easier. Has anyone asked whether this fantasy might be about his baptism—which after all was a form of immersion and which did facilitate his academic career? Was the ox, known to be a beast of strength and sullen stupidity, the gentile?

anti-Jewish prejudice or to some prearrangement with Ostwald; in any case, Haber felt ill-treated and sought other jobs.

In August 1901 Haber married Clara Immerwahr, two years younger than himself, a highly talented woman, also from Breslau, also of Jewish descent, who had converted in 1897. She came from an affluent secular family and Haber had known her as a student when she received her doctorate in chemistry *magna cum laude* in Breslau, probably the first woman to do so at that university. After an exceptionally difficult pregnancy she gave birth to a son, Hermann, on June 1, 1902. Three months later Haber left his family for a five-month professional trip to the United States—an unusual disappearance from the family even in an age when a husband's vocation enjoyed unquestioned primacy. We can glean a picture of growing difficulties in the marriage from the amazingly candid correspondence that Clara Haber carried on with her old teacher and her husband's friend, Richard Abegg. In 1909, she wrote to him:

> What Fritz gained in these eight years, that—and much more—I have lost, and whatever remains of me fills me with the deepest dissatisfaction . . . and if I must blame a part of . . . [my dissatisfaction] on a particular trait of my character, the major part must be placed unquestionably on Fritz's smothering assertiveness for his person in the home and in the marriage, next to which any being which is not even more inconsiderate . . . would go to pieces. . . . All of Fritz's other human qualities except this one [the will to work] are close to shrinking and he is, so to speak, prematurely old.[27]

The letter bespeaks fiercely formulated resentment and is in striking contrast to the view others had of Haber, and we may view her indictment with a certain skepticism. In his circle of colleagues, students, and friends Haber was considered lively and scintillating. But if he was brilliant among others and then exhausted at home, the discrepancy would have been

wounding to this intelligent woman who had her own ambitions. But it is also true that it was a marriage between two
extravagantly difficult people, contracted at a time of exceptional stress for both. During that period Haber was involved
in a bitter, critical dispute with the great Walther Nernst.
Months before his marriage and for years thereafter, Haber
apologized to Abegg for his excessive "irritability" and extreme nervousness, and blamed these on overwork and the
fact that he had had no vacation for years.[28]

But it was also the period of Haber's scientific triumphs at
the Technical Institute of Karlsruhe, capital of the liberal
grand-duchy of Baden, where he worked from 1894 to 1911.
Much later he recalled his "impression of greater political maturity . . . [in Baden] and greater willingness to be considerate
. . . than in the more class-oriented North."[29] He became a respected member of the international scientific community, an
internationalist with a strong Germanic core and a notable German bearing.

Haber also became ever better known in the world of chemistry. In 1902 the German Electrochemical Society appointed
him its delegate to a convention in the United States, charging
him with assessing the state of chemical training in America.
Endowed with a society's grant and a personal subvention of
2,000 marks from the renowned chemist Jacobus van't Hoff,
Haber set sail in September—the trip that took him away from
Clara and the baby.

At the time the United States was a great, enigmatic mag-
net for cosmopolitan Europeans: a distant power in dynamic
ascendancy. Haber gathered impressions in America and—
despite his faulty English—established collegial relations.
Upon his return, he published a report that attested to his intellectual acuity and precision and his clear command of language: "Today there is no country in the world to which we
devote more attention and concern." Grasping the connection
among social mores, scientific development, and technology,
he emphasized the peculiarities of the American character:

"The self-confidence . . . of the individual as well as of the people is perhaps the most important trait of the American spirit. It is documented in . . . the early independence which the young demand, in the hypersensitivity of the mass of the people, which we note with great surprise as it is mirrored in the daily press." He noted that American professors had to teach more for lower compensation and less prestige than their German counterparts. Critical of much about the American system, he defined his own ideal for measuring the achievement of the teacher; by how far "the student's capacity for independent thought is developed." Haber had an abiding interest in what he himself excelled in: pedagogy.*

Haber sketched the ever-closer developing relations between the United States and Germany—and yet the two countries still knew little of each other: "We all know the caricature of the American, who tirelessly runs after the dollar and who because of his wish for self-enrichment loses the sense for law and order as well as the interest in any kind of intellectual culture." But Americans also have a caricature of the Germans: "We are looked upon as a people that bow to the top and are rough to the people below, that regard medals and civil service positions as the most devoutly wished-for goals, that are comfortable in voluntary political nonage and that pass on the pressure which they gladly accept from officialdom to their wives and daughters, whom in marriage as in life they shortchange when it comes to freedom and educational rights." He understood America's economic challenge: "Bismarck's avowal that the Germans fear no one but God is gradually but seriously amended in business circles: 'and a little the United States.'"[30]

On his return from America, Haber faced new frustrations because of his slow advancement. The next step was a full professorship; his hopes for a chair in Vienna were dashed when

* From the mid-1920s, he encouraged my mother in her work on child education, her modifications of Montessori thought and methods; she dedicated her two books on education to him.

he informed his principal supporter there that he was a "baptized Jew." To a colleague in Frankfurt he wrote: "It is very difficult for me to get a chair anywhere. Religion and—if it is not immodest to say—achievements equally obstruct my way. Jews or baptized Jews are not wanted in the major positions." In the other positions, scientific productivity intimidated colleagues *in situ*. He needed a laboratory big enough for him to have a few students, one assistant, some equipment, and a salary that would be above the 3,300 marks "which I get here, *tout comprise*. And *last not least* I must be independent. Because I don't want to be anybody's assistant."[31] He wanted to be a leader. And he was impatient.

Meanwhile Haber taught, published, carried out his own experiments, obtained patents, and continued to give expert opinions to industry and public authorities. He was best at the intersection of theory and experiment, of scientific research and technical applicability. He began to work with some of the leading industrial firms in Germany. In 1904, he signed a contract with Carl Zeiss of Jena, the world-famous optical company, assigning to them the rights to develop a discovery of his, which, if commercially successful, was to yield him a 5 percent royalty for the fifteen-year term by which German law protected patents.[32] In 1905 appeared his *Thermodynamics of Technical Gas Reactions*, hailed as an important milestone. In 1906, he was made a full professor at Karlsruhe, thus at the age of thirty-eight attaining his academic goal.[33] In 1907, he received a call to Zurich and Karlsruhe responded by a generous counter-offer. He stayed—to the great satisfaction of students and colleagues.

Together with his British colleague Robert Le Rossignol, Haber now turned to what was to become his greatest single achievement: the fixation of nitrogen from the air. For some years this task had been regarded as a tremendous challenge— scientific, economic, and commercial. In 1898, in his presidential speech to the British Assocation for the Advancement of Science, Sir William Crookes, distinguished chemist, had raised a Malthusian specter of terrifying magnitude: "The world's demand for wheat—the leading bread-stuff—increases in a crescendo ratio year by year." Prospective demand far outstripped prospective production; the two leading producers of the time, the United States and Russia, would have to cut back on exports in order to feed their own peoples, he guessed, and the likely supply of new arable land would be inadequate to meet the demand. "For a long time guano has been one of the most important sources of nitrogenous manures," he went on, "but guano deposits are so near exhaustion that they may be dismissed from consideration." Britain was particularly vulnerable because it was dependent on wheat imports, which in wartime might be jeopardized. This would be disastrous because "the very first and supremely important munition of war" was food. Germany's needs were equally great—though Crookes did not say so. Its agriculture depended heavily on the use of saltpeter, half of which it imported from Chile. Between 1902 and 1904, the price of Chilean saltpeter rose by 25 percent; experts believed the supply would be exhausted in thirty years.

Crookes called on chemists to come to the rescue: "The fixation of atmospheric nitrogen therefore is one of the great discoveries awaiting the ingenuity of chemists. . . . Unless we can class [the fixation of nitrogen] among certainties to come, the great Caucasian race will cease to be foremost in the world, and will be squeezed out of existence by races to whom wheaten bread is not the staff of life."[34]*

* Following custom, Sir William also surveyed scientific progress in other realms. At the end he reaffirmed his own belief in psychic research, above all in telepathy, "with the fundamental law . . . that thoughts and images may be transferred from one mind to another without the agency of recognized organs or sense." In support he cited the work of Breuer, Freud, and William James. He ended with a peroration to science: "Steadily, unflinchingly, we strive to pierce the inmost heart of Nature, from what she is to reconstruct what she has been, and to prophesy what she yet shall be. Veil after veil we have lifted, and her face

Chemists of many countries were after the big prize, as were the major chemical firms. There was good reason for Germany to win the race: its chemical plants were preeminent in the world. By 1900, they had a virtual monopoly on the production of dyestuffs. In this burgeoning field there was bitter competition—and the beginning of rationalization amongst the principal firms. In 1906 the Badische Anilin-und-Soda Fabrik (BASF), Bayer, and AGFA (the last having been founded by Paul Mendelssohn Bartholdy, son of Felix and a relative of the family controlling the famous Berlin banking house) formed an Interessengemeinschaft, which historians call the little IG—forerunner of the later giant IG, a cooperative arrangement whereby the three firms shared profits and some business intelligence.[35] In this second Industrial Revolution, led by chemical and electrical firms, the unique German mixture of competition and cartelization proved remarkably successful.

The chemical industry was indeed the prime example of Germany's economic triumph: the industry itself, which had close links to banks and thus to credit, sought out leading scientists; the state supported its academic-industrial dynamism; and German labor performed its tasks with incomparable skill and dedication. The world gradually grasped the magnitude of this emergent force, though "it was a long time before it occurred to some observers that the attitude of the German people was as important as technical or educational causes."[36] Here was born the academic-industrial-banking complex so characteristic of imperial Germany, forerunner of its still vaster military-industrial-academic complex that emerged in the First World War.

Germany's industrial magnates had an exquisite eye for scientific talent; they competed for it, both in the technical universities, which carried less prestige, and in the old humanistic

grows more beautiful, august, and wonderful, with every barrier that is withdrawn." Sir William Crookes, "Address," *Report of the British Association for the Advancement of Science*, 1898, vol. 68, pp. 30–31, 33.

the electrochemical division of Hoechst, BASF's rival, had visited his laboratory and made clear to his assistants that Hoechst would be interested in Haber's patent for the production of ammonia.[43] Haber was shrewd: competition is the spice of business.

With astounding speed, Haber's letter, obviously itself the result of prior negotiations, was converted into a formal five-year contract. BASF would finance any special needs for laboratory apparatus and grant Haber 6,000 marks annually. (His professorial salary was 4,000 marks plus a housing allowance of 1,200 marks.) In short, he doubled his salary—even without the projected profit-sharing. In return, Haber would "support the interests of BASF insofar as his official and scientific work allows it" and place the results of his research at its disposal; the work would remain Haber's literary property, but its commercial utilization became "the unlimited and exclusive property" of BASF. It was up to BASF to decide whether a given process would be patented or manufactured in secret (industrial espionage, even within Germany, was common at the time), and either way Haber would receive 10 percent of the net profits. These were to be calculated in a most intricate fashion; that is, they would be the differential between the profits obtained by using a Haber process as against possible profits obtained by some other process. BASF retained the right to calculate these profits and Haber renounced any claim to examine its books. Finally, and contrary to Haber's earlier proposal, BASF retained certain rights concerning the publication of important research results and some control over Haber's relations with other firms.[44] The contract was signed in March 1908 and greatly boosted Haber's work and income. It also exemplified the ever closer and never uncomplicated relations between industry and academic scientists.*

* Another example: In 1912 Schering, the pharmaceutical firm, offered Hermann Staudinger, an associate professor at Karlsruhe, a position as third director (presumably the No. 3 position in the firm), on the following terms: a five-year contract with a salary of 10,000 marks, 1.5 percent of annual profits, with

A week after signing the contract, BASF registered Haber's first patent concerning the synthesis of ammonia. But the technical difficulties of actual production were awesome. Even before they could be seriously addressed, Haber in October 1909 told BASF of a competing offer he had received: the chairman of the supervisory board (*Aufsichtsrat*) of Deutsche Gasglüh-licht, also known as Auer, had asked him to resign his professorship, become a company director, establish a scientific-industrial laboratory for it, with a completely free hand in regard to equipment and collaborators and virtually unlimited capital. The 30 million marks that BASF thought it needed for the production of ammonia the new company could easily match. His annual income, commensurate with his responsibilities as head of such a laboratory, would be "a six-digit number." For those days or ours, this was an astounding figure—roughly eight times his annual income at the time.

The chairman of Auer's supervisory board was Leopold Koppel, a self-made man, born in 1854 in Dresden, of Jewish descent and evangelical faith. By the end of the century Koppel had become a major Berlin banker, investor, and philanthropist. In 1905—with imperial consent—he established a Koppel-Foundation for the promotion of collaborative international research in the sciences, especially with the United States and France, in explicit consonance with Andrew Carnegie's philanthropic work and with the kaiser's wish to establish exchange programs with the United States. Koppel's fortune was officially estimated at 20 million marks. He was prodigiously

---

a guarantee of 15,000 marks annually (Prof. Dr. Bernhard Lepsius to Staudinger, June 8, 1912, Deutsches Museum, Munich). Staudinger refused the offer and accepted a call to Zurich as Willstätter's successor instead. Somewhat later he negotiated for—and declined—a position in a state institute in Hamburg, with a top civil service salary for that kind of position of 13,000 marks (Von Melle-Staudinger, December 19, 1919, Deutsches Museum). Clearly industry offered more lucrative employment than either university or state. After the war, Haber and Staudinger had a violent falling-out over the latter's public attacks on the criminality of gas warfare.

wealthy, led a quiet life, enjoyed the company of artists and intellectuals, and accumulated great works of art.* He and Haber became close friends.[45] We have no record of how August Bernthsen, the head of the BASF research division, received Haber's news. After all, Haber was asking to renegotiate a contract that had been signed but eighteen months earlier and still had three and a half years to go. The gentlemen of BASF might have been taken aback: by glance or spoken word the managers at Ludwigshafen may have wondered about the pushiness of certain "chosen people." Once again Carl Engler used his good offices to facilitate an agreement between BASF and Haber, but it took BASF ten typewritten pages to explain to Engler what they were prepared to do, why they resented certain "suspicions" that Haber had voiced concerning royalty arrangements, and "in future we would want to set certain limits to Mr. Haber's somewhat unrestrained ideas."[46] By November 15, a new agreement was initialled: Haber would receive 23,000 marks annually, of which 8,000 marks were designated for his expenses involving instrumentation and assistants; he would be allowed to advise Auer on their gas-lamp enterprise, but all other research would first be offered to BASF. The new contract reiterated that Haber would submit to prepublication review and would not enter into any new commercial relationship without advising BASF first. The contract was to run for five years and be automatically renewed if neither side declared its intention to end it.[47]

Haber had transformed his financial situation: his university salary had increased, his arrangements with BASF had grown by 150 percent, and Auer was going to pay him for advice as well. He was on the way to becoming a wealthy man—and to receiving ample recognition as a scientist.

* Some years ago, I wrote to Ted Koppel, star newsman of ABC television, asking whether he was related to Leopold Koppel and in possession perhaps of family papers; the New York Times Magazine had reported that Koppel, secretive about his private life, had been born of rich German-Jewish refugees in England. I received no reply.

The first visit by BASF directors to Haber's laboratory in July 1909 began with mishaps and proved a comic failure. It took several years, the ingenious work of Carl Bosch, chief BASF chemist and engineer, helped by Alwin Mittasch, and the collaboration of Krupp and other firms, before a BASF factory for the commercial production of ammonia was erected in 1913. To translate Haber's discovery into full-scale industrial production "involved many new and formidable problems, and their successful solution under the leadership of Bosch stands out as perhaps the most difficult and brilliant feat of chemical engineering ever achieved."[48] Carl Bosch and his colleague Friedrich Bergius shared the Nobel Prize for this in 1931.

A year after industrial production began, it became clear that the Haber-Bosch process, as it came to be known, was bedrock for the survival of Germany's war effort: without a steadily increasing supply of ammonia, German production of munitions and fertilizers would have been throttled. Like other great discoveries of our time, Haber's invention was the response to a great scientific challenge and an overwhelming practical need, and it had unanticipated consequences.

The Haber-Bosch process, essentially still used today, was originally a scientific-industrial triumph for Germany. It also brought Haber fame and a growing fortune, and it furthered his laboratory, where thirty to forty young scientists came from many countries to work with him. He was at the height of his powers. He was devoted to his own research and to the collegial effort that was science; unstintingly he gave encouragement and direction to his associates and colleagues. He was also an incisive, scrupulous judge of their work and promise, an ever more important voice in matters of academic appointments.[49] Ambition and the will to succeed were his, as was his driving genius, and the time was ripe. His years in Karlsruhe clearly demonstrated Haber's pedagogical skills and his ever-practical bent; Richard Willstätter thought those years his time of greatest brilliance.[50] The autodidact had become a major presence in the scientific world—and of course in Karlsruhe, where he also enjoyed the special esteem of the Grandduchess Louise.

ALBERT Einstein also came from a secular Jewish family, but of Swabian, rural origin. He was born on March 14, 1879, in Ulm, a quiet Swabian town on the Danube—geographically and perhaps culturally almost as distant from Haber's Breslau as the confines of the German Empire allowed. Einstein's birth certificate identified his parents, Hermann and Pauline, née Koch, as "belonging to the Israelite faith," the then-customary formula. The Kochs and Einsteins had lived for many generations in Wurttemberg, a largely Protestant realm which Napoleon had elevated into a kingdom. They had worked in small towns and villages as artisans and shopkeepers; none of them acquired either fame or notoriety. Albert's parents were fairly prosperous and, according to all accounts, remarkably harmonious.[51]

A year after Albert's birth, the Einsteins moved to Munich, where Hermann fell in with a plan of his younger and more enterprising brother, Jakob, to start a gas and water installation business. A few years later, they began an even more ambitious venture, the production of dynamos in an electrotechnical business; the Einstein family moved into a comfortable villa in a Munich suburb, with a large garden and old trees.

Einstein's early years were incomparably easier than Haber's had been. A loving mother presided over a contented family. The father was an amiable failure, always accommodating; people liked him. There was none of the Spartan severity or relentless expectation that marked Haber's youth. Pauline fostered the child's independence, even as later she occasionally tried to fetter the grown man. In 1881, the Einsteins had a daughter and named her Maria—Maja was the name by which she was known in the family. All his life, Albert felt closest to her.

One similarity marked both households: these were nonreligious, assimilated Jews. The Einsteins seem to have had a kind of defiant pride in not being religious, in not following religious customs or observing Jewish holidays. The very names—Albert and Maria—bespoke assimilation. As in so many German homes of the time, literature and music had a special place in the family. Hermann Einstein read aloud from the German classics; Albert's mother was musical and started him on violin lessons at the age of six, and by the time he was twelve or thirteen he played Mozart and Beethoven sonatas with his mother at the piano. The violin was to be a companion and a solace for life. The family provided intellectual stimulation as well. His Uncle Jakob gave him mathematical problems and Albert delighted in them. At the age of twelve he was given a book on Euclidean geometry: "The lucidity and certainty of its contents made an indescribable impression on me."[52]

Formal education proved rather less congenial—though not related to his celebrated reticence in speaking for the first three years; his difficulty with learning foreign languages and his mistakes in computation have been a source of endless comfort to the similarly afflicted or to their parents, though affinity in failure may not suffice for later success. Albert did well in elementary school and at the age of nine entered one of Munich's renowned gymnasia, the Luitpold Gymnasium. The instruction was strict: Greek and Latin, German, history, in short, the humanities narrowly conceived; mathematics and the natural sciences received less attention. He was not happy at school, and he hated anything that resembled mindless drill: "the teachers in the elementary school appeared to be like sergeants and the gymnasium teachers like lieutenants."[53] He had already conceived a hatred for everything military, for coercion of any kind. Still, the young Einstein imbibed something from those school years: somewhere he learned and practiced a clarity of expression, a mastery of the German language, that appeared early and never left him, not even after two decades of living in America. He had a rich fundament in German classics and he continued to read the great novels; he was remarkably indifferent to works of history.[54]

He had a brief, intense moment of "deep religiosity." In a thoroughly secular home, he refused to eat pork. It passed quickly; he did not receive bar mitzvah, nor did he ever learn Hebrew. Decades later he recalled that the moment of orthodoxy had left him "with the impression that youth is intentionally being deceived by the state through lies."[55] In his early twenties he expressed a view that he clung to for the rest of his life: "The foolish faith in authority [*Autoritätsdusel*] is the worst enemy of the truth."[56]

Independence encouraged an autodidactic quality in Einstein's life; as a youth he had turned to mathematics and philosophy on his own. "Between the ages of twelve and sixteen I made myself familiar with the elements of mathematics, including differential and integral calculus."[57] When he was only ten, he became friends with Max Talmud (later Talmey), an impoverished medical student who introduced him to popular works on philosophy and science. In time, Talmey gave him Kant's *Critique of Pure Reason*, which Albert read at the age of thirteen. From a very early point, then, Einstein sought friends who shared his interests, and from that early age knew, too, that he had to be "apart," immersed in his own thought. From adolescence till his death he pondered the necessary tension between the "I" and the "Thou," as he often put it, between the need for solitude and the desire for companionship.

In 1894, when Albert was fifteen, his parents abandoned the languishing business in Munich, hoping to find better conditions for an electrotechnical business in Italy. They sold their Munich villa to a developer, and Albert saw his cherished trees felled even before the family had departed.[58] It was a harsh introduction to the dynamism of capitalism; his later affinity to undogmatic socialism had deep roots.

The parents left Albert in Munich under the care of distant relatives, believing that his education should not be interrupted. A few months later, Albert, depressed by the school's authoritarianism, and encouraged by one of his teacher's extreme hostility—and with only a doctor's certificate to satisfy the school authorities—decided to leave Munich, leave Germany, and join his startled parents in Italy.

Einstein left Germany as a voluntary exile, thus escaping German military service. (According to German law, if a boy left the country before the age of seventeen he was absolved from military service without being categorized as a deserter.) Everything about the army—enforced conformity, mindless drill—enraged him. Upon formal petition, the Wurttemberg authorities released him from citizenship, and for a number of years he remained stateless. (In those halcyon days, a passport was of minor consequence.) His first political act, then, was a withdrawal from the claims of the German state, a rejection of subservience. In the course of his life, he lived in many countries; I believe he found the Swiss temper the most congenial, the Swiss passport the most cherished. In 1901, he became a Swiss citizen, having declared himself as belonging to "no religious denomination." (Swiss citizenship made him liable for military service, but he was disqualified for medical reasons.) He had no tie to the Jewish religion or Jewish rituals, but he never ceased being aware of his Jewish descent or of the antagonism that Jews—whether religious or agnostic—encountered in most parts of Europe.

After a brief stay with his family in Italy, Einstein returned to Switzerland, where he spoke the language and learned to fend for himself. Though underage, he was given dispensation to take the entrance exam to the ETH; he did well in mathematics and physics but failed the exam as a whole. Luck brought him to the cantonal school in Aargau, near Zurich, and he boarded with the family of Jost Winteler, himself a teacher at the school, much interested in questions of relativity regarding linguistic studies. Decades later Einstein remembered the school "because of its liberal spirit and the unaffected thoughtfulness of its teachers."[59] The Winteler family provided a perfect home; Frau Winteler became a second mother to the six-teen-year-old Albert, who fell in love with the daughter, Marie, slightly older than he. After a year or so, he ended the relation-ship, writing to Marie's mother that he regretted the pain he had already inflicted on Marie.* In a celebrated passage, the eighteen-year-old added: "Strenuous intellectual work and the contemplation of God's nature are the angels which, recon-ciling, fortifying and yet implacably severe will guide me through all the turmoil of this life."[60]

In the fall of 1896 in his final examinations, Einstein had to write an essay in French about his future plans; he wrote that he hoped to study mathematics and physics at the ETH and become "a teacher in those branches of the natural sciences, choosing the theoretical part of them," citing his "disposition for abstract and mathematical thought." The scientific field would also afford "a certain independence . . . which I like a great deal."[61] He passed his examinations and a week later began his studies at the ETH. There were only twenty-three students in his section concentrating on mathematics and the natural sciences.

By and large the angels of work prevailed during Einstein's four years at the ETH, but there was alternate turmoil and sol-ace as well. His beginnings there coincided with the failure of the Einsteins' business in Pavia, and he had to rely on a modest allowance from well-to-do relatives. He wrote to his sister:

> The misfortune of my poor parents, who for so many years have not had a happy moment, weighs most heavily on me. It also hurts me deeply that as an adult I have to be

* The ties between Albert and the Winteler family remained exceptionally close. In 1898, Albert's close friend Michele Besso married Anna Winteler; in 1911, Albert's sister Maja married Paul Winteler. In 1906, a terrible tragedy be-fell the family: the son, Julius, deranged, killed his mother, a brother-in-law, and himself. In a poignant letter to the father, Einstein expressed the shock that he felt at the thought "of the dreadfulness which blind fate brought about. The dear deceased gave me so much that was good and from me experienced only pain and suffering." Einstein to Jost Winteler, November 3, 1906, *CPAE*, vol. 5, p. 44.

a passive witness . . . . I am nothing but a burden to my
relatives . . . . It would surely be better if I were not alive.
Only the thought that I have always done what my feeble
strength allowed and that year in and year out I do not
allow myself a pleasure, a diversion except what my studies afford, keeps me going and must sometimes protect
me from despair.[62]

But he also formed life-long friendships in Switzerland with
a few men of his own age and in Zurich found a paternal
friend, Alfred Stern, a historian at the ETH and a student of
Ranke, thirty-three years older than himself, whose father had
been a famous mathematician and the first Jewish professor in
Göttingen. (Both Stern and Winteler had strong liberal convic-
tions, strengthening Einstein's own predilections.) When he
left Zurich in 1901 he thanked Stern for "all your kindness and
paternal friendliness. . . . More than once I came to you in a sad
or bitter mood and with you always regained cheerfulness and
inner composure." Einstein added that he knew, of course, that
he was mostly a chipper and amusing character. In fact he
could be harsh and melancholy as well; his future wife Mileva
regretted his being "malicious," his having "an evil tongue,"
because it harmed his career.[63] Any kind of authority he
treated with irony and a certain sarcastic arrogance, often his
fellow beings as well. The violin was his steady, serious
delight.

At the ETH he became close friends with two fellow students, Marcel Grossmann and Michele Besso. Both shared in
his work and both helped him at difficult junctures of his life.
Heinrich Zangger, a physician and a major presence in Zurich's academic life, befriended him. He needed friends and he
needed solitude—and by and large, he knew how to balance
the two.

Einstein's section at the ETH contained one woman student,
a rarity in those days: Mileva Marić, three years older than Albert, of Serbian parents and Russian-Orthodox faith, daughter

of a prosperous Hungarian civil servant. They met in 1897, and after she left in the winter semester of 1897–98 to study in Heidelberg, they began writing to each other. After her return to the ETH in the spring of 1898 the two drew closer. Einstein delighted in the intellectual companionship; in one of his first letters in August 1899, he wrote, "When I read Helmholtz for the first time I could not—and still cannot—believe that I was doing so without you sitting next to me. I enjoy working together very much, and find it soothing and less boring."[64] That letter still was couched in the formal manner, addressing her as "*Sie.*"

Sometime in the winter of 1899–1900 their companionship turned into an affair. In the summer of 1900, his mother asked him what would become of his friend and he answered instantly: "My wife." Maternal tears ensued and warnings that Mileva was but another bookworm and not a likely wife, that he was destroying his future, that Mileva could not be brought into a decent family. Einstein was undeterred, his assertive self—perhaps made more stubborn by parental objections, which he thought philistine. His mother was not to be the only woman who had to suffer his imperious wish for independence. And still he wanted to spare his parents' feelings without sacrificing an iota of his love. He wrote Mileva: "If I do not have you, I actually feel as if I did not entirely have myself. When I sit, I want to walk; when I walk, I would wish myself home; when I am conversing, I want to study; when I study, I can't sit still and concentrate; and when I go to sleep, I am dissatisfied with how I spent the day."[65]

Einstein's love letters expressed his sensual and intellectual yearning, and also his ruminations about scientific issues. They also bespeak his many different moods: from high exuberance to deep melancholy. But the depth of attachment is crystal clear: she gives him strength and happiness, she is his "sacred treasure." The frequent separations are painful: "Whoever has tasted freedom cannot bear chains anymore. . . . Except with you I am alone with everybody." The conflict with his parents persisted: "[They] cry over me as if I had died."[66] He tried to reassure Mileva: his stubbornness would prevail over the lament of his parents.

He needed all the toughness he could muster. He encountered discouragement everywhere, and still the unemployed youth of twenty-one carried on mental arguments with the scientific giants of his time. While Einstein received his diploma, allowing him to teach mathematics and physics in a high school, Mileva failed her examinations twice. Like his friends and fellow students, Einstein hoped for an assistantship at the ETH but was rejected, and for two years continued to depend on financial help from his family. It was a time of great exertion—he published his first paper in the most distinguished journal of the time, *Annalen der Physik*, in 1901—and immense anxiety. He began to suffer from stomach disorders, which his sister attributed to malnutrition.

In March 1901, Einstein sent a reprint of his first paper to Friedrich Wilhelm Ostwald, in Leipzig, asking whether he "might have use for a mathematical physicist who is familiar with absolute measurements."[67] There was no reply; a month later, Einstein's father wrote on his son's behalf, asking whether Ostwald might not read the reprint and at least send Albert a few words of encouragement. Nothing happened. Having failed in various places, Einstein wrote Mileva that he would try for an assistantship in Italy: "First of all, a major difficulty would be avoided, i.e., anti-Semitism, which in the German states would be as unpleasant for me as it would be a hindrance; second, I have rather good connections there."[68]

In the spring and fall of 1901 Einstein had two stints as a substitute teacher. An odd vision: hours in the classroom, the rest of the time spent brooding and thinking about the work of the great physicists of the day—Boltzmann, Ostwald, Planck, and Paul Drude, whom he wanted to engage in a major dispute. But by turns he was exhilarated: "It is a glorious feeling to perceive [*erkennen*] the unity of a complex of phenomena which to direct sensory observation appear as completely separate entities." Max Planck said much the same—and in a wholly different realm, Theodor Mommsen had recognized it as the greatest accomplishment for a historian.[69]

The uncertainty, however, gnawed at him, and he wrote Mileva: "It is a stupid thing, this starvation business, but otherwise he is a splendid character, your treasure, if a bit of a hangdog."[70] Einstein's friend Marcel Grossmann mentioned that his father could perhaps get him a position at the patent office in Bern, but again nothing came of it—in the short run.

Einstein met failure with alternating moods: "God created the ass and gave him a thick skin."[71] He knew that anger came from wounded vanity—and still he was exasperated: "What obstacles these old philistines place in the path of someone who is not of their sort is really horrible." They saw in intelligent youth a danger to their "brittle dignity." He knew whereof he was complaining, having offered himself to all physicists, as he put it, "from the North Sea to the southern tip of Italy."[72] He wrote and submitted a doctoral thesis for the ETH, but it was not accepted. "This setback was the last one in Einstein's career," as Abraham Pais noted.[73]

Einstein's professional disappointments cast a deep shadow over their private life: In May 1901, Albert and Mileva found out that she was to have a child—which in advance they dubbed "Lieserl." In July he wrote Mileva that he had decided to settle for any kind of job and promised her that as soon as he had one they would get married. They would ask no one; the respective families would simply have to accept a *fait accompli*.[74]

During Mileva's pregnancy, she saw very little of Einstein, perhaps only once, and sometime in January 1902, Mileva's father informed him of Lieserl's birth. Einstein inquired after Mileva's health and the child's looks. He did not join her nor apparently did she ask him to do so. Even at this difficult moment in Mileva's life and, after all, in his own, he preserved his "apartness" in a literal sense.

In February, a month after Lieserl's birth, Einstein moved to Bern—before his appointment at the patent office, facilitated by the intervention of Marcel Grossmann's father, had been confirmed. He earned a meager living by private tutoring and in June began at the patent office as a technical expert third class, without tenure, at the respectable annual salary of 3,500 Swiss francs. At last he had found a perfect niche for himself.

And yet the year 1902 was overshadowed by terrifying events in his personal life. We know from an anxious letter of Albert to Mileva that Lieserl contracted scarlet fever; Albert was worried about the aftereffects of the disease. In the same letter he asked how Lieserl was registered—presumably for adoption.[75] But there the thread disappears. We have no certain record of what happened to Lieserl—there is no evidence of her death, and the likeliest conclusion is that the child was given away. We can only guess at the motives for this decision, which was never alluded to in any subsequent utterance that has survived.

In the fall of that year, Einstein's father fell ill; his many misfortunes had taken a toll on his health. He suffered from heart disease, and Albert traveled from Bern to Milan to be with him at the end. On Hermann's deathbed he consented to Albert's marriage. "When the end was near, Hermann asked everyone to leave so that he could die alone. It was a moment his son never recalled without feelings of guilt."[76]

A few months later, on January 6, 1903, Albert and Mileva married. All his life, Einstein recalled his unease about this step. There would have been reasons for his anxiety at the time: unease, perhaps even guilt, at his desertion of Mileva during her pregnancy and at the abandonment of their child; regret that his marriage had made his mother angry; and finally, probably most importantly, fear of the commitment, the first yielding to what he later called the *Nurpersönliches*, the merely personal, which he always tried to escape.[77]

Yet it was an astonishingly mature man of twenty-three who settled in Bern. The overriding impression of his formative years is controlled independence, of dedication to thought, to work, to physics, a calling from which he never strayed. I believe that the need for solitude came to him intuitively, though we know that in 1901 he read Schopenhauer's aphorisms "with great pleasure," and these aphorisms were a call to solitude, a warning against worldly and corrupt pursuits. He was congenially self-protective, and he also had a remarkable sense of people's frailty, *especially* men's;* one of Einstein's friends noted that he was simultaneously cheerful in a childlike fashion and cynical. Einstein himself thought that his "sassiness" was his guardian angel: it was certainly shield and sword at once.[78]

The years in Bern were the most peaceful and most creative time of his life. In January 1903, weeks after his wedding, he wrote: "So I am now a married husband," a rather peculiar formulation for so precise a writer. Mileva, he added, cared "superbly for everything, cooks well and is always cheerful."[79] In May 1904 their first son, Albert Jr., was born. Einstein enjoyed him; a second son was born six years later.

Bern was also a time of friendly, simple companionship; he met regularly with two friends, Konrad Habicht and Maurice Solovine—the three celebrated their meetings by calling themselves the Akademie Olympia; together, they read and discussed Spinoza, Hume, Mach, Poincaré, Sophocles, Racine, and

* At the time—and probably before and after—it was customary to think of women as morally superior to men, though in the very years in which Einstein singled out *men's* wretchedness, writers like Strindberg or painters like Munch depicted women as eternal tempters and embodiments of evil. That fathers had different expectations of sons and daughters is a related deformation; my friend Martin Schwarzschild, distinguished astronomer and son of a distinguished astronomer, told me of a note that his father had once written: "A pretty daughter I have but I am still without a competent [*tüchtig*] son." This common view—not regarded as a prejudice in those days—aside from discouraging the vast majority of daughters or condemning them to acquiescence, might also have spurred a few to still greater exertion, inspired them with a greater will to succeed.

Cervantes. In 1904 he persuaded the patent office to give Michele Besso a post, thus bringing an old friend and intellectual companion to his side.

It was in Bern—far from the centers of science—that the obscure Einstein wrote the four papers that revolutionized modern physics and cosmology. His *annus mirabilis* of 1905 has always been celebrated, and the wellsprings of his genius inspire puzzled awe. "In this one year, a young man of twenty-six years of age changed forever our accepted view of the physical world."[80] This was the crowning achievement of what Thomas Nipperdey has called "the iconoclastic modernity of German physics around 1900."[81] The papers were again published in *Annalen der Physik*. They paved the way to fame—first among scientists and eventually in the world at large. There is a marvelous discrepancy between the obscure clerk at the Patent Office—who was gradually advanced in bureaucratic stages and by 1906 received a promotion and a salary of 4,500 Swiss francs—and the young genius on the verge of fame.

In the scientific world, Max Planck was the first to recognize the power and originality of Einstein's work. Einstein began to correspond with other eminent scientists: Philipp Lenard and Johannes Stark—who after the First World War were to become his foremost enemies—as well as Wilhelm Wien and Max von Laue. Above all, the great Dutch physicist Hendrick Antoon Lorentz took a strong interest in Einstein's work. Some were eager to meet him: Planck, for example.[82] In 1906 he received a doctorate from the University of Zurich. His academic progress was slow compared to that of ordinary or mediocre students. He tired of his eight-hour work day and worried that "soon I come into the stationary and sterile age where one laments the revolutionary thought [*Gesinnung*] of the young."[83]

But slowly the Swiss academic world began to realize the treasure in their midst and the need to recognize the revolutionary field of theoretical physics. In 1908 he became a *Privat-dozent* at the University of Bern, offering lectures to few listeners, while continuing his work at the patent office. He found formal lecturing uncongenial (his former teacher, Alfred Kleiner, professor of physics at the University of Zurich, attended a lecture of Einstein's and thought it disappointing).

Still Einstein could not be measured by the usual criteria. In 1909 Kleiner formally proposed that a new associate professorship in theoretical physics be created for Einstein, who "today ranks among the most important theoretical physicists and has been recognized rather generally as such since his work on the relativity principle . . . uncommonly sharp conception and pursuit of ideas . . . clarity and precision of style." Kleiner's colleagues needed his reassurances about Einstein's person "since," as the faculty report recorded, "Herr Dr. Einstein is an Israelite and since precisely to the Israelites among scholars are ascribed (in numerous cases not entirely without cause) all kinds of unpleasant peculiarities of character, such as intrusiveness, impudence, and a shopkeeper's mentality in the perception of their academic position." The faculty report acknowledged that not all Israelites were of such character and not all non-Jews free of such fault.[84] Without further ado and, as far as we know, without Einstein ever hearing about these collegial objections, the University of Zurich offered Einstein an associate professorship and he accepted.

To friends he reported, "I am now also an official member of the guild of the whores" and "So now I too am a great schoolmaster . . . but I remain a simple guy who does not demand anything of the world—only one's youth is gone, the delightful one, when every day one sees the heavens full of violins."[85] This was Einstein's way of announcing that his academic career had begun in earnest.*

* In the same letter, in May 1909, Einstein expressed his own views about Jews in academe—particularly German Jews. A colleague, Jakob Laub, had reported about the lamentable careerism of a young Jewish student: "The *rich* German Jews must become *professors*, their parents simply educate them in this way." Einstein replied regarding "the dear wretched boy. . . . How every regular artisan is a splendid character as compared to this poor devil who in dealing with officialdom loses every last trace of self-respect. . . . Why do they fawn in such a humiliating fashion on the state? . . . For the state's treasury this is all

After an absence of some eight years and at the relatively young age of thirty, Einstein moved back to Zurich and into a position of considerable public distinction. Zurich was a liberal, tolerant city, traditionally hospitable to foreigners, indeed even to political exiles.*

Einstein's scientific fame spread rapidly throughout the scientific world. In 1909, in his lectures at Columbia University, Max Planck said: "In its breadth and profundity, this principle [Einstein's special theory of relativity] is comparable only to the revolution in the physical world-view occasioned by the introduction of the Copernican world-system."[86] In 1910, Planck's colleague in Berlin, Emil Fischer, one of the first Nobel laureates in chemistry, wrote Einstein that a leading figure in the German chemical industry had offered—anonymously—a gift of 5,000 marks a year for three years to support his work, believing "it a duty of wealthy people in Germany to support such brilliant work." The donor was Franz Oppenheim, director of AGFA, a major German aniline-dye producer.** Einstein gratefully accepted.[87]

In 1911 he accepted a position as full professor at the German University in Prague—and had to confront his religious status. Imperial Austrian authorities could not accept someone who claimed to be "without religion" [konfessionslos], which he had signified on his Swiss citizenship application a decade

---

very advantageous. Also it is easier to run things with dogs than with wolves." *CPAE*, vol. 5, Jakob Laub to Einstein, May 16, 1909; Einstein to Jakob Laub, May 19, 1909, pp. 186–190.

* There had been another candidate for his new position: Friedrich Adler, a fellow student from the ETH days, and the son of one of the great leaders of the Austrian Social Democratic Party. Adler withdrew in favor of Einstein. Years later, in November 1916, Friedrich Adler shot and killed the Austrian premier Count Karl Stürgkh. Einstein made various efforts, private and public, to help Adler, whose death sentence was commuted and who was freed in 1920.

** The Oppenheims had a celebrated home in the Wannsee part of Berlin, where amid a brilliant art collection, they entertained their close friends, among them Haber, Moellendorff, Max Liebermann, and Ludwig Justi, director of the National Gallery in Berlin.

earlier. To a friend he wrote that in taking the Prague oath of office, "I resorted to the reacquired Jewish 'faith.'"[88] He was a nonbeliever, and it is a tribute to his honest exactitude that when discussing fellow Jews he never used the common term *"Glaubensgenossen"* (co-religionists) but the less common, almost strange-sounding *"Stammesgenossen"* (members of the tribe). Einstein declared himself "of the Mosaic faith," as the then-prevalent formula prescribed. A man who had been stateless and *konfessionslos*, and married to a Slav, was suddenly plunged into a milieu where nationality, race, and religion were burning issues.

In Prague, Einstein was totally absorbed with his work on gravitational theory—and still appeared at the major scientific meetings of the time. In 1911, he spoke at the annual meeting of German natural scientists in Karlsruhe—where for the first time he met Fritz Haber; by November of that year he wrote to his friend Zangger, "At present I have an active correspondence with Haber, who is of uncanny agility. . . . In any case, one has to admire the fertility of ideas"—the reference being to questions concerning atomic theory.[89]

In his miraculous if often impecunious years in liberal Switzerland, Einstein had neither time nor need to concern himself with politics. In Prague he saw a new version of "the German problem." Prague, a city of historic beauty, was now one of historic conflict. In the last decades of the nineteenth century, its population had doubled: by 1910, it was close to half a million, of whom over 90 percent were Czechs. The German minority, still powerful in economic life and, in its own eyes, superior to mere Czechs, had shrunk to 7 percent, and nearly half of them were Jewish. The dominant conflict was between Czechs and Germans, with the latter feeling embattled and resentful; they had once been the unquestioned rulers. Prague Germans—unlike Germans elsewhere in Bohemia—were largely upper and middle class; they remained liberal and tolerant in an age where political liberalism was in decline in Austria. Ethnic conflict had led to the division of Charles

University, the oldest of central Europe; separate German and Czech entities had been established. By the time Einstein arrived, the ever greater hostility between the two national groups disturbed university life as well.

German Jews in Prague had to contend with rabid anti-Semitism on the part of Czech *and* German nationalists, but the well-to-do Jews clung to their German identity, and leaders of the German community tried to preserve the German-Jewish symbiosis, while many lower-class Jews decided to declare themselves Czech—a different version of assimilationist intent. In this charged, confused, and nationalistic atmosphere, some Jews, both among the intellectual elite and among less privileged groups, embraced the nascent Zionist movement, despairing of the old hope for an assimilated existence, free of prejudice and bigotry.

For all his capacity for "apartness," Einstein could not be oblivious of the political conflicts surrounding him. The city and his work he loved, but not the people, whom he found simultaneously proud and servile.[90] We know that he had a few Czech students in his classes. We also know that Mileva had a very difficult time adjusting to life in Prague. She was a Slav among embattled Slavs, a Russian-Orthodox among Catholics, and married to a German-speaking Jew with Swiss citizenship: these external difficulties added to the internal ones.

Einstein acquired a new assistant in Prague, Otto Stern, an experimental physicist who many years later—on Einstein's nomination—also received the Nobel Prize. Stern recalled, "Einstein was completely alone in Prague. . . . The only truly intelligent man there was [Georg] Pick," who had once been Ernst Mach's assistant and who refused to accept the existence of molecules, thinking the notion a superstition. Einstein's intellectual milieu in Prague was more Jewish than it had been in Bern or Zurich. Pick and Stern were Jewish, as was a technical assistant named Emil Nohel, who came from a farmer's family in a small Bohemian village, and who told Einstein about Jewish life in the countryside (including the piquant detail that many Jewish peasants used Czech as their everyday language and German for the Sabbath—as their substitute for Hebrew). But Einstein lamented "the lack of interest among the students for my beautiful subject."[91]

Einstein's fame grew steadily in his short months in Prague, as invitations and formal calls poured in. In early November 1911, he gave the final paper at the famed first Solvay Congress of physicists in Brussels, where he saw again the great Lorentz, whom he revered, and met for the first time the French contingent, including Henri Poincaré, Marie Curie, and Paul Langevin. He belonged and he knew it.

Most important, Marcel Grossmann, now dean of the mathematics-physics section of ETH, persuaded his colleagues that Einstein should be offered a professorship there. By the winter of 1911–12 the decision had been taken; Einstein, overjoyed, returned to Zurich in August 1912.

But just before his return to Zurich, Einstein's life was dramatically transformed: he had fallen in love with his divorced cousin, Elsa. They had known each other as children and in the spring of 1912 they had met again in Berlin. In his first letter to Elsa, from Prague in April, he declared his love, confessing at the same time his difficulties with Mileva. (Relations with Mileva had been troubled for some time; in 1909, he wrote to Michele Besso: "My equanimity of soul, lost because of M., not regained.") To Elsa he avowed: "But I must love someone, otherwise it is a miserable existence. And that someone is you."[92*]

In August 1912, the Einsteins moved back to Zurich, and he wrote his second letter to Elsa, a letter of renunciation. For both their sakes, he wrote, it would be best to terminate their relationship. But, in true lover's fashion, the letter avowing a break also reassured her that she would always have a cousin who

---

* In the same letter to Elsa, Albert explained why at an earlier time he had been fond of her younger sister, Paula: "Actually it is quite simple. She was young, a girl, and accommodating. . . . The rest is done by an amiable imagination that deceives." We now know that Einstein succumbed rather often to that "amiable imagination."

deeply cared for her—and who gave her a clandestine address for reaching him in Zurich.

The new professorship at the ETH coincided with yet another period of intense creativity. His teaching responsibilities were light, and he "never really prepared for the lectures, but still after all he was Einstein," recalled Otto Stern, his chief assistant, who also remembered the brilliance of Einstein's colloquium.[93] Einstein immediately plunged into collaboration with his old friend Grossmann, and arrived at the mathematical foundations of what was to become the general theory of relativity.

In March 1913 he wrote Elsa: "In the last half year I have worked more strenuously than ever before in my life and a few weeks ago I now finally solved the problem. It is an audacious continuation of the relativity theory together with a theory of gravitation. Now I have to give myself some peace or I shall go *kaput* right away." Earlier he had written her that he worked all day, every day "without giving myself any rest at all. *Noblesse oblige*—this fame is linked to a certain wretchedness."[94] But fame engulfed him—and would bring him to Berlin after all.

HABER and Einstein met for the first time in September 1911, when both men were on the move: Haber to Berlin and Einstein to Zurich, though he also began to think of an eventual move to Berlin, then probably the center of the natural sciences, with a university that "could arguably be called the best in the world."[95] What happened next illustrates the human drama of biography, the connections between deep historic forces and private aspirations and sheer contingency.

By 1912 Haber and Einstein drew much closer because both their lives became enmeshed with a historic development in German science: the creation in 1910 of the Kaiser-Wilhelm-Society, which sponsored a growing number of semi-autonomous institutes for "basic research" in the natural sciences. In the fall of 1911 Haber had moved to Berlin as director of the Kaiser-Wilhelm-Institute for Physical Chemistry and Electrochemistry, and not many months later, he became a decisive collaborator in the campaign to bring Einstein to Berlin as well.

The founding of the Kaiser-Wilhelm-Society is a story in itself, a characteristic drama in the history of a Germany that was half-modern and half-feudal, and all ambitious. The personae involved the kaiser himself, his ministers and entourage, leading scientists and industrialists, and the immensely rich of that country in ascendancy—especially immensely wealthy Jews—all of whom contributed to a multi-million-mark effort to establish and support research institutes outside the universities, so that Germany could remain competitive with the privately financed institutes in the United States and elsewhere. The Kaiser Wilhelm institutes constituted clusters of excellence until Hitler's seizure of power, when they cowered and collaborated with his regime; the Kaiser-Wilhelm-Society was reborn in 1948 as the Max Planck Society, once again taking its place among the best institutes in international science, once more collaborative and competitive with other countries, especially the United States.[96]

In October 1910, at the centennial celebration of the founding of the University of Berlin, the kaiser proclaimed his intention to call into being new institutes that would be independent of but collaborative with university and academy, an implicit reference to the two institutions in Berlin. The occasion was one of unimaginable pomp: imperial majesty and academic regalia, the German professoriate as the emperor's academic "Guard's Regiment." The pomp was historic, the speech itself moderate, for it had been written by Adolf Harnack, the renowned liberal theologian and a favorite of the kaiser. (Four years later he was ennobled.) The kaiser announced that nine million marks had already been collected, and that he would serve as "protector" of the new Society—whose coffers, he was confident, would become fuller still, and he paid special tribute to the generosity of Leopold Koppel.

The imperial announcement was both a culmination and a beginning. German scientists—and Harnack, who had become the leading spokesman for *Wissenschaft*—had long feared that Germany was losing out to other countries in the promotion of basic research. German preeminence—in this case in all the *Wissenschaften*—and German fears seem always joined. Scientific luminaries, especially Nernst and Ostwald and the renowned chemist Emil Fischer, believed that research, ever more expensive, had to be carried out in independent institutes, with scientists freed from academic obligations. The chemists had a model: the Imperial Institute of Physical Technology, established in 1887, as a joint effort of Werner von Siemens, industrial scientist, and the imperial government.[97] They were awed by such institutes in America, most especially the Carnegie Institute, even as they hoped that Andrew Carnegie's *Gospel of Wealth* would open hearts and pockets of the German super-rich.

One of the early and decisive proponents of this plan for free-standing institutes was Friedrich Althoff, who for several decades had been a kind of enlightened dictator of Prussia's universities, with a passion for attracting the best talent to them. Althoff quickly saw that the new plan could give substance to his old dream of establishing a German Oxford in Dahlem, an undeveloped suburb of Berlin, that was still then largely a royal domain. Althoff died in 1909, and others realized his hopes.[98]

Harnack prepared the formal petition to the kaiser, stressing that military prowess and *Wissenschaft* constitute "the two strong pillars of German greatness" and warning against the threat of foreign nations; in an age of imperial rivalry and fear, this nationalist argument weighed heavily.[99] We know from American experience that rivalries with foreign powers, deemed hostile, will loosen purse strings for scientific progress.

Harnack hit upon a characteristically German hybrid form of organization: the new institutes should have a mixed paternity: the imperial or the Prussian state and a semi-autonomous foundation in which scientists, industrialists, and government bureaucrats would be represented. In Harnack's language, the aim was to have them independent of "clique and wealth."[100] Harnack was sufficiently orthodox so that the many skeptical professors, especially among humanists who still took a fearful, condescending view of the new and extravagantly expensive sciences, had to accept his reassurance that these institutes would supplement, not subvert, the original Humboldtian notion of a university that combined teaching and research. Harnack had a more benevolent view of the state, that timeless entity above all parties, than he did of industrial capital, hence the co-directing presence of the government. The German states had traditionally assumed financial responsibility for higher education, and faculty had civil service status. The much-vaunted ideal of academic autonomy at times clashed with the reality of state dominance.

Harnack and his associates knew, of course, that the project would appeal to the emperor and that imperial sponsorship was needed for the raising of private funds. Kaiser Wilhelm was a curious mixture of feudal dreams and modern desires; he proclaimed himself as ruler by divine right and craved popular approval, indeed love—as none of his ancestors had before. He was the imperial epitome of the modern insecure and anxious man, but however much the memory of absolute monarchical power filled his dreams and shaped his self-image, he was also an intensely modern man, proud of German science and industrial might. In the new society, the emperor would have the right to appoint half the senators, the other half to be elected by the dues-paying members.

The imperial nimbus and the governmental initiative were both in place before the massive effort at fund-raising began. The government then ordered its provincial administrators to draw up lists of the most affluent persons in their areas; tax returns were scrutinized. One Rhenish official reported back to Berlin, "The encirclement of the finest game [*Edelwild*]" had begun.[101] We can reconstruct the subtle method of extraction: the rich prey would be reminded that a proper contribution would be in Germany's national interest as manifested by the direct involvement of the All-Highest, and in their own interest. Thus began an organized competition for coercive volunteering.

Germany's business magnates had their own interest in the institutes, for they were expected to contribute to German productivity. The wealthiest of them, Gustav Krupp von Bohlen und Halbach, signed up for the largest gift (1.4 million marks), but notable also were the co-owner of the Bleichroeder Bank (300,000 marks) and Eduard Arnhold, coal magnate and outstanding art collector (250,000 marks). Mendelssohns and Rothschilds also appeared quite prominently.[102]

Benefactors were rewarded with imperial recognition. The society's senators—and some of the largest contributors became senators—were given a special medal to wear with the emperor's portrait and were invited to an annual reception at the palace. Status and distinction were at stake.

One group in Prussia was disproportionately wealthy and disproportionately eager for social recognition: Jews, baptized or not. Some thirty-five percent of the original contributions came from Jews, who made up less than one percent of the population. In turn, Jews became directors and members of the new research institutes and often received subsequent "honorary" professorships. The wildly anti-Semitic kaiser had a weakness for rich Jews, and for his weakness he was vilified by rabid, incorruptible anti-Semites.

Leopold Koppel was the second largest contributor, promising 700,000 marks, provided Haber would be the director of the new institute for physical chemistry and Koppel the sole contributor. On Haber's demand, Koppel added another 300,000 marks and also agreed to provide 35,000 marks for annual upkeep, provided the state would contribute the director's salary of 15,000 marks plus a housing allowance of 5,000 marks and another 35,000 marks for expenses—and of course the land on which the institute and director's villa were to be built. The state assumed the director's salary, thus accepting Haber's demand for the status of a civil servant and giving the state continuing involvement. (That the economics ministry balked at every turn was a normal part of innovation.)

Haber used his customary acumen in negotiating for his new post; the fact that the scientific community assumed he would win a Nobel Prize for the fixation of nitrogen helped. He demanded a free hand in the choice of personnel and projects, the absolute right to decide on matters pertaining to patents, and also "the right to give advisory and expert opinions to industry." He also asked for more freedom regarding short-term leaves, citing his fragile health.[103] What Koppel had wanted to give Haber within the confines of the Auer company he now enabled him to have with an imperial aura.

The institute formally opened in the kaiser's presence in 1912; by this time, Haber had also been appointed an *Honorarprofessor* at the University of Berlin; the kaiser had given him the title of *Geheimrat*, or Privy Councillor. A few years later he was elected to the Prussian Academy of Sciences. But beyond titles and office, Haber quickly became a recognized member of the Berlin community of science, respected for his work, the acuity of his judgment, and the wealth of his connections. More: he helped to create a Kaiser-Wilhelm-Institute for Chemistry and more than anyone else was responsible for the appointment of Richard Willstätter, organic chemist and at the time a professor in Zurich. The institutes were built next to each other—and Willstätter became Haber's closest friend.

The lure of scientific Berlin became ever greater, and some scientists sought to exploit it. Planck and Nernst had their eyes on Einstein, on the new "Copernicus." Haber first raised such a move with Einstein in December 1912 and in January 1913 wrote to Hugo Krüss, aide to Althoff's successor in the Prussian Ministry of Education, Friedrich Schmidt(-Ott), that he thought Einstein would be willing to come to Berlin. In the summer of 1913, Nernst and Planck traveled to Zurich to offer

Einstein an incomparable position in Berlin, made possible by the death of Jacobus Van't Hoff, who had been one of two salaried members of the Prussian Academy: the offer was for a salaried membership in the Prussian Academy (12,000 marks, half of which to be paid by Koppel), a professorship at the university with no teaching duties, and the directorship of a Kaiser-Wilhelm-Institute for Physics to be especially established for him—with the possibility of attracting a key colleague to Berlin as well. Right after their visit, Einstein remarked to Otto Stern: "You know, the two appeared to me as if they were people who wanted to get hold of a rare postage stamp."[104]

In the ensuing months Haber was the chief impresario for Einstein's Berlin debut. Only he knew that Einstein had his own private reasons for the move; the rest of the world assumed, also correctly, that Einstein saw the offer as providing freedom from teaching in an exceptional milieu. And yet he had intermittent misgivings. Not everyone in Berlin had the intellectual openness of Lorentz, for whom Einstein felt such reverence. Planck and Laue, he mentioned to his friend Besso, found his gravitational theory uncongenial: "The free, uninhibited view is generally something alien to the (adult) German (blinders!)." No wonder that he added: "I feel a certain apprehension [*Unbehagen*] as the Berlin adventure draws closer."[105]

He was afraid of what he feared might become his "Berlinization." More sharply, he inveighed privately in his letters to Elsa against the philistine, the *Spiessbürger*, the conformist—in short, against the German professor, as he appeared in caricature and all too often in reality. He wanted to be different; he wanted, he once wrote Elsa, "a gypsy household."[106] Within a few years, he was to become a major presence in Berlin, fame and controversy swirling about him. He made his concessions: a would-be gypsy in the occasional frock coat.

Haber had been the organizer of Einstein's appointment, and he was his sole comfort when Einstein insisted on a separation from Mileva, on sending her to Zurich, thus losing his sons as well. That loss—that murder, as he once called it, self-inflicted, and yet, he thought, the price of survival—came at the very end of July 1914. And days later, in the words of Sir Edward Grey, "The lamps are going out all over Europe; we shall not see them lit again in our lifetime."

IN Germany the outbreak of war in August 1914 precipitated exultation and national rejoicing, a celebration of the nation rallying in the face of foreign aggression, banishing domestic conflict. The instant sacrifices that the war imposed were hailed as acts of purification, as a means of redemption. But the actual war, and not the chimera of a short and victorious battle, brought unimaginable sacrifices and, finally, angry suspicion and sharp internal conflicts.

Scientists faced a new challenge: it was the first war in which their talents were desperately needed, and not only their talents, but their public prestige. Before 1914, German scientists, like scientists elsewhere, were patriots, some even nationalists, but proud to belong to science's international community. The war changed all that: it inflamed an ever more bitter conflict between German and Allied intellectuals. Germany's elites, and most especially the professoriate and the priesthood, hailed the heroism of what they believed was their country's defensive war, even as much of the rest of the world was appalled by Germany's invasion of neutral Belgium. Allied outcries against German atrocities prompted an instant, fierce German response. The Manifesto of the 93—which denied that Germans had committed atrocities, asserted Germany's innocence in causing the war, and insisted that Germany's culture and military tradition were one and the same—so fully expressed the prevailing attitude that some distinguished scholars signed it first and read it later. It had been drafted by Ludwig Fulda, a popular writer and a Jew, and among the other greats, Haber, Willstätter, and Paul Ehrlich signed it.[107]

They were responding not to a text but to a mood. A question, hitherto unexplored, I believe: did these German academics and clerics, themselves misled, carry a disproportionate share of responsibility for the emergence of this new intellectual conflict, as their political-military leaders did for the outbreak of the war itself? In any case, the manifesto evoked the opposite reaction from what had been intended. The very neutrals to whom it had been specially addressed recoiled from it, while intellectuals in the Allied countries proclaimed that German academics had proven themselves traitors to the truth, traducers of elementary scholarship. This escalated the ideological conflict that accompanied the war and was to poison European culture for decades to come.

Somewhat later and independently, a number of other writers and scholars, including Thomas Mann and Ernst Troeltsch, insisted that Germany had chosen its own path, a *Sonderweg*, to freedom, different from and superior to Western freedom, which they considered corrupted by formal mechanisms and materialist values. As the war dragged on, some of these writers began to see the dangers of this special path, the annexationist unreason that clamored for a total victory; they began to urge moderate war aims and long-overdue domestic reforms that would expand suffrage and strengthen parliamentary power. But these moderates became more and more marginalized during the war.

Haber and Einstein instantly moved in opposite directions.* Haber sought to place all his immense and brilliant energy at the service of Germany's war effort; now he could demonstrate the depth of his patriotic commitment; and he believed—for a very long time—in Germany's ultimate victory. Einstein, from the beginning, thought the war a kind of suicidal drama in Europe's history, an eruption of insanity. He sensed the terrible

---

* But close personal ties remained: during the early months of 1915, Einstein gave the thirteen-year-old Hermann Haber "lessons in mathematics," because he had been "quite sick and couldn't go to school." Some tutor! Einstein to Hans Albert Einstein, January 25, 1915, *CPAE*, vol. 8A, pp. 84–86.

immediate and permanent costs; he grasped that Europe's civilization was being torn apart; and he saw through the patriotic exhortations to the reality of slaughter and death. He believed that Germany was responsible for the outbreak and prolongation of the war; greed and madness had afflicted most Germans, he thought, and infected the other combatants as well. He was shaken that so many of his colleagues so readily chimed in with the chorus of hatred. In the third week of the war he wrote to Paul Ehrenfest in Leiden: "Europe in its madness has now begun something beyond belief. In a time like that one sees what a wretched animal species we belong to. I am quietly, sleepily pursuing my peaceful ruminations and feel only a mixture of pity and disgust."[108]

Einstein did indeed continue his ruminations: they culminated in the general theory of relativity in 1915. But even at the time of his most intense intellectual effort, he expressed his dismay at the raging madness. To his fellow pacifist Romain Rolland he explained that the German victory of 1870 had left the country with "a religious faith in power which found in Treitschke an appropriate, not an exaggerated, expression. This religion dominates the minds of almost all of the cultured elite; it almost completely extruded the ideals of the Goethe-Schiller era."[109]

In October 1914, G. F. Nicolai, né Lewinstein, a Berlin physician, sought to launch a counter-manifesto, appealing to all Europeans to mobilize their influence "so that the conditions of peace do not become the source of future wars," and to "create an organic unity out of Europe.... Should Europe, too, as Greece did earlier, succumb through fratricidal war to exhaustion and destruction? For the struggle that is raging today will hardly leave a victor but only vanquished behind." It was the first political plea that Einstein ever signed, but for want of requisite signatures it was never published in wartime Germany. (It was included in Nicolai's book Die Biologie des Krieges, which, following its appearance in Zurich in 1917, was quickly translated into many languages and found an international audience.)[110] In November 1914 he was one of ten founding members of a small democratic, reformist group, Bund Neues Vaterland. German authorities banned it in 1916, and it was refounded in 1922 as the German League of Human Rights.

Einstein loathed German imperialism and quietly hoped for its defeat; a decisive German victory he thought would be a disaster for Europe, and especially for Germany. But in a letter to Lorentz in August 1915 he also mentioned that his faith "in the politically more progressive states" had declined; they too were governed by all-powerful oligarchies who controlled the press, and the mighty ones "have no heart for the many." These were his views, and he clung to them, but he may have also thought it opportune to remind a great neutral mind of the commonality of sin in the war-torn world. Still, Einstein was closest to what was perhaps imperialism's most exaggerated form, that of Germany, and I doubt that he was quite so alive to the Allies' rapacious aims.[111]

Neither his physics, in this his most creative period, nor his intermittent ill health kept Einstein from the effort to find ways of expressing opposition to the war and to German policies. He thought the silence of the moderates sinful. Anti-militarist views filled his correspondence—enough to make German authorities fear him as a dangerous pacifist with international commitments and friendships.* When in November 1915, the Goethebund of Berlin asked Einstein and others for their views of the war, Einstein's reply was characteristic. He began: "The psychological roots of the war are in my opinion biologically founded in the aggressive characteristics of the male creature." Invoking Tolstoy he insisted that patriotism was the source of all evil; in wartime, it was the warrant by which the aggressive instinct would be allowed to commit mass murder. Thus in peacetime the individual should purge himself of these patri-

---

* By January 1918 the Army Command of the Marken ordered the head of the Berlin police to consult the military before giving certain pacifists, Einstein included, permission to travel abroad. *Albert Einstein in Berlin, 1913–1933*, ed. Christa Kirsten and Hans-Jürgen Treder, vol. 1 (East Berlin, 1979), pp. 198–199.

otic-aggressive sentiments. He hoped for a supranational organization that would eliminate European wars. "As in the past,
power-hunger and greed should be treated as despicable vices,
ditto for hatred and bellicosity." He revised this text several
times, but not its last sentence, with a malicious formulation
that he intuitively knew would inflict maximum, memorable
pain: "But why many words, when I can say everything in one
sentence and, moreover, in a sentence which is particularly fitting for me as a Jew: Honor Your Master Jesus Christ not in
words and hymns, but above all through your deeds."[112]

Throughout the war Einstein thought of himself as a Swiss
internationalist, aware that the longer the war lasted, the
greater the hatred it spawned. In 1915 he welcomed his election to a Dutch-sponsored antiwar organization that hoped to
prepare plans for a durable peace.[113] During the war he frequently traveled to neutral Holland and Switzerland, kept up
his contact with colleagues, especially Lorentz, often serving as
a bridge between Planck and Lorentz.

His work remained passion and solace. Neither the disaster
of war nor terrible worries about family matters could deflect
him. He feared, not without reason, that Mileva was encourag-
ing his sons' estrangement from him. In 1916, Mileva fell seriously ill, with the doctors misdiagnosing her breakdown as
brain tuberculosis. Einstein thought that his youngest son,
Eduard, had succumbed to scrofula and blamed himself for
having disregarded Mileva's earlier symptoms.* Meanwhile

---

* In 1946, in a correspondence with an old friend and physician interested in
eugenics, Einstein acknowledged the importance of selecting partners with favorable heredity prospects, but rejected any collective effort of improving the
human race. "Perhaps there is something benevolent in the wasteful sport that
nature, seemingly blind, places on its creatures. Still it can only be beneficent if
we try to persuade young people how critical that decision [marriage and repro-
duction] is, taken at a moment when nature leaves us in a kind of drunken sensual delusion so that we least possess our power of judgment when we most
need it. I had to experience this drastically in myself and in my son." Einstein to
Hans Mühsam, June 4, 1946, Einstein Archives, Hebrew University, Jerusalem,
file 43.

he worried about the boys, who were in the care of a nurse-maid.[114] Mileva recovered, but by February 1917 Einstein became very ill, with liver and gall bladder troubles and, later, an ulcer. Wartime rationing exacerbated the difficulties of a pre-scribed diet, but Elsa's care proved indispensable, and pack-ages from Switzerland that he received as a Swiss citizen helped as well.

He detested the war, though he once helped the German navy to develop a better gyroscope. In politics he was isolated, but he could endure this aloneness and accept, often with an ironic smile, peoples' wrongheadedness. He had rather low ex-pectations of people, a kind of distant contempt, deepened by the war, that shielded him from disappointment. But he had intimations that the promise of science could turn to terror—later, of course, this fear was to haunt him. To Zangger he wrote: "Our entire much-praised technological progress, and civilization generally, could be compared to an ax in the hand of a pathological criminal."[115]

Haber, on the other hand, helped to forge a powerful axe. Immediately after the outbreak of the war, he abandoned his own work and dedicated himself totally to the war tasks at hand. Indeed, he was among the first to grasp the novelty of these tasks: he was the scientific complement to Walther Ra-thenau and to his friend Wichard von Moellendorff, both of whom directed the war ministry's division for raw-material al-location. He understood, as Germany's military commanders did not, that a German victory depended on withstanding the British blockade, that German science would have to contrib-ute alternative sources for the indispensable raw materials that the nation had once imported. Haber believed that science had multiple responsibilities in wartime, enhancing the country's fighting capability among them. The army, on the other hand, believed that one could fight the war with the means of 1870, and it took the kaiser's personal intervention to make a reluc-tant military establishment appoint Haber to the rank of cap-tain, thus giving him requisite authority and recognition.

Haber became the most important organizer of science in wartime Germany. As his son, a historian of science, wrote decades later, it had been a good choice: "In Haber . . . [the High Command] found a brilliant mind and an extremely energetic organizer, determined, and possibly also unscrupulous."[116] He reveled in rank and uniform and easy access to the highest quarters of state and army. To concentrate all one's energies in a cause one believes in and to do so in the shadow of danger is a heady experience. Haber proved to be a brilliant organizer, even an empire-builder, and he drove his subordinates relentlessly, as he drove himself. At last he could assume the role of "leader," which he thought was ideally suited to him.[117]*

Haber put his institute on a wartime footing, a kind of Manhattan Project before its time, enlisting 150 "scientific co-workers" and a far larger number of other staff. The institute organized the hugely expanded use of the Haber-Bosch process for the fixation of nitrogen so that the production of nitric acid for explosives and fertilizers would be adequate for the vastly increased need. In 1916 Haber reported to Rudolf von Valentini, chief of the Imperial Civil Cabinet and from its beginning a member of the institute's board, that the production of synthetic saltpeter, nonexistent in Germany before the war, now reached 25 million tons per month; delivered to the army at cost by seven chemical plants, it "has made possible the conduct of the war in the last few months."[118] (At cost? Given the prevalence of war profiteering, this seems a dubious assertion.) Without this effort, Germany's military capacity would have been exhausted by the spring of 1915 for lack of munitions, and the German people would have been starved for lack of fertilizers.

---

* Perhaps even more than his colleagues, Haber had a special penchant for celebrating great men as *Führer*. In Wilhelmine and Weimar Germany, the term was unburdened and endemic. By the end of Weimar, there was a growing hunger for *Führertum*. An innocent yearning for the exercise of responsibility eased the path for the corrupting triumph of villainous power, an elitism that led to nihilism.

Haber's best-known and most ambiguous wartime contribution was the preparation of poison gas. As he explained to Germany's foremost industrialist, Gustav Krupp von Bohlen und Halbach, after the first few months of the war it was clear that the offensive capabilities were weaker than the defensive ones on both sides, and only a new weapon could break the murderous stalemate of trench warfare. In experimenting with various kinds of gas, he narrowly escaped a deadly cloud of gas himself. His friend Willstätter prepared a gas mask adequate to protect German soldiers from Allied retaliation and from German gas drifting back into their lines because of prevailing westerly winds. Haber called on other young scientists, including Otto Hahn and James Franck, to help in preparations. When the Germans first used chlorine gas on April 22, 1915, they did so, under Haber's supervision, against Franco-Algerian troops at Ypres. It was an initial but far from decisive success. On the eastern front, Haber reported later: "The panic which the first attack at Ypres had caused among the enemy occurred among the Russians in the East only after repeated attacks at the same spot but then regularly."[119] The army never fully exploited the weapon—or so argued proponents of gas warfare.

During and after the war, Haber tried to explain his work in developing a weapon that outraged many people—in Germany but especially abroad. The Hague Conventions of 1899 and 1907 had prohibited the use of poisoned weapons. Haber believed that the use of gas would bring the war to a quick conclusion; he argued that the gas, which immobilized but usually did not kill, was a more humane weapon than the artillery bombardments that had become routine; he pointed out that the Allies had their own plans for introducing gas warfare, and Germany had merely anticipated them.[120] It would appear that neither Haber nor those closest to him, like Willstätter, worried about the legal and moral issues involved, such was the brutish atmosphere of war. Gas warfare did not prove decisive, though its horror—the terrifying choking, the blinding, the deaths, the experience even for survivors of a living death—has become an inextinguishable part of our collective memory, an early instance of science put to satanic service.

In a long, handwritten letter of January 1915 to Arnold Sommerfeld in Munich, Haber explained his new wartime life. He thanked Sommerfeld for his consoling words about the death of Otto Sackur in December 1914, a brilliant young physicist who died in an explosion in Haber's institute while experimenting on a new shell casing for the army: "He died as a soldier on the battlefield in the attempt to improve the technical means of warfare with the help of our discipline. My own scientific work has stopped. I spend my days as adviser to the war department when I don't travel to shooting ranges and factories."[121]

Otto Sackur had been a friend of both Habers. Clara Haber had known him since her student days in Breslau some fifteen years earlier. His death was a shock for her and immediate, terrifying proof of the horror of the war and of the dreadful participation of her husband—who had been at Sackur's side moments before the explosion. She was appalled at the human losses, appalled perhaps at her husband's total commitment of self and scientific knowledge, to war purposes. But there are hints of more intimate marital trouble as well. Haber returned to Berlin following his observation of the German army's first use of poison gas on April 22, and in the night of May 1–2, after a stormy argument, Clara shot herself with Haber's army pistol. No explanation of hers has survived, neither for the son who found his dying mother nor for her husband.

Can later generations have a sure sense of what drives an unhappy person to death? All the overly precise efforts at explaining a suicide—quite aside from any efforts to exploit such a tragedy for political or ideological purposes—are usually unsatisfactory.[122]* The oft-repeated assertion that Haber reacted coldly or indifferently to his wife's death is erroneous. He did

* Hermann Haber, son of Clara and Fritz, took his own life in 1947 in the United States, and Hermann's oldest daughter did the same a short time thereafter. Though the immediate circumstances of these deaths were different, the tragedy was the same.

what his character and the conditions seemed to dictate to a man such as himself: he threw himself *in extremis* back into his work. In fact, he left the next morning for his assignment at the Eastern front.*

By all accounts Haber was an indefatigable worker for the German cause, which he found physically exhausting, but psychologically exhilarating.** By mid-summer 1916, the now almost omnipotent Army Command recognized the need for still greater mobilization efforts, and Haber, given his experience and temperament, urged a centrally planned economy. The immediate need was for better allocation of manpower; in early September Haber discussed the matter with his friend Wichard von Moellendorff, who then sent him a memorandum outlining the need for and functions of a labor mobilization office within the war ministry. Such a plan was close to Moellendorff's conception of a corporate state in which labor and industry would collaborate with the state as an active partner and sometime arbiter.

By "temperament" Haber believed himself to be a "pessimist," but continuing to hope for a German victory, he opposed any kind of compromise peace. In early 1916, he wrote Valentini: "I am hoping for peace [in the next few months], though I would not want a peace by which France and Belgium would remain foes with a military capacity. Because quite aside from all ethical and political considerations, a peace that would oblige us to arm against a formidable enemy in the

---

* In October 1917, Haber married Charlotte Nathan in a church wedding at the Kaiser-Wilhelm Gedächtniskirche in Berlin, having insisted that Charlotte, a secular and emancipated woman of Jewish descent, convert to the Evangelical faith. The physical attraction to Charlotte, twenty years younger than himself, apparently was very strong, but soon Charlotte was suffering from her husband's total absorption in work that alternated with nervous exhaustion.

** In 1939, in his memorial lecture, Haber's one-time British student, J. E. Coates, put it well: "The war years were for Haber the greatest period of his life. . . . To be a great soldier, to obey and be obeyed—that, as his closest friends knew, was a deep-seated idea. . . . It must not however be supposed that he exalted and enjoyed war as such—on the contrary in his heart he hated its wastage and suffering." *Journal of the Chemical Society*, 1939, p. 1661.

West as we had to do so carefully in the past would impose on us material burdens that apparently today are not yet recognized." He then sketched the dangers of another war, dominated, as he believed it would be, by the airplane. But would any but a Carthaginian peace have given Germany a continental dominance? In early 1917, Haber still thought that unrestricted submarine warfare would force Britain to end the war. A year later he gradually lost his faith in a decisive German victory.[123]

Some Germans realized after the battle of the Marne in 1914 that a clearcut German victory on the western front was highly improbable. But the German military command deliberately misled the German people as to the odds: it also opposed all political demands for electoral reforms designed to mitigate the inequalities of the class system. The kaiser finally promised such reforms at Easter 1917; Haber sensed the dangers if these reforms were not promulgated. In February 1918 he wrote to Carl Duisberg, the head of the chemical giant Bayer: "I feel that the Conservatives' resistance to the [proposed] electoral reforms is most likely to lead us into the greatest internal difficulties and that our masses will not recover their good faith if they are now disappointed." By now, he was close to the Moderates, who were pleading for a reasonable peace and domestic reforms.[124]

The reforms were not adopted in time. Worse, the military dictatorship which by the end of the war had come to govern Germany in all but name did not prepare the people for the rapidly deteriorating military situation. Ludendorff's demand in September 1918 that a new government ask for an armistice without delay came as an unimaginable blow, even to Germans very close to the government, including Haber. At that moment German armies were everywhere on enemy territory and the people still thought that the recent triumph in the East would prove to be a prelude to success in the West. Only a people so deluded could have been persuaded later that indeed the armies had been victorious but had been "stabbed in the back" by internal enemies, by pacifists, socialists, and Jews.

This was the dreadful legacy that Germany's military-authoritarian leadership left a hapless people. The war that ended in Germany's defeat continued at home in bitter discord. A deeply divided people faced an overwhelmingly hostile world: the moral and physical consequences of the war were to be even more devastating than Einstein had anticipated.

IN the war Haber and Einstein had become fraternal opposites, but their friendship persisted despite their radically different views.* The war had awakened both of them from earlier apolitical slumbers; like the German people as a whole, they had become politicized. The armistice of November 11 that ended the killing was probably the last day of universal rejoicing. Germany's defeat and revolution, however, meant different things to Haber and Einstein. For Haber, it meant devastation, for Einstein, liberation. In 1918 Haber's world was shattered; Einstein's seemed in auspicious ascendancy.

The revolution of November 1918, which ended the German empire and established a republic, was a revolution in form but not in substance. At first the new Germany was led by

---

* Thus in January 1918 Haber wrote Einstein a long handwritten letter because he feared that his manner of meeting a request of Einstein's might have displeased the latter. Einstein wanted to have help for his friend Gunnar Nordström, a Finnish physicist, to travel to neutral Holland: Haber had gone to the very top with the request and apparently Einstein had rebuked him. Haber reassured Einstein that "nothing was further removed from my mind . . . than [to feel] pleasure at your unfamiliarity with military custom. . . . It is not only in the field of mathematical physics that life depends on the knowledge of and acceptance of certain formal connections and not only in the field in which you work miracles is it usually impossible to achieve success without the formal laws. For myself I merely ask that you believe that I am pleased and happy to be useful to you, that I have too much respect for your person and achievement to ever make fun about something you do and that I personally am extremely fond of you [*ich Sie persönlich lieb habe*]." Haber to Einstein, January 1918, Einstein Archives, Institute for Advanced Study, Princeton.

moderate and radical Socialists and headed by the deeply moderate Friedrich Ebert. Haber and Einstein, along with some scientists like Planck and humanists like Ernst Troeltsch and Friedrich Meinecke, accepted the new regime, if often with misgivings, and sought to work with it to salvage what could be salvaged. Of these major German figures, Einstein was no doubt the most sympathetic to the new rulers, but they all realized that the Ebert government needed support in battling disorder and social radicalism at home and revanchism abroad, liquidating a war that right-wing annexationists had heedlessly prolonged. By contrast, much of the German professoriate turned sullen; the dignitaries of the old order felt diminished by Germany's defeat, deprived of some of their exalted prestige, estranged from a democratic republic. Recurrent struggles broke out between the tiny band of reasonable men and the great mass of resentful discontents.

Haber was destined to undergo in private life what his compatriots were suffering collectively: he, too, was "demobilized" and had to find his way back to civilian life; he, too, suffered from the humiliations that the Versailles settlement imposed on all Germans.* All through the war he had driven himself ruthlessly; exhaustion and crushing disappointment led to something akin to a nervous breakdown.[125] When his name appeared on the Allied list of war criminals to be extradited for trial, his safety was threatened; for a brief time he sought asylum in Switzerland. In those dark days even a letter from the minister of war, Heinrich Scheüch, acknowledging Haber's resignation from his post, brought little comfort:

During the long duration of the war you put your broad knowledge and your energy unrestrainedly in the service

---

* On May 10, 1919, Richard Willstätter wrote to his erstwhile student and friend, the Swiss chemist Arthur Stoll: "Now that the terms of the peace have become public we live in the deepest depression, almost in despair." I am grateful to Arthur Stoll's son to have given me access to his father's important correspondence.

of the fatherland. Thanks to your colleagues' high esteem
you were able to mobilize German chemistry. Germany
was not destined to emerge victoriously from this war.
That it did not succumb already in the first few months to
the superiority of its enemies because of shortages in munitions, dynamite, and other chemical compounds of nitrogen is in the first place due to you. . . . Your brilliant
successes will always live in history and remain . . . unforgotten.[126]

Fifteen years later, by decree, they were forgotten.

Haber had long been worried as well about Germany's desperate economic plight; the country was bankrupt and ill-fed
because of the continued Allied blockade. Moellendorff, working together with Rudolf Wissell, the Socialist minister of economics, was preparing a radical revision of the economic
order, hoping to establish a corporate system, a *Gemeinwirtschaft*, which the ministry defined as a "national economy that
is systematically managed and socially controlled for the
benefit of the national community." Haber wrote to him in December 1918, affectionate in tone, if skeptical that such a plan
would find popular support:

I don't believe it will be possible to spare our people . . .
the hard sacrifices, the oppressive unhappy conditions
after the war. The people do not want to see this, and
tough, strict coercion will be required. If we get an enemy
occupation, then that coercion will come for certain. If we
are spared an occupation, we must achieve feats of self-
discipline that we today seem incapable of inspiring in the
large masses. . . . I think that the present state of the world
has as much to do with the original Christian ideas as the
future economic society [will have] with the ideas which
you now advocate. Unmistakable influence but very feeble likeness. The Revolution was a popular indictment
[*Vehmegericht*] of the political system, not of capitalism.
The nation is "bourgeois" to its very depths.

Hence, he believed, Germany would reject the idealistic, communal vision that Moellendorff and Wissell sought to realize.[127] And indeed, a few months later, the Wissell-Moellendorff scheme was dead. Haber had been right in his pessimism: the nation *was* bourgeois, egoistic, not ready for the sacrifices that Moellendorff's 'Germanic Socialism' would have imposed. Haber also knew that there had been a deeper reason why Germany had not stood the test of war. In the Seven Years' War, he wrote, Frederick the Great had triumphed against a ring of enemies: "But such a test can be mastered only by a state that signifies for all its members honor and well-being, a meaning for life and a faith for the future. The Industrial State [that is, imperial Germany] which for thirty years lived in enmity with its factory workers does not pass such a test."[128]

At the time Einstein, who had detested the old regime, celebrated the revolutionary change. In early December 1918 he wrote to Michele Besso, "Something great has truly been attained. The religion of militarism has disappeared. [The disappearance of the old order] is for the likes of us . . . a liberation. . . . I am enjoying the reputation of an unblemished Socialist."[129] At the same time he warned students against revolutionary excesses: he opposed violence or dictatorship of any kind, at least for his own country. For a brief moment, Einstein was in step with German politics—and angered at Allied vindictiveness.

In December 1918 Einstein wrote Arnold Sommerfeld: "If England and America have enough sense to be close to each other, then there can be no more wars of any magnitude. The economy dominated by military considerations which I find so repugnant will also disappear. . . . I am firmly convinced that culture-loving Germans will soon be allowed to be proud of their fatherland again—with more reason than before 1914."[130] By July 1919, he wrote a close friend that if the social difficulties could be alleviated, "then we could be pleased with the country we live in. Then it would once again be confirmed that

failure and deprivation are the best educators and purifiers."
For the time being the tendency was to blame the foreign
enemy and too little was done to "expose the old sins."[131]

For Einstein, the year 1919 marked a unique triumph that
transformed his life. In March, a British expedition headed by
A. S. Eddington had observed the solar eclipse; another group
went to Sobral in Brazil. In November, Royal Society president
and Nobel laureate J. J. Thomson announced that the results
showed the gravitational light deflections that Einstein had assumed, thus confirming the general theory of relativity. Thomson hailed Einstein's work as "one of the greatest—perhaps *the*
greatest of achievements in the history of human thought."[132]

Almost overnight Einstein became a celebrated hero: the
German press, or at least its liberal-democratic segment, fea-
tured him prominently, and his picture, often reproduced, became familiar. The new cult of the tousled genius was symptomatic of a deeper change: once dignitaries of the old order,
preferably bemedaled and in uniform, had appeared; now appeared the picture of this solitary sage in his meticulously cultivated informality. He was an asset in a country that was on
the brink of bankruptcy and deliberately shut out of the international community of scientists.

He was celebrated abroad as well: a scientific genius, untainted by wartime chauvinism and of dubious nationality,
had revolutionized man's conception of the universe and
newly defined the fundamentals of time and space, and he had
done so in a fashion so recondite that only a handful of scientists could grasp the new mysterious truth. French and English
scientists could celebrate him, anoint him as the first "rehabili-
tated" German; these were accolades taunting to other Germans. In fact public renown generally and Allied acclaim in
particular did not sit well with some of Einstein's German
colleagues.

However differently, Haber and Einstein became important
representative men in the Weimar Republic. Haber served German science with all his energy and ambition; Einstein, by his

mere presence, became, unwittingly, a national asset. They drew closer again, despite remaining differences, held together by ties of respect and affection, by common pursuits, by private needs—and by the anti-Semitic vilifiers of Einstein, who, Haber feared, might drive Einstein to accept an offer from abroad.

Acclaim engendered controversy: some notable German scientists expressed their reservations about Einstein's relativity theory in an ad hominem, anti-Semitic fashion. Einstein realized anew that the nationalist-racist element in German life was very much alive, made still more dangerous by what he called the Germans' "inborn servility."[133] Haber had no such suspicions, but he too encountered the dark underworld of German life in the calumnies directed at friends and sometimes at himself. In those years of public attacks, Einstein found in Haber a solid friend and counselor.

In February 1920, Einstein's university lecture was disrupted, allegedly because the students protested the presence of nonstudents at the lecture, but the press emphasized anti-Semitic undertones. In August the press played up a public meeting that denounced Einstein's theories; Einstein replied publicly and—to the distress of his friends—polemically, asserting that the attacks sprang not from a desire for truth but from political-racial antagonisms: "If I belonged to the Deutsch-Nationale Partei [the right-wing party of Germanic nationalism], with or without swastika, instead of being a Jew of progressive international commitment, then . . . ." He omitted the obvious conclusion: then there would have been no attack. None of this pleased Einstein's colleagues, but Laue, Nernst, and Rubens published a statement saying that no one surpassed Einstein "in the recognition of others' intellectual property, in personal modesty, and in distaste for publicity."[134]

In September 1920, at a formal meeting at Bad Nauheim of German natural scientists, the Nobel laureate Philipp Lenard resumed his attack on relativity; he hated the publicity glorifying what he thought a dubious scientific achievement. (In later years, he said outright that relativity was "a Jewish fraud," a position that the Nazis readily espoused.)[135] Haber wrote to Willstätter about the Bad Nauheim meeting: "Its scientific yield for me was not particularly great, its results in other respects depressing. . . . Nernst and I had to lead the defense" against a large group led by the physicist Willy Wien that sought to dislodge the existing board composed of Berlin members. He continued: "Planck told me unambiguously that in the negotiations Wien was motivated not by considerations of substance or the effect on science but by his anti-Semitic, right-wing attitude. . . . I am in agreement with Planck and Sommerfeld, both of whom are truly well disposed toward me, that from now on I shall remain in the background." Haber also mentioned that Carl Bosch had given a lecture, ignoring Haber's part in the fixation of nitrogen, focusing almost entirely on the achievements of his own firm—from which Haber had become estranged. No wonder he was depressed. A few months later, Haber hurried to his father's deathbed; they were reconciled and he grieved greatly.[136]

Like Planck, Haber was concerned to preserve the constellation of scientific genius in Berlin, with Einstein its most brilliant star. When in 1919 Zurich sought to recapture Einstein, Haber insisted that the state and Koppel raise Einstein's salary in Berlin. Fearing that Einstein might mind this intervention, he wrote to him: "Our life has had a confusing character [*bunten Inhalt*] since we moved more closely together at the Karlsruhe meeting [in 1911]. . . . But I think that though the war years drove us apart, they still left me the moral right to ask you for information as to what caused you to negotiate with Zurich about a return there." In order not to lose Einstein, Haber would try to create "satisfactory conditions" in Berlin:

Satisfactory at least in regard to history which will some day demand an accounting of the conditions under which you had to labor to continue Newton's work. . . . If you should have the idea that you don't want that much money—and I believe you capable of this—then you still have the option of using the money for the expenses of the Institute you head. . . . I think it important that you remain silent about your supplementary income. . . . So scold me, but don't make me angry, because I am supposed to rest and I must be right.[137]

(Einstein's supplementary income included royalties on his writings; for a fifteen-page lecture in 1920 he received an advance of 3,000 marks and by 1922, nearly 6,500 copies had been sold).[138]

Like most people, Einstein probably had a complicated, ambivalent feeling about money.* He was both indifferent to and at times covetous of it—or at least his friend Haber was covetous for him, and his second wife as well. Money was a necessary but never a sufficient condition—not for Einstein and not for Haber.

In 1920, the press reported that Einstein, angered by the attacks on him, had decided to leave Germany. At once, Haber urged him to disregard the anti-Semites:

This combine of nullities . . . [cannot] balance the collective admiration . . . which all serious scientists accord you. . . . All judicious people have attributed a leadership capacity to you and in such great measure as has not been true since Helmholtz, and the anger induced by the stupid fellows can lead an irritable nervous cripple like me to act *ab*

---

* In January 1903, Einstein wrote to Michele Besso that his sister Maja "at the bottom of her heart, deep in the tiny chamber of her unconscious" might have different feelings than she herself would acknowledge or be aware of about some putative pecuniary obligations she had to a former employee of their father's. *CPAE*, vol. 5, p. 11.

Haber wanted money for Einstein. In 1920, he charged a Dr. Lieber in New York with coordinating Einstein's schedule for a projected (and then postponed) trip to the United States: "Herr Einstein would not undertake this trip and these lectures in America if he were a rich man." He had originally hoped to earn $30,000 in his six-month stay, but Haber thought $25,000 a more likely figure. Clearly Einstein's fame was profitable, especially in wealthy and culture-hungry America. Haber to Dr. Lieber, November 30, 1920; Einstein to Haber, October 1920, Einstein Archives, Institute for Advanced Study, Princeton.

irato but not you, [with your] Olympian peace. . . . Not the push of stupid fellows but inadequate stimulation by others could drive you away. Everyone uses up people for intellectual nourishment and I understand that Berlin has become a kind of empty plate.[139]

However, if it was not intellectual companionship but, rather, material conditions that were wanting, then Haber wanted to help.

Einstein turned down all the enticing offers from abroad precisely because he appreciated the Berlin circle. In 1918 he described to Besso, and to others later,

how between my closest colleagues (especially Planck) and myself, beautiful relations have developed, and *how* here everybody has always been forthcoming and still is toward me, and if you further realize that my labors have found their fruition only because of the understanding I have found *here*, then you will understand why I could not bring myself to turn my back on this place. . . . Here people reach out to me while keeping a certain distance and thus life proceeds almost without tension; I have learned that in life.

In 1928, he wrote to Laue: "I see at every occasion how fortunate I can consider myself for having you and Planck as my colleagues."[140]

Haber and Einstein were honored and became ever more prominent. In 1920, Haber received the Nobel Prize in chemistry for 1918—much to the chagrin of the public in Allied countries.* In late 1922, Einstein, while traveling to Japan, learned

---

* But coincidental with the Nobel Prize for Haber came a wounding academic setback. In September 1919, Emil Fischer, the renowned organic chemist, committed suicide. Haber hoped that Willstätter would accept the call to Berlin as Fischer's successor, but he declined, at which time Haber was proposed as the leading candidate. However, Carl Duisberg, the most influential chemical industrialist of the period, used all his power to thwart the appointment on the grounds that Haber was not an organic chemist, hence of less value to the

that he would be awarded the Nobel Prize for physics "for his discovery of the law of the photoelectric effect"—not for the theory of relativity. A complicated comedy ensued: Einstein being away could not receive the medal himself; custom prescribed that the diplomatic representative of the honoree's country would receive it in his place. Swiss and German representatives vied for the honor—both of them with good claims. Einstein had clung to his Swiss citizenship and, when traveling, flaunted his Swiss passport; but his appointment in Berlin as a civil servant had automatically conferred German citizenship on him. After long bureaucratic wrangling, the Swedish ambassador to Germany delivered the medal to Einstein in Berlin—and Einstein was now formally allowed to keep his double citizenship.[141] A year earlier, Einstein had accepted a signal German honor: he was elected to the Arts and Science Division [Friedensklasse] of the Orden Pour le Mérite, the highest German distinction, with a membership restricted to thirty Germans and thirty foreigners.*

Haber and Einstein now served the Weimar Republic in important if very different ways. Haber became the driving force behind the founding in 1920 of the Emergency Committee for German Science, its purpose to raise funds for basic research from the German government and the Länder governments, and, above all, from private sources at home and abroad. It would distribute these funds as well. A steadily worsening inflation threatened to reduce state support for German science, and German industry was expected to open its coffers. But scientists like Haber came to realize that the indispensable help of industry brought with it the danger of excessive industrial authority. Meanwhile, individual scientists suffered from

---

chemical industry. From then on Haber regarded Duisberg—with whom he had multiple contacts—as "enemy in seeming friendship." Haber to Willstätter, January 7, 1926, HC.

* He seems to have made a habit of not wearing the insignia of the Orden at the prescribed meetings, a defiance at no cost. Harry Graf Kessler, Tagebücher 1918–1937 (Frankfurt am Main, 1961), p. 457.

inflation and the effects of the Allied isolation of German science; in February 1920 Willstätter complained that he was cut off from the great scientific journals from abroad.[142] Haber invested a huge amount of time in this new committee, a continuation of German *Wissenschaftspolitik*. He was organizer and spokesman:

> The collapse of our country as a great political power will in the future continue to be a warning that our existence as a people depends on the maintenance of our intellectual great-power standing, which is inseparable from our scientific enterprise. Whether the Committee remains the executor of this idea will depend on whether within the academic community the three enemies of every scientific self-administration—prejudice, self-seeking, and administrative incompetence—will be limited to the harmless realm of individual personal malcontents.[143]

Ambitious, and afflicted by various somatic and psychosomatic ailments, Haber directed his institute with restless energy at his usual furious pace.* And again he put his scientific talent at the service of his country. This time the idea was to extract gold from the ocean—in order to liberate Germany from the crushing burden of reparations, just as at an earlier time he had successfully fixed nitrogen from the air in order to liberate Germany from a potential enemy stranglehold on nitrates. German science would restore German fortune. The new idea first came to him in 1920; in 1923, he set sail on an ocean trip with a floating laboratory. But the search proved futile: the gold in ocean water was not economically extractable, and he had to abandon the effort.

Haber's intense involvement in every aspect of German science was public knowledge. He had contacts everywhere—with officialdom, with politicians (he was closest to the Democratic Party), and with people of rank in the private world. But

---

* My father, at the end of his medical residency, worked at Haber's Institute for Physical Chemistry from 1921 to 1923.

he worried about Weimar's future in the shadow of Versailles. In the early years he renewed his ties to the army and may have been involved in the super-secret deliberations about the use of poison gas in a future war. His former associates in the army apparently told him of Soviet-German collaboration in this field, which by the mid-1920s ceased; I doubt whether even his closest friends—Willstätter, say—knew of this part of Haber's life.* Likewise Haber and his institute experimented with pesticides and developed a deadly substance that came to be known as Zyklon B. The horror of Haber's involvement with the gas that later murdered millions, including friends and distant relatives, beggars description.[144]

In the meantime Einstein, the new world sensation, embarked on a whole series of trips to foreign countries, lecturing and visiting old friends and new colleagues. He traveled within Europe, most importantly to Paris in March-April 1922, where, at the express urging of Foreign Minister Walther Rathenau, he had accepted an invitation to lecture at the Collège de France. He was received in the grandest style, and his friend and colleague Paul Langevin took him on a tour of devastated northern France, to the rubbles of Reims. The German embassy in Paris reported to Berlin that "Einstein, who after all had to be recognized as a German, brought German culture and German science new attention and glory."[145] Einstein's triumph annoyed many of his German colleagues who were still suffering from a kind of quarantine imposed by Allied scien-

* In a remarkable letter of October 8, 1933, written from Switzerland in English, Haber reported to the Paris representative of the Rockefeller Foundation—which had supported his institute—that a new Nazi-appointed director of the institute was likely "to study chemical warfare with the Institute. . . . You will remember that in war time I have been the leader of the chemical warfare in Germany and that I have been proud to work for the military authorities with the institute as experimental basis. But after the Armistice, I have cancelled every such work and fully declined to renew it in whatever form." Haber was imperfectly fluent in French, uncertain in English—a common priority in those days. The letter is part of the Rockefeller Foundation Archives, R.G. 1.1 717D Kaiser Wilhelm Institute, 1929–35 (box 13, folder 110), Rockefeller Archive Center.

tists. Einstein covered the globe, traveling to Japan, Palestine, to North and South America, and to most European countries.

Successive German governments were alert to Einstein's triumphs abroad and considered him a great emissary. When the very first attacks on Einstein had taken place in Germany, the German chargé in London, Friedrich Sthamer, reported that the English press were closely watching these events, speculating that Einstein might leave Germany. Sthamer warned: "With such a man we can make real cultural propaganda and we should not drive him out of Germany."[146] The German Foreign Office had the greatest interest in keeping Einstein at home so that he could help abroad.

One of Einstein's first trips reflected a political passion of his own—and brought to the surface a great difference between Haber and Einstein. In the spring of 1921 Haber learned that Einstein planned to go to the United States with Chaim Weizmann, leading Zionist and distinguished chemist at Manchester University; the purpose was to raise money for a Hebrew University in Jerusalem. Haber, as we know, had converted; Einstein identified with the oppressed everywhere, but most especially with the oppressed of his own "tribe." In May 1914, for example, he had refused an important invitation from the Imperial Academy of Sciences in St. Petersburg: "I find it repugnant to travel without necessity to a country in which my tribesmen are so brutally persecuted."[147] He had always been aware of the pervasive strength of anti-Jewish feelings in Europe. Gerald Holton has written of Einstein's "vulnerability to pity." Late in life, Einstein claimed that when he first came to Berlin, he saw Zionism as "the only solution" in the face of the servile attitude of German Jews. In October 1919 he wrote to a colleague that "the Zionist cause is very close to my heart. . . . I am very confident of the happy development of the Jewish colony and am glad that there should be a tiny speck on this earth in which the members of our tribe should not be aliens. . . . One can be internationally minded, without renouncing interest in one's tribal comrades." For assimilationist

German Jews he had bemused contempt, expressed most forcefully in a letter of 1920 to the Central League of German Citizens of the Jewish Faith. He mocked the very name of the league, which he thought expressed the view "I don't want to have anything to do with my impoverished Eastern Jewish brethren," and, second, "I don't want to be regarded as a child of my people but only as a member of a religious community." He demanded "more dignity and independence in our own ranks!" He was neither a German citizen nor did he possess anything akin to a "Jewish faith." There would always be anti-Semitism as long as Jews and non-Jews lived together: "Perhaps it is thanks to it that we have been able to preserve our race. . . . Let us leave the *goj* his anti-Semitism and preserve for ourselves the love for our kind." He thought German Jews peculiarly susceptible to servility.[148]

On matters Jewish and on questions concerning Germans and Jews, Haber and Einstein differed—and retained their friendship. In 1921 Haber pleaded with Einstein not to go to the United States just then, not to sail on an Allied ship or to associate himself with former enemies. He recalled their friendship, adding: "Everything you have done, as long as I have known you, has sprung from the nobility of your human nature and the goodness of your heart." But his doings now had the significance that "the acts of princes" had in earlier times. Germans would consider such a trip as an act of treason:

> So many Jews went into the war, perished, became impoverished, without complaining, because they thought it their duty. Their lives and deaths have not eliminated anti-Semitism from the world but, in the eyes of those who make up the dignity and greatness of our country, have demeaned it to something odious and undignified. Do you want by virtue of your conduct to wipe out all that we have gained from so much blood and suffering? . . . You sacrifice definitely the narrow ground on which the existence of academic teachers and students of Jewish faith in our institutions of higher education rest.

Einstein answered on the same day, insisting that he must
go, especially "after I have seen lately in countless examples
how perfidiously and unlovingly one treats superb young Jews
here and seeks to cut off their chances for education." Nobody
could accuse him of being unfaithful to his German friends, he
claimed, not after he had turned down offers from all over the
world. "I did this by the way not out of attachment to Germany but to my dear German friends, of whom you are one of
the most outstanding and most benevolent." "Dear Haber,"
the letter ends, "An acquaintance has recently called me a
'wild animal.' The wild animal likes you and will visit you
before his departure."[149] Einstein went with Weizmann to
America, pleading for the Zionist cause and giving well-paid
lectures at American universities. He spoke at Columbia, for
example, and in 1923, at the time of Germany's terrifying inflation, the university made him an extravagantly generous
offer, which he refused.[150]

Neither Haber nor any of his other friends could restrain
Einstein from his new political involvements. He took his fame
as a warrant to make public utterances on a number of subjects; he had come to realize during the war as well as in his
scientific work that the outsider, the *Einspanner*, may intuit
truths that are at odds with conventional wisdom. Among academics, he had been almost alone in his absolute if quiet opposition to the war—and he had been right. After the war, and in
a sense justified by its end, he espoused pacifism, internationalism, Zionism, and a mild brand of socialism. These were
causes that his scorn for German imperialism had taught him:
they were the reverse of chauvinism and German nationalism.
Postwar progressives in many countries held similar views
(with the exception of Zionism), and they were anathema to
most German academics.

Throughout Weimar, Einstein stayed close to "progressive"
groups in politics and culture. He favored the underdog, he
signed manifestos for what he assumed to be humanitarian
causes, and he supported organizations that sought to improve

Soviet-German relations. (Unbeknownst to him, the Reichs-wehr and the Red Army were already conspiring to translate such pious hopes into hard reality.) His politics were vaguely socialist; capitalism spelled greed and inequality to him. He was impressed by the progress he thought had been made in the Soviet Union, though he was largely oblivious to the price. A few times, he denounced repression there, too. Like so many others, Einstein continued his wartime antipathies into the peacetime period, usually without acknowledging the deeper source.

Right-wing colleagues and frightened German bourgeois de-tested Einstein. But even friends were dubious about the pro-priety of a physicist's pronouncing so freely and so radically on issues of politics and morality. He was not deterred; he gave speeches and wrote articles and did so in his curious philosophical-polemical style, with its ironic regret at the folly and frailty of man, especially of Germans. He knew how to wound the German soul and encountered enough provocation to practice his skill. He was no longer heeding his own injunc-tion, in November 1918, to Leo Arons, when the latter asked him to sign a radical petition. At that time, Einstein explained that the loud pronouncements of German academics about politics should have taught everyone that the first imperative was "MAUL HALTEN," or Keep Your Trap Shut.[151]

Einstein's occasional radical pronouncements notwithstand-ing, both he and Haber moved in the highest circles of Weimar political and social *Prominenz*. Berlin was full of flourishing sa-lons where the elites of wealth and power, of artistic and intel-lectual eminence, met. The mingling of diverse personalities, of Christians and Jews, for example, of the esoteric with the con-ventional, of people with often passionately and wildly oppos-ing political views—all this created a fascinating, entrancing, supercharged, if at times superficial atmosphere for Republi-can Berlin. Harry Count Kessler's *Diaries* document this buf-feted, brilliant milieu. Haber and Einstein also encountered each other at the Prussian Academy, whose meetings Einstein attended with astounding regularity, and at other scientific sessions. They lived and worked very much in the public world, on intimate terms with the great of their times. Both men seemed securely anchored in Berlin's institutional life as well, though Einstein remained both an idol and a recluse; Haber was neither.

And yet the glitter and elegance were only part of the story: both men encountered the resentful viciousness that also crept around Weimar. Haber's correspondence and Einstein's life make clear that neither of them was shielded from the anti-Semitic impulses that were both silently and noisily endemic in Weimar Germany, strong in the upper classes though largely absent in some notable families, among them Laue, Planck, and Bonhoeffer. In Weimar, Jews reached positions of new prominence—and the anti-Semitism that had turned more vile and popular toward the end of the war now became part of the battle cry of the radical viper. And still, the signals were hard to read. Many German Jews thought that anti-Semitism was an aberration that would vanish; others took a darker view, and some turned Zionist. In most it kept alive a perpetual unease, an ambivalence about self and countryman.

Haber and Einstein knew that anti-Semitism and anti-republicanism were closely linked in Germany. Einstein, however egregious himself, agreed at times that the enemy need not be goaded, and in 1921 warned Walther Rathenau—whom he had known for years—against accepting the portfolio at the Foreign Ministry because of prevailing resentments against Jews. The murder of Rathenau in 1922 was the most shocking anti-republican and anti-Semitic outrage. Einstein wrote for *Neue Rundschau*: "That hatred, delusion, and ingratitude could go so far—I still would not have thought it. But to those responsible for the ethical education of the German people for the last fifty years, I would want to call out: By their fruits you shall know them."[152] There was ample reason to fear that Einstein might be the next victim of a nationalist assassination.

Richard Willstätter, also a Nobel laureate and a fervent German patriot, was another German-Jewish scientist who repeatedly encountered the anti-Jewish prejudices of the time. In 1915, King Ludwig III of Bavaria signed Willstätter's appointment as a full professor but admonished his minister, "This is the last time I will let you have a Jew." In 1924, when the Munich faculty objected to the appointment of Victor M. Goldschmidt, who was the most qualified successor for a particular vacancy, Willstätter knew that the opposition was based entirely on presumptive racial reasons: the same evening, he resigned his professorship, never to enter his university laboratory again. Haber wrote him instantly: "The blow will echo throughout the world. I can understand that in the matter of Victor Goldschmidt you encountered more Hitlerism than you can bear."[153] Willstätter withdrew, believing—wrongly—that at least in the private realm he would be insulated from the passions of his time. He never returned to the university, the unanimous pleas of students and colleagues notwithstanding. A faithful assistant carried on his experiments, which he would discuss with her in daily conversations.

Public issues troubled Haber and Einstein; private disappointments kept them close. Both suffered from the sorrows and sufferings that no one is spared, but which to them came in serious blows. Haber's health was extremely fragile, his insomnia a constant affliction, and his second marriage came apart in the mid-1920s, roughly at the same time that he lost a major part of his wealth in bad investments in South America. The divorced wife's onerous demands coinciding with his shrinking income from investments caused him financial worries, greatly worsened after the onset of the Great Depression.[154]

He had his many moments of self-doubt, of lacerating dissatisfaction with self. Medical solicitude—often in the form of comprehending, compassionate encouragement—helped, but only work restored psychic well-being and full engagement on

behalf of science or friends; he had a passion to lead, to organize projects that would transform vision into reality. In good
times and in bad he indulged his passion for chess and detective stories. In 1920, together with a friend, he bought a run-
down estate *cum* farm in southern Württemberg, near the Lake
of Constance. He mocked his own role as rural renovator—in
fact his feats of light-hearted self-mockery, often scribbled in
verse form, lightened his own dissatisfied disposition.

Einstein's life was different—and somehow easier. He
viewed the world with bemused irony, skeptical about individuals and everyday arrangements, strangely confident that
the world could be ordered harmoniously and justly. His
views on public issues were often a mixture of high seriousness
of motive with the mischievous note of the clever, rebellious
child. The trappings of fame and his amiable imagination facilitated his indulgence in a succession of erotic attachments. The
most serious of these was his love for his one-time secretary
Betty Neumann in 1923–34, but there were other women, much
to the chagrin of his wife.* In March 1928, he suffered a serious
circulatory collapse; his recovery took many months.

Haber had an exceptional capacity for friendship, a gift of
character that he cultivated. Friendship, I think, had a special
place for creative and vulnerable people in an age when seeking pastoral or professional help was hardly thought of. Letters—then more highly prized than now—were means of
unburdening oneself. In those years Haber remained the paternal, practical friend to Einstein and a key intermediary between him and his former wife. He advised, even mildly lectured Einstein about his financial obligations to Mileva and he
also helped to instill greater compassion for the woman who
was caring for his friend's children. (The younger Einstein son,

* In my work in the Einstein Archives in Jerusalem I was once given by mis-
take the primitively wrapped (but closed) file of his correspondence with Neumann. Before I might have been tempted to tamper, the file was quickly
snatched away from me, but I seem to remember that in the head archivist's
office I saw a photo of Einstein inscribed to "Betty" with a poem.

Eduard, called Tede, was diagnosed as schizophrenic in 1920 and had to be institutionalized; he died in the Bürghölzli Sanitarium in 1965.)

Both men had their share of suffering. Haber lost one wife to suicide, another in divorce; Einstein occasionally mused about the difficulties inherent in marriage and in later years acknowledged his failure as husband. Einstein cherished his solitude, but there was loneliness, too, and intermittent yearning for companionship. A letter from Haber to Einstein in December 1928 suggests the intimate candor between them:

> Ever since I separated from my second wife in the fall of 1926, something inside me was broken. . . . I needed [the separation] for survival. But that earlier I had led my life in such a way that at the age of almost 60 I could not endure my marriage any longer and had to separate myself from beloved children, that gnawed at me and humiliated me in my own eyes. [I recall] the proofs of warmest sympathy from those whom I quietly love. And it matters a great deal to me, my dear Albert Einstein, that you have a good opinion of my usefulness and it encourages me in my depressed hours or more exactly in the long days in which I am wholly filled with a sense of superfluity and mediocrity.[155]

Haber and Einstein shared one other major effort: they both hoped, jointly and separately, to repair the breach in the international community of scientists. In 1919 representatives of the leading scientific academies in the Allied countries established a new organization, the International Research Council, an umbrella organization for a number of international unions covering different branches of science. A contradictory aim burdened the new organization from its inception: it was to promote international cooperation *and* exclude Germany—and the other Central Powers—from its ranks. This deliberate breach in what had always been an international commitment on the part of scientists bespoke the mood of the moment—and

continued to hang over the decade of the 1920s, one more instance of missed opportunities. Scientists in Allied countries
continued to boycott German scientists, that is, they refused to
admit them to international meetings or organizations. The *re-
vanchiste* sentiments of Allied scientists had their counterpart
in the resentful, sullen *Trotzigkeit* (truculence) of the Germans
themselves. If foreigners did not want to deal with Germans,
Germans *a fortiori* did not want to deal with them, either. Einstein thought the Allied boycott and the German counterboy-
cott detrimental to science, hence irrational; he had contempt
for nationalist narrowness in any form. Haber considered the
reciprocal boycott detrimental to the fatherland, to its recovery; strangely enough, the inventor of poison gas warfare
emerged as the most important and ultimately successful scientist in unpoisoning the atmosphere in the scientific community, if anything more successful in neutral and Allied countries than among recalcitrant Germans.[156]

In 1922, Einstein accepted a request from the League of Nations to serve on its International Committee on Intellectual
Cooperation, a feeble forerunner of UNESCO. The committee
had distinguished members, including Marie Curie and Lorentz, Henri Bergson and Gilbert Murray; the League chose the
members and they were not designated as official representatives of their nation. Still, Einstein was uncomfortable in his
new role—despite his affection for Curie and Lorentz. After
the murder of Rathenau in June 1922, he thought a Jew should
not serve as even an unofficial representative of Germans who
would not want him in that position; in 1923, at the time of the
French occupation of the Ruhr, he resigned altogether, expressing his disappointment with the League itself, which "discred-
ited the ideal of an international organization." Madame Curie
(and others) sought to persuade him that existing imperfec-
tions did not warrant complete withdrawal, and in 1924 Einstein rejoined the commission. In 1925 he urged Planck to organize a German commission for international cooperation, but

Planck hesitated for three months, torn by conflicting loyalties, and finally declined. Einstein explained to Lorentz that he had not persisted because Planck's response sprang from some deep inner conviction, which was primary, and his unsatisfactory rational explanation was secondary. Einstein continued his intermittent involvement with a distinguished and ineffectual body. A committee person he was not.

Meanwhile he continued his frequent travels to foreign countries, always gratefully monitored by German embassies, who were delighted with the *éclat* with which he was received. In 1925, in Buenos Aires, Einstein wrote in his diary: "Funny people, these Germans.I am a stinking flower for them and still they keep putting me in their buttonholes."[157]

Haber meanwhile worked incessantly on behalf of German science policy—at home in connection with the Emergency Committee for German Science and abroad with friends and colleagues in neutral and Allied countries. At times the two facets of his activities were linked: he worked with the Rockefeller Foundation, which awarded his institute various grants within its program of support for German science; in 1924, he attended the centenary of the Benjamin Franklin Institute in Philadelphia as the German delegate of the Prussian Academy of Science and Berlin University. His chief effort was to heal the breach symbolized by the International Research Council (IRC) and its exclusion of German members. He negotiated simultaneously with Dutch colleagues who sought to soften the Allied boycott and German "hotheads" of right-wing persuasion who relished Allied vindictiveness as confirming their own view of Allied envy and duplicity. Gradually the anti-German sentiment among British and American scientists softened.

In all his work over these years he was—again—in closest touch with the relevant German ministries, with Foreign Minister Gustav Stresemann and occasionally with German chancellors directly. He paralleled Stresemann's efforts to deepen the Locarno spirit of 1925, followed by German entry into the League of Nations in 1926, working toward a genuine reconciliation with France. In December 1925, Haber sent Chancellor Hans Luther two handwritten letters regarding the negotiations concerning the IRC. The French-Belgian contingent had obstructed Anglo-American efforts to lift the exclusionary clause against Germany, but a final and favorable decision would most likely be taken in June 1926. Haber worked closely with French scientists and politicians (especially with Paul Painlevé, mathematician and left-centrist politician who in the late 1920s was minister of defense); these efforts led to a change in the French position. Meanwhile German scientists were likely to make strong preconditions before accepting an Allied invitation to join the IRC, and some even wished to start an entirely new organization, but Haber warned the chancellor: "The world wants again to *work with us*, but the Western powers don't want *our leadership*, only *our participation*." He added further that some Germans favored a Russian initiative that would lead to a German-Russian counter-organization, something that would flatter German pride but injure German interests; the important scientific developments occurred west of the Rhine.

Successive German governments were far more supportive of Haber's efforts than were the various scientific organizations within Germany. In the summer of 1926, the IRC repealed the exclusionary clause, but it took another five years before German organizations were ready to join the IRC. All of this repeated in miniature the political conflicts on a worldwide scale. After the occupation of the Ruhr in 1923, governments on both sides worked toward reconciliation, while a large part of the German public wanted to repay earlier Allied vindictiveness with their own continued defiance. (German scientists had practiced nationalist obduracy; it prepared them for their later support of Hitler.)

Haber simultaneously worked for German entry into the International Union of Pure and Applied Chemistry—and again the negotiations with the three German chemical societies proved more difficult than with foreigners; time and again Haber had to battle German stubbornness until finally in 1930 German scientists joined the International Union. In fact, Haber was designated as president of the union; he hesitated to accept because of ill health but wanted to secure this honor for a German colleague, and when this proved impossible, he was formally elected to the office in 1933—at which time he had to decline because as a Jew, he explained, he could not accept such an office on behalf of German science. That incident is but a part of the later tragedy.[158]

Haber also developed a special interest in Japan, recognizing the ambition and potential of a nation that already in prewar times had looked to German science, especially medicine, as models to emulate or imitate. Weimar's first ambassador to Japan was an old close acquaintance of Haber's, Wilhelm Solf, a scholar-statesman of liberal views. With Solf's help, Haber became an ever closer associate of Hajime Hoshi, head of a Japanese pharmaceutical company. Hoshi contributed a great deal of money to promote German scientific research, some of it funneled through Haber. In 1924, after Einstein's visit to Japan, Haber accepted Hoshi's invitation, and he and his wife spent two months in Japan, a mixture of a Roman triumphal tour and a missionary's preaching, as he reported to Willstätter.[159] Solf and Haber became good friends; Solf wrote him of his exasperation in the late 1920s with the public style, bureaucratic wrangling, and incompetence *cum* arrogance of the Japanese. Haber reported on German political developments and tried to advance Solf's ambition to become Germany's first ambassador to the League of Nations. In 1926, a Japan Institute was founded in Berlin, a piece of bilateral cultural relations that Haber had tirelessly worked for. In short, Haber enjoyed his role as a roving ambassador for Weimar, for German science, for global cooperation, always in close touch with German officialdom, always true to his own faith that science should serve as the conciliator of nations. In that same spirit, he agreed to

Einstein's request that he should replace him on the League's Committee on Intellectual Cooperation. It proved short-lived work.[160]

Haber's work on the international front came on top of all his other responsibilities: the Emergency Committee, Kaiser-Wilhelm-Society, the Prussian Academy, and above all his own institute. He caught himself living between overexertion and exhaustion, high spirits and despondency. At times he thought of escaping altogether; this mood seemed to seize him most often in 1926, the year of his separation from his second wife. In January he wrote Willstätter that he was thinking of leaving Berlin. The many institutions he served no longer meant much to him; they were largely run by mediocrities who preferred routine to innovation. All that remained was his own institute: "But in scientific matters I am too ambitious. . . . What I can do, is not enough for me, and what I can't do, I can no longer learn or acquire." He needed to be needed. In October 1926 he wrote Einstein in very much the same vein: he was thinking of leaving Berlin and retiring to the country. He had doubts about his own scientific capability, and his involvement in the affairs of science or in scientific policy gave him no joy. To have "influence" was not enough: "I either want to direct things or let them go. I am needed in particular moments, when difficulties appear, and subsequently the old traditionalists continue."[161] Still he carried on and found contentment in being useful. And the director's villa in Dahlem, Faradayweg 8, remained the meeting place for friends and notables, with Haber as the scintillating host, ever curious about all that was happening in the world. Or at his country home in Witzmanns, to which he invited Einstein in 1929 to spend some weeks with Willstätter, James Franck, and my parents.

He was most fully himself as director of his institute and more specifically as head of his world-famous fortnightly colloquium. There, by dint of his celebrated relentless probing— often in the presence of Planck and Einstein or visitors from elsewhere, such as Bohr and Willstätter—he would help colleagues to grow beyond themselves as men and as scientists. These sessions were major events, attracting foreigners as well as Germans, scientists in Haber's field and in related ones. As Karl Friedrich Bonhoeffer recalled it: "How often did it not happen that at the end of an unclear, too specialized lecture, [Haber] would take the floor and in two, three sentences formulate the problem discussed? And how often did the group not get more from those two or three sentences than from the entire hour before? . . . And then with a smile [he posed] the Socratic questions which lifted the discussion into lucidity." He was obviously happiest when wrestling with scientific questions.*

Dahlem was, as Althoff had wanted, a kind of German Oxford—rich, remote, full of often eccentric talent—with the further advantage of being at the end of a subway line from the heart of a great capital. Haber was part of Weimar's glory, of what made Berlin, in Erwin Chargaff's words, "the very empyrean of science."[162]

HABER and Einstein both experienced the death agony of the Weimar Republic close up. Stresemann's death in the fall of 1929 was instantly, if coincidentally, followed by the onset of the Great Depression; by July 1930, the National Socialists scored their first electoral breakthrough, and by 1932 *lucifer ante portas* was a common saying, though most Germans thought—or thought at times—that Hitler could still be averted. In those final years of mounting disorder, massive unemployment, and the virtual dissolution of republican government, in that strange interlude after Weimar had ceased to function and before Hitler took over, in those two and a half

---

* In March 1931 Willstätter wrote my father that Haber was visiting him in Munich. He found him "in brilliant shape: healthy, in a good mood, satisfied with his work and hence with all the world." He rejected any notion of vacation. "At the moment he is interested only in physical-chemical problems, which he discusses pacing for hours about my room. He is at present a bit superhuman [*übermenschlich*]." A mere two years later, his world and his health were destroyed. Willstätter to R. Stern, March 8, 1931.

years from Chancellor Brüning to Chancellor Schleicher, almost anything seemed possible: illusions abounded in what became an increasingly desperate, uncertain world.

Characteristically, Haber and Einstein had categorically different views and prescriptions. Haber's views can be gleaned from a letter he wrote to Hermann Dietrich, Brüning's minister of finance, in May 1931, when the full dimension of disaster was still unclear. The present outlook, he wrote, was no less bleak than that during the last year of the Great War, when "the connection between the leaders and the people was lost . . . and in the fall of 1918 we were presented with the bill." The same gap was opening up between the heads of Germany's economy—who swore by the need for private enterprise while praising the achievements of the Soviet Union—and the increasingly hard-pressed masses. The government, Haber thought, should act now rather than yield to duress later: "That is, to detach the power of the state from the parliamentary system and the power of the economy from private leadership, and to adopt a dictatorship and a planned economy as its own program." He explicitly recalled Moellendorff's earlier vision of a planned economy, now more timely: "The new generation is here. It fills the streets and pushes aside the old parties. . . . It looks for a German form for what in a different manner has already been realized in Russia and in Italy. It has lost confidence in the liberalism of our grandfathers and in the slow evolutionary path of trade-union social democracy."[163]

Unlike party leaders and many of his friends, Haber saw the depth of crisis and the profound change in the public mood of Germany. He publicly supported the founding of a successor party to the Democratic Party and retained his friendship with Rudolf Hilferding, whom the Nazis murdered. The economic crisis, he thought, demanded a radical, dictatorial-authoritarian solution and a temporary abandonment of the rule of the market economy. He failed to realize that there were no men, no de Gaulles, who could transform the nation's decaying democratic system into a more efficient constitutional regime.

But to call for an authoritarian solution was consonant with his *Lebensauffassung*: a year and a half later, General von Schleicher as chancellor had a few weeks in which to grope for such a program and to get support for something that bore a remarkable resemblance to Haber's hopes.

As German politics moved to the right, Einstein became more outspoken in his left-wing pacifism. Between 1930 and 1932, he spent much time at the California Institute of Technology in Pasadena, and in America made his most radical statements—to the discomfort even of his friends there. He spoke before pacifist groups, signed even more manifestos, and at one time urged citizens to refuse military service, thus disabling states from waging wars. (This was also the time when Einstein and Freud exchanged public views about the causes of war, the physicist blaming the nationalist state and urging the virtual abolition of sovereign states in favor of a supra-national government.) But events in Germany demanded more specific remedies and in July 1931 he wrote to Haber: "Don't you think that the present situation will necessarily lead to an almost complete stoppage of the imports of foodstuff (similar to what happened in the war) and that therefore it is necessary to make sure that the existing food supplies be controlled and that equity of distribution must be secured." He suggested an early introduction of a "rationing system" as a way of avoiding the creation of even greater social injustice; in actuality, nothing was done; unemployment and economic misery mounted—with disastrous consequences.[164] Haber and Einstein agreed that the economy could not be left solely to market forces.

Einstein went beyond private warnings and public statements about militarism. Where Haber sought an authoritarian answer, Einstein favored an antifascist coalition of Communists and Socialists. In June 1932, in anticipation of the July election (at which the Nazis scored their greatest victory before the assumption of power), Einstein joined Heinrich Mann and Käthe Kollwitz in urging a common electoral front and a single list of candidates for Communists, Socialists, and trade unionists. A few days before the election, a mass meeting, also supported by Einstein, reiterated the call for what later came to be called a popular front but at the time was a fantasy without a shred of practicality. The Communists, in their Stalinist phase, vilified all other parties, branding the Socialists as "social fascists," as the worst betrayers of the working class; the socialists, in turn, hated the Communists. (The conflict between the two was sealed in the Revolution of 1918–19. The Communists blamed the murder of Rosa Luxemburg and Karl Liebknecht in 1919 on the Socialists; posthumously they were invoked to divide what they had meant to unite—the German working class.) In the best of worlds, German workers and social-democratic voters from all classes would have practiced the unity Einstein preached; in the worst of worlds, the one in which Einstein lived, National Socialists and Communists collaborated, as for example, in the transportation strike in Berlin in November 1932. In one of the momentous dramatic dialectics of our century, National Socialists and Communists killed and helped each other by turns; for decades Communists won left-wing sympathy by default, given the brutal horror and crude irrationalism of their opponents.

Both Haber and Einstein were abroad when frivolous conservative intriguers brought Hitler to power on January 30, 1933. Einstein was in Pasadena, en route to a semi-annual appointment at the Institute for Advanced Study in Princeton, which was to begin in the fall of 1933. On doctor's orders, Haber was at Cap Ferrat in France, waiting for more clement weather in Berlin. He may have briefly thought—as so many people did at the time—that Hitler would constitute a mere interlude, that he was simply a puppet of his conservative allies, that in any case the aged Hindenburg was still there to prevent the worst. Politics is always seen through the prism of the past; Haber had belonged to the establishment of the past.

For Einstein, Hitler's appointment was confirmation of his deepest suspicions about Germany. He lost no time in attacking the new regime; by mid-March, he vowed not to return to Germany, to a country of intolerance, unless conditions changed. He also called for a worldwide "moral intervention" against "the excesses of Hitlerism."[165] The new rulers in Berlin, still exceedingly nervous about unfavorable publicity abroad, were enraged by Einstein's denunciations. But Einstein, fiercely uncompromising, continued his imprecations after his return to Europe at his temporary refuge in Coq sur Mer in Belgium, as guest of his friend Queen Elisabeth of Belgium. His wife asked for police protection, afraid that the Nazis might assassinate him. He resigned from the Prussian Academy— even before he had received a letter from Planck urging such a step. The Nazi authorities demanded that the academy expel Einstein, and in an official communiqué the academy announced Einstein's resignation "without regret." Further internal debates ensued and in one session—in Planck's absence— Otto Hintze, a renowned historian of the old Prussia, was perhaps the only one to speak out against the extrusion of Einstein: "His words were greeted by silence. Only later, at the coat-check and as he put on his coat, did a few furtively shake his hand." Haber regretted Einstein's political utterances. Einstein meanwhile replied to the academy that there had been no hate campaign against Germany in foreign countries, only reports and comments about government actions and "the program regarding the destruction of German Jews by economic means." He acknowledged that he had urged civilized people everywhere to do all that could be done to restrain "the mass psychosis" in Germany, the threatened "destruction of all prevailing cultural values." In June, Einstein empowered Laue to have his name withdrawn from various German organizations, including the Orden Pour le Mérite, where his continued membership could embarrass his friends.[166]

Einstein's books were burned, his property was confiscated, and in 1934 his German citizenship revoked.* In the summer of

---

* The Gestapo sent the Einsteins a detailed listing of their savings at the Dresdner Bank—roughly 50,000 marks in cash, saving accounts, and stocks, which—citing various laws and decrees and "in defense against still to be

1933 Elsa Einstein wrote: "The Nazis took over the house in Caputh [Einstein's weekend home near Berlin] and confiscated everything they found there. That was the beginning of the last campaign in the war between Einstein and Germany."[167]

For Haber, the coming of the Nazis marked the end of his active career. He returned to Berlin weeks after Hitler's appointment, and for a short while his life continued to revolve around his Kaiser-Wilhelm-Institute. His letters to friends and family make clear that he understood the noose was ever tightening: he instantly grasped the threat of the emergency decrees set forth at the end of February, when after the Reichstag Fire all constitutional liberties were suspended. Nazi storm troopers began a reign of terror against political opponents, and the regime started taking its first measures against Jewish officials, especially Jewish judges. Haber feared that professors would be next and wrote to Willstätter that he needed to consult with him: his immediate inclination was to remain at his post for as long as possible, if only to shield those for whom he considered himself responsible. Within days of the Enabling Act of late March 1933, which gave Hitler's government full decree power, a new law was promulgated for the "Restoration of the Professional Civil Service." Non-Aryan professors were to be removed (exceptions made, in order to placate Hindenburg, for veterans and other special categories). Haber and James Franck, for example, could have stayed at their posts but would have had to dismiss many of their subordinates. In mid-April, Franck wrote to Haber, obviously in answer to a letter: "Don't scold me prematurely or without reflection. I asked the ministry today to release me from my obligations. I gave as reason 'the attitude of the government toward German Jewry.'" He felt that he could not face the students at the be-

---

anticipated Communist activities endangering the state—were to be expropriated in favor of the Prussian State." Gestapo, May 10, 1933, signed by Diels, head of the Prussian Gestapo. The same day in the Berlin book-burning ceremony, Einstein's works were burned. Copy in the Yahuda files, Hebrew University, Jerusalem.

ginning of the semester and pretend that their agitation did not touch him: "Nor will I make use of the scrap of charity which the government offers veterans of the Jewish race. I honor and understand the position of those who wish to remain in their office today, but there also have to be people like me."[168]

It has perhaps been insufficiently noted that while the Nazis instantly purged the German civil service of Jews, including most scientists in academic positions, they were slower in their campaign against Jews in the private realm, especially in business. Planck's warnings about the consequences of expelling scientists did not move Hitler, whose contempt for pure science coincided with his anti-Semitism and with his avowed intent that Jews should not remain in positions of authority in Germany.

Haber was anguished, as his letters of the time make clear. He felt torn: worries about his own material existence and his commitment to the institute clashed with his sense that he could not dismiss Jewish colleagues and stay at his post at the same time. Then, at the end of April, in a letter to the Nazi minister of education he asked to be relieved of his directorship, effective October 1. He noted that he could have stayed despite being

a descendant of Jewish grandparents and parents. . . . My decision to ask for my retirement derives from the principle of research with which I have lived until now and the different views which you, Herr Minister, and your ministry represent as the carriers of the present great national movement. . . . You will not expect from a man in his sixty-fifth year a change of mental outlook which in the preceding thirty-nine years directed his academic life, and you will understand that the pride with which he has served his German homeland for his entire life prescribes this request for retirement.[169]

Planck still hoped to find some compromise between the government and Haber, but the Nazi minister publicly denounced the anti-regime attitudes of institute directors (this was clearly aimed at Haber) and thus frustrated any last-minute efforts.[170]

For a brief moment, Haber felt relieved that he had taken a decision—and never doubted it had been the right one. But his life had been destroyed—his battered health made it almost impossible to consider prospects of a new future—to say nothing of the psychic bonds that tied him to his home and work in Dahlem and that for sixty-four years had made Germany his sole home.

Days after his resignation, he wrote to Hermann, his oldest son in Paris (in a letter transmitted by a Swedish friend), that his angina pectoris had worsened, "but the liberation that a decision taken brings about will improve my condition." He noted that "the definition of Aryan and non-Aryan descent causes difficulties. . . . The practical difference is that [those] Aryans who are decent people feel ashamed and prophesy an early change [in the regulations], while the non-Aryans have pessimistic views of the future."[171] His friend and successor at Karlsruhe, Georg Bredig, also of Jewish descent, when told to retire, asked Haber for help in recommending a successor. Haber indignantly refused, considering such cooperation with officialdom as demeaning. He wrote to Bredig that his own resignation had been regarded by his Aryan colleagues "as honorable resistance . . . while the deferential acceptance of assignment to the ghetto [i.e., staying on in an ostracized position] only strengthens their disrespect for non-Aryan colleagues."[172] How quickly this new terminology of racial separation came to be used!

Haber's resignation had something poignant and paradigmatic about it. It may be wrong to single out one man's misfortune at a time of calamity, but Haber's fate exemplifies the psychic and to some extent the physical destruction that was to mark the life of German Jewry. His fate prefigured much of what was to come but that was yet indeterminate.* Even the

---

* In the spring of 1933, fearful of what might happen to him and his children, Haber turned to his former collaborator in the army, Hermann Geyer, who in

Nazis improvised most of the time. A few days after his resignation, he wrote to Willstätter:

> I am bitter as never before. . . . I was German to an extent that I feel fully only now and I find it odious in the extreme that I can no longer work enough to begin confidently a new post in a different country. . . . From the I. G. Farben circle [a firm with which he had had very close connections] there has been no one who has talked to me or visited me concerning my request for retirement. . . . Planck makes every effort to show me respect and affection.[173]

And Planck continued to do so.

Of course there were exceptions aside from Planck, but it is clear that the great silence surrounding Haber's last official weeks marked callous indifference or perhaps fear or shame. In those days, a private letter of solidarity would not have required any particular courage. Days after the newspapers carried the story of Haber's resignation, Karl Friedrich Bonhoeffer wrote to him of his sorrow at the loss for German science: "But at least I want to assure you—what I hope you would know of

---

the meantime had advanced to being a major-general. In a handwritten, cordial letter Geyer testified that Haber had not only been a "frontline fighter of merit" but also: "In the months before the first great gas attack (April 15) you lived for weeks or months at the front and sat not only with the high staffs but with full commitment of your person. You also were in the furthest front line in order to help and learn and to study the conditions for using the gas process [*Gasverfahren*] of every kind." Geyer mentioned "a particularly impressive occasion" when both men stood in the "furthest front line" on March 21, 1918, at the moment of the "great attack in the west" under heavy fire. In his reply, only partially preserved, Haber thanked Geyer for his note, which he would use to enable his children "to remain in their school"—if that should become necessary. At the same time he mentioned: "I received directly and indirectly the army suggestion that I should again put my Institute in the service of gas warfare and gas protection, as had happened during the war, and I evaded the suggestion." His reason: "a garden suburb [*Villenort*] such as Dahlem was inappropriate for such purposes." Generalmajor Hermann Geyer to Haber, May 14, 1933, Haber to Geyer, May 15, 1933. Haber papers in possession of Mrs. Agnes Lévy, St. Sulpice, Switzerland.

me in any case—that I will always proudly and gratefully ac-knowledge that you have been my teacher and that I shall tell the future generation of your achievements on behalf of German science and technology."[174] There were very few such letters.

Haber's health and spirit were broken; his institute, his work, his place in the life of others had been the center of his life. He fell into moments of despair. "I have lived for too long," he wrote to my parents in June 1933.[175] He found fleeting solace in what had always helped him: work. Despite his own burden, He became an unofficial organizer for friends and colleagues who needed to emigrate. This endeavor brought him close to Chaim Weizmann, who hoped that some of Germany's great scientists would come to his Daniel Sieff Institute in Rehovot (today's famous Weizmann Institute); he would, he told Haber, accept "Aryan" scientists as well. Haber assumed that Germany would lose its leading position in chemistry: "My fate and that of my Institute will not constitute a unique situation. To continue to pursue great developments in Germany with the help of people selected principally for their political conviction seems to me to be hopeless."[176]

Weizmann tried to help where he could; he was disappointed that so many scientists preferred positions in places like Turkey to settling in Palestine. Willstätter, who visited the institute in Rehovot, declined Weizmann's invitation. "It is very kind of you to worry about my remaining in Germany, as Haber tells me you do. You must not do it; I think you have enough worries to bear for other people. The philologist [Karl] Vossler said to me: 'For our government you are a big bedbug. If one steps on it, it gives off a big stench. That is why one doesn't.'"[177] Neither man could have grasped the horror of the formulation: within a few years, the Nazis did step on Jews because they considered them vermin, Willstätter included; they had learned that they could do it with impunity. Germans, on the whole, did not so much applaud as avert their eyes.

The German horrors had their ironic impact on old friends. In May 1933 Haber sought to enlist Einstein's ever-ready help for displaced scientists, and Einstein's response contained wounding taunts: "I can conceive of your inner conflicts. It is somewhat like having to give up a theory on which one has worked one's whole life. It is not the same for me because I never believed in it in the least."[178] Einstein was equating Haber's faith in Germany with a scientific theory one has worked out and cherishes; Einstein himself never had that faith, in fact found his theory about Germans confirmed by their eager or servile response to Nazism.

A few months later, Haber sought to mediate between Weizmann and Einstein, who had had a falling-out over the Hebrew University in particular and Zionist disregard of Arabs in general. Haber wrote to Einstein that his own plan to visit the Hebrew University was being impeded by the controversy. "I have the impression that the public quarrel between you and Weizmann renews the misfortune that the internal conflicts in Jerusalem signified in the days when Titus and his legions besieged Jerusalem." He begged Einstein to talk with Weizmann and concluded, "In my whole life I have never felt so Jewish as now!"

Einstein replied instantly—and even more woundingly. He attacked Weizmann, and warned Haber against working with the Hebrew University. But he was

> pleased that . . . your former love for the blond beast has cooled off a bit. Who would have thought that my dear Haber would appear before me as defender of the Jewish, yes even the Palestinian cause. . . . I hope you won't return to Germany. It's no bargain to work for an intellectual group that consists of men who lie on their bellies in front of common criminals and even sympathize to a degree with these criminals. They could not disappoint me, for I never had any respect or sympathy for them—aside from a few fine personalities (Planck 60% noble, and Laue

100%). I want nothing so much for you as a truly humane atmosphere in which you could regain your happy spirits (France or England). For me the most beautiful thing is to be in contact with a few fine Jews—a few millennia of a civilized past do mean something after all.[179]

In the remaining months of Haber's life in exile, Weizmann proved a far more solicitous and compassionate friend than Einstein. Weizmann never taunted him about his former Germanism, though obviously aware of the cruel historic twist. In fact, Haber and Weizmann formed a poignantly close relationship, with Haber at one point pleading with Weizmann to resume his battles for the leadership of the World Zionist Organization, and promising that he would visit Palestine as soon as his health would permit it.* Haber's affective closeness to Weizmann—fellow scientist and the principal leader of Haber's rediscovered community in suffering, Jewry—had a symptomatic quality: the official Haber had always lived and prospered in the German world; the private Haber had always found his closest friends (and wives) in families of Jewish descent.[180]

Haber's hope to visit Rehovot came to naught, but his library has found an honored home there. Einstein continued his quarrels with Weizmann, but willed that his papers should ultimately go to the Hebrew University.[181] He became a critical friend of Israel's, hence Ben Gurion's remarkable offer to Einstein to become Weizmann's successor as president of Israel. These changes in friendship are also part of the fate of German Jewry.

---

* In this he was encouraged by his son Hermann, who in Paris worked for Joseph Blumenfeld, Weizmann's cherished brother-in-law. Haber's doctor—my father—also encouraged him to visit Palestine and all manner of specific arrangements were being planned. Joseph Blumenfeld and his family fled to New York in 1940, and I gratefully remember his friendship. In the fall of 1933 Dr. Weizmann intervened with French authorities, including his friend Anatole de Monzie, minister of education, to facilitate my father's negotiations for a medical license in Tunis. Margarethe Haber to Weizmann, October 6, 1933, Yad Chaim Weizmann.

In the fall of 1933, Haber found a temporary refuge in Cambridge, England.* His stepsister, Else Freyhan, cared for him—as she had for years—but his physical condition steadily deteriorated.** Sir William Pope, who had developed mustard gas for the British Chemical Warfare Service during the war, offered Haber a laboratory, where the latter tried to resume his research, but as he wrote to Willstätter: "I have fallen into a state of decline here. . . . The capacity for building up a new life in one's mid-sixties is a rare gift and for me in any case a most uncertain one." Willstätter could hardly bring himself to respond: "What I see and feel about your fate does not lend itself to writing. . . . That you have worked again and have brought the examination of Hydrogen Peroxide Catalase to important results pleases me greatly as proof of your improved health and capacity for work because it is incontrovertible that for you life means work."[182]

Haber carried on a lengthy correspondence concerning his emigration from Germany; if he left formally, he would have to pay a special tax (Reichsfluchtsteuer) on all his property, assessed not at current but past elevated values. Such an arrangement would leave him, and above all his divorced wife and their children, who were still minors, in precarious straits. And still he spent immense thought and energy in trying to help friends and colleagues less fortunate than himself. By now he, too, had lost any illusions about the Germans. In early

* Offers came from other places as well. In 1933 Hajime Hoshi's company, Hoshi Pharmaceutical, suffered financial difficulties and therefore Hoshi had to wait till January 1934 before he could send an official invitation to Haber: "Dr. Haber! You have done great works. Every nation in the world must recognize your works and respect you. I am convinced of the fact that Japanese people is only the race which able to recognize your greatness exactly, because Japanese people is superior in Fairness, Generousity [sic], Kindness to everybody than other nations in the world." Haber was dead before the letter could reach him. H. Hoshi to Haber, January 26, 1934, Haber papers in possession of Mrs. Agnes Lévy, St. Sulpice, Switzerland.

** Her youngest son, Dieter, died in the Dachau concentration camp on February 6, 1945, having been transported there from Budapest on November 14, 1944. Archive, Dachau concentration camp.

January 1934, a few weeks before his death, he wrote to my father: "Lucky the person who did not grow up in the German world and is not growing up there now! But the people on the far side of the Rhine will have greater difficulty in getting rid of the debts against humanity which they are now incurring than they imagine, and your children and their children will profit more from the sufferings of their parents than we profited from the well-being of our own forebears."[183]

Haber died of a heart attack on a visit to Basel on January 29, 1934. He had gone there to meet his son and son's wife as well as my parents. Family and friends felt bereft. He had had a genius for friendship; in his own life, marked by sorrow and success, he had found fulfillment in enriching the lives of others. His friends and colleagues felt the historic injustice as well and saw him as the victim of National Socialism. James Franck wrote to my father and to Haber's son from the United States:

> It is simply an inextinguishable shame that this man was morally forced into exile. . . Much of what happened and is happening at home [in Germany] I am able to forgive and try to see what is good, even if that is sparse, but in my whole life I will not be able to forgive forcing a man like Fritz Haber, who did more for his country than is almost imaginable, to end his life in exile. Since it was not given to your father to survive the harsh time, I wish that he had never even seen it in the first place.

And Weizmann wrote: "The only thing one must have faith in is that just as his life will remain unforgotten so his death as a martyr will have a deep importance for us and for the world in years still to come."[184] I have not found Einstein's letter to Haber's son Hermann, but the latter thanked him for the expression of his friendship and sympathy. In ensuing years, Einstein often reaffirmed his friendship with Haber; after the fall of France in 1940, he repeatedly wrote to my father offering his help to get Hermann Haber and his family—caught stateless in

France—out of that country.[185] After Hermann Haber's suicide in 1947, Einstein wrote his widow a letter of warmest sympathy, offering whatever help he might be able to provide.[186]

In January 1935 Planck organized a memorial service for Fritz Haber—despite the protest of a regime that wanted to extinguish Haber's memory. And Haber's old Institute for Physical Chemistry now bears his name, even though in recent years people have objected to this because of his part in the First World War and because feminists depict him as the sole culprit in the tragic fate of his first wife. The memory lives on—dimly and in distorted controversy.

The openness of Berlin's scientific community—in the academy, in the Kaiser-Wilhelm-Society, in the university, and in impromptu settings—had brought Haber and Einstein into close companionship, and it was Haber's genius to convert collegiality into friendship. For Haber, his institute had been home; for both men the scientific cluster of activity in Berlin guaranteed the deepest kind of nurturing. They found and kept alive a place of human decency, an oasis even in its own time, an oasis before Hitler destroyed all that was valuable and destroyed the faith that had been the precondition of these deep bonds.*

Haber, the sometime poet, would have cherished the words that Einstein, who had a deep religious vein, spoke at the graveside of Rudolf Ladenburg, a fellow physicist, in Princeton in April 1954—words that recalled the life that Einstein and Haber once shared:

> Brief is this existence, as a fleeting visit in a strange house. The path to be pursued is poorly lit by a flickering consciousness, the center of which is the limiting and separating I.

* Unlike other émigré scientists like James Franck, and unlike Thomas Mann, Einstein refused all subsequent contact with Germany. For him, genocide was Germany at its most demonic; after Auschwitz he could muster no magnanimity. Even the righteous could not redeem the "country of mass murderers," as he called Germany.

The limitation to the I is for the likes of our nature un-
thinkable, considering both our naked existence and our
deeper feeling for life. The I leads to the Thou and to the
We—a step which alone makes us what we are. And yet
the bridge which leads from the I to the Thou is subtle and
uncertain, as is life's entire adventure.

When a group of individuals becomes a We, a harmonious whole, then the highest is reached that humans as
creatures can reach.[187]

4

Walther Rathenau and the Vision of Modernity

❖❖

An earlier, shorter version of this essay was written for a *Festschrift* for Edzard Reuter, the former, visionary, progressive head of one of Germany's best-known firms, Daimler-Benz (now DaimlerChrysler). Rathenau and Reuter, different in character, similar in their public roles, sketched remarkably similar visions of a more just society. In revising it, I was struck by the thought that Rathenau's analysis of the deficiencies of capitalism has acquired a new topicality. The end of Communism signified for many the triumph of capitalism and seems to have inspired a globalized idolatry of the market. Social critics, on the other hand, grapple with the problematic aspects of the culture of capitalism, as did Rathenau in his prescriptions and prophecies.

❖❖

WALTHER RATHENAU was not like anyone else. Blessed with an abundance of talents, driven by contradictory ambitions, he became a public figure of achievement and renown, while remaining a private person of terrifying complexity. He was ever conscious of his inner conflicts; he analyzed them, brooded about them, and drew inspiration from them. Usually reticent, even secretive, he could astound his friends with self-dramatizations of his divided being. In 1917, on the occasion of his fiftieth birthday, in the presence of friends whom he addressed as the true representatives of the higher, the spiritual Germany, he acknowledged, "My being has always been marked by an internal struggle." He then referred to Plato's *Phaedrus*,

where that wonderful metaphor of the charioteer and the two steeds appears. Every time I have read this metaphor and the magnificent description, it has given me a peculiar feeling and a sudden illumination. You know that the metaphor speaks of human passions and drives, but for the moment I am not talking about these. The comparison depicts a Greek chariot with two noble, strong-necked Greek thoroughbreds. One sees how one horse rears, pulls at the reins, sweats and foams, pulls itself together, bends, stands on its hind legs, stops short, and then flies off again; the charioteer has to curve to one side and then re-peat the game with the other steed on the other side. This magnificent picture is too grand for a minor life, but I al-ways had to appropriate it in order to understand some-thing of what was given to me.[1]

I was stopped by the multiple presumptions of that passage: the unfathomable complexity of my being can be grasped only in a celebrated passage from Plato? Rathenau may have ex-ceeded the norm of human inexplicability (as if there were such a thing), and his astounding public career, despite and because of that unfathomable self, should tell us something about the culture he lived in, in which he wanted to excel, and which he thought needed total renovation.

At other times, Rathenau characterized his inner conflict as being between his "urge to reality" and his "yearning for the spiritual."[2] He was in continuous conflict with his father, who exemplified the former and from whom he had inherited the urge—and perhaps the talent—for success in the practical world. Emil Rathenau, after managing various enterprises in-differently, had founded the Allgemeine Elektrizitätsgesell-schaft (AEG) in 1883, based initially on his acquisition of the Edison patent for Europe, a brilliant move and, incidentally, a recognition of America's growing presence in the ever-expanding world market. The older Rathenau was a practical visionary: he foresaw and helped to realize the age of electricity. By dint of single-minded energy and entrepreneurial dedication, he made the AEG into one of the preeminent international concerns of the time. His son wanted still more: he wanted to emulate his father in the practical world; to surpass him by gaining public recognition and prominence, even power; to transcend him by spiritually and intellectually comprehending the real, practical world and, in so doing, by transforming it. He believed in the superiority of the aesthetic-spiritual realm, indeed in the supremacy of the spirit. He was half-Hegelian, half-romantic—and all, very self-consciously, German.

A father-son conflict is a favorite old theme, perhaps especially in German life and literature. Walther was sixteen when his father founded the AEG; he grew up in an atmosphere of intermittent uncertainty,"not of want, but of anxiety," as he later wrote.[3] After his university studies, Walther worked in and eventually managed several electrochemical enterprises in remote towns in Switzerland and Germany. It was a double apprenticeship, at once practical and emotional, designed to achieve technical expertise and personal independence. After ten lonely years away, he returned to Berlin and finally made his way in the world of international business.

Both Rathenaus were ideal-type "captains of industry." They also exemplified the network that existed between German banking and industry, as well as the presence and success of Jews in German life. Walther once said that there were three hundred men, all known to each other, who did Europe's business. He relished belonging to that world; by turns, a major industrialist and a financier, he served as a member on almost one hundred corporate supervisory boards. In the marvelously disciplined society of Wilhelmine Germany he was an acknowledged and important presence, as was his father. But the son, while exemplifying German ascendancy in the economic realm, also expressed German unease about the spiritual worth of material achievement. Perhaps he was the only

German captain of industry who excelled in capitalism and condemned it; usually achievement and denigration came separately. He was an employer of multitudes, yet he called for the abolition of the proletarian class and the emancipation of workers. And he was ambivalent about his success in the material world: he had to prove himself there in order to justify himself before his father, to achieve early independence from him, to satisfy part of his ambition; but it never sufficed; he also needed to understand it, to explicate its spiritual suffering. Almost all his writings turned on what might be called the social and spiritual elements in the modern economy and in modernity itself.

Rathenau's deepest ambivalence sprang from his Jewishness, which marked his life and determined his death. Given his mockery of Jewish speech and customs and his vilification of the public conduct of wealthy German Jews, he has often been cited as a prime example of German Jewish self-hatred, an unappealing prototype of the servile German Jew. But he also felt deep pride in belonging to what he considered the Jewish race, to what he thought of as "the salt of the earth." Like other German Jews, he loved his country and sought to serve it, yet he knew the pain of unalterable apartness and in 1911 wrote: "In the youth of every German Jew, there comes a moment which he remembers with pain as long as he lives: when he becomes for the first time fully conscious of the fact that he has entered the world as a second-class citizen, and that no amount of ability or merit can rid him of that status."[4] He had a deep—probably even erotic—attraction to what he thought of as the virile, courageous Nordic man; the Prussian officer was his ideal, and his utterly unsurprising failure to become an officer in the elite regiment, the *Garde Kürassiere*, in which he did his one-year military service, brought home to him his complaint about Jews as second-class citizens. Ambivalence and ambition marked Rathenau's very being; it was a prescription for fragility.

His grand ambitions Rathenau had to realize on *his* terms. Money was incidental; necessary, but not sufficient. He wanted to be more than a great financier or industrialist, more than a man of influence and connections, more even than a writer; he wanted more than a ministerial post, though at certain moments he coveted all of these roles. At times, I think, he dreamed of becoming a German Disraeli, a latter-day Earl of Beaconsfield, a princely and exotic presence. In later years, he acknowledged this dream model. I think that, all his life, he hoped to grasp a vision of the future, knowing that an old world was being superseded, wishing to help construct a society that would accommodate and humanize the unleashed forces of modernity.

His Jewishness was both spur and brake. In the public realm he could have achieved even more than he did, at a cost that some of his fellow Jews had accepted: conversion to Christianity. He thought the price demeaning, even though he may have felt greater affinity for Christianity and for Germanness than most of the Jews who did convert. James Joll, in his exemplary portrait, spoke of the "dehydrated mysticism of Rathenau's own eclectic religious views."[5] He did not want to sacrifice pride for triumph, and his pride, his Nietzschean imperatives, demanded that he retain his formal Jewishness *and* reach unprecedented heights. He rejected conversion, as he himself often said, because it was a form of opportunism—and an acceptance of the state's injustice. He knew, then, from bitterest experience, that state and society could throttle a man's soul, and he dreamt of a future polity that would allow the human soul to experience and fulfill itself. Out of some amalgam of intellect and of his own suffering, he created a social vision that in some ways was prophetic.

Rathenau had a multiplicity of gifts and interests; he tried to cultivate them all and to give up none for any single-minded pursuit. He had a great practical bent and extraordinary intellectual power; he understood the world of business, the web of

interests, the connections between science, technology, and national power. He excelled in that world and was regarded as
an economic wizard. He had read voraciously in world literature and carried his *Bildung* none too lightly. In his twenties he
had already discovered his gifts as a writer, though with characteristic ambivalence he used pseudonyms for many of his
early efforts. He also cherished his artistic and literary talents:
his drawings and paintings demonstrated skill and originality,
and to the end of his life he played the piano. And still, he
probably devalued what he did best. He was an economic man
and yearned to be a latter-day philosopher-king.

He was irresistibly drawn to the world of power—as many
entrepreneurs were at a time when the kaiser was receptive to
their attentions. Even a pseudo-feudal regime could not ignore
that Germany's power derived from its immense economic
strength, a fact that Rathenau kept emphasizing. Rathenau met
Chancellors Bülow and Bethmann Hollweg—on the first occasion he approached Bülow in an embarrassingly self-abasing
fashion. He accompanied Germany's colonial secretary (a converted Jew) on an official visit to Southwest Africa; he con-
versed with Wilhelm II once or twice a year. He was on the
fringes of power—and wanted more. But assessing German society at the time and seeing power in its imperial guise, he also
became a critic of this fabulous machine that seemed to him to
have neither soul nor purpose. He wrote (but did not publish
until after the war) a sharp portrait of the kaiser, of whom he
said: "An enchanter and a marked man. A nature rent, yet not
feeling the rent. He is on the road to disaster."[6] Could Rathenau have felt a certain affinity with him? Each had his own
smashing insecurities, but they were wildly different men, the
kaiser and himself. And only Rathenau suffered from the oft-
grating gift of self-awareness.

Rathenau balanced his precarious closeness to the highest
ranks of officialdom by cultivating friendships with the heads
of what we would now call the counterculture, with the artistic

representatives of modernity. Years ago, there was an exhibition at the Guggenheim Museum in New York called "Expressionism: A German Intuition." German poets and painters, the Berlin Secession, founded in 1898, did have an intuition of the new; many of them understood the inner deadness of the prevailing life.

Rathenau lived in many worlds, unusual for an economic man, but congenially possible in the Berlin of his time. He had close ties with the poet Richard Dehmel and the young Gerhart Hauptmann, whose plays were regarded as scandalous caricatures of society. He became a friend of the expressionist playwright Fritz von Unruh, whose prewar plays, produced by Max Reinhardt, another of Rathenau's friends, caused great conservative consternation. An anti-militarist before the war, Unruh became an embattled pacifist during and after the war. He was friends with avant-garde painters, most notably with Edvard Munch, who painted his portrait. Rathenau bought a Max Pechstein picture. Peter Behrens, his contemporary, who believed in the complementarity of art and technology, designed an AEG factory. Rathenau was a cherished oddity, a *Fabeltier*, for the great Berlin publisher S. Fischer, whose salon of artists and writers he liked to frequent.[7] He relished the great performances in theater and opera. During the war, he joined his friend Max Reinhardt, Hauptmann, and the much-decried Frank Wedekind in a group to support new playwrights, a group called "Das junge Deutschland." He was always attracted to the young, to the *idea* of youth and renewal. His longest and perhaps most intimate friendship was with Maximilian Harden, the fiercely intelligent, courageous, unstable Jewish editor of *Die Zukunft*, who for attacking the kaiser and the scandals surrounding the imperial entourage was imprisoned several times. Years later, after the First World War, Harden and Rathenau had a violent falling-out, and Harden wrote virulent, tasteless polemics about his erstwhile friend, even after the latter's murder.

Rathenau needed, found, and sometimes dropped friends; in seemingly self-revelatory letters he reached out to friends, usually women-friends—to whom he never came closer than by these letters. One can only guess at the reasons for his feeling that he was "the loneliest man I know," for his categorical need for independence which he feared would be lost if he yielded to erotic commitments.[8] After his father's death in 1917, he saw his mother every day that he was in Berlin. For all his private torments, he was and he intended to be a fascinating person for others: his friend and later biographer, Harry Count Kessler, likened him in appearance, in his early years, to Stendhal's Julien Sorel in his black suit.[9] He was a captivating presence, radiating elusive brilliance, and long before the Great War he was a welcome guest in the best salons and the most diverse circles and a ready, if famously frugal host to his artistic friends. He exuded wealth, vast knowledge, fluency, and perhaps some form of transfigured sensuality.*

He had an extravagant admiration for the Prussian ethos; to him, the Prussian officer was an incarnation of that ethos, as was the classical architecture of Friedrich Gilly and Karl Friedrich Schinkel. He should have lived in Prussia's great Era of Reform. In his own time, he worried about the continued dominance of Prussia's declining feudal caste over a modern, industrialized Germany. Others had similar misgivings; Max Weber, for one, or Thorstein Veblen—but Rathenau's views were complicated by his affective attachment to a caste to which he did not belong and which in its declining phase became an ever more desperate political power.

* Gustav Radbruch, a great if now largely forgotten jurist and minister of justice in Weimar, remembered Rathenau, his one-time ministerial colleague, as always trying to hide behind a mask: "I never met a person whose essence was so thoroughly and to the last detail formed as his was, and if nobility is a personal and unpretentious life style, then the occasionally used term of 'Jewish nobility' applies." He added that superficial observers mistook the finely fashioned personality for vanity. By whatever name, it was a persona different from German norms. Gustav Radbruch, *Der Innere Weg. Aufriss meines Lebens* (Stuttgart, 1951), p. 158.

Rathenau typically thought in antinomies and often wrote in aphorisms. One of his most revelatory essays was entitled "On Weakness, Fear and Purpose," in which he opposed two types of men, those whose basic impulse is fear and those whose basic mode is confidence and courage. The latter resembles David Riesman's description of the inner-directed man, the former suggests Rathenau's fear of what he might be or become himself. This lamentable—often successful—person he calls "*Zweckmensch*," that is, a man of purpose, of mere intentionality. The *Zweckmensch* would often be the instrument of great progress but he was never satisfied: "He desires, he demands, and he begs for recognition. . . . he feels malicious joy [*schadenfroh*] and pity simultaneously."[10] In this essay, and others in the prewar period, he would also cast his imagined opposites in racist terms, asserting that the blond Nordic man, the prototype Aryan, was the man of courage—challenged and often bested by the non-Aryan *Zweckmensch*. The *Zweckmensch*, of course, resembled his father—at least in his single-minded ambition. Before the war, Rathenau echoed some of the cruder stereotypes of the anti-Semites; he had imbibed the pervasive racial thought of his day, having assimilated some of the ideas of the Comte de Gobineau and of Houston Stewart Chamberlain.

In 1913 Rathenau published *Concerning the Mechanism of the Mind or the Realm of the Soul*. This exquisitely ponderous book was characteristic of some of his early writing; Carl Fürstenberg, great banker and wit, once remarked that Rathenau's books are more easily written than read. (In later years, after his father's death, his style became simpler, less florid.) The book elaborated his dread of the deadening effect of mechanization, of a soulless modern existence. In many ways, his thoughts recall Max Weber's contention that the modern world was one of disenchantment, pervasive, spreading rationalization and bureaucratization. And, like Weber, Rathenau had deep misgivings about the character of imperial politics in Germany. For both men, Marx and Nietzsche were titans to be reckoned with; I suspect that Weber sought to fight off Nietzsche, clinging to the austere belief that analysis and empirical argument must prevail over intuitive insight and passion. Rathenau, I believe, yielded to the inescapable Nietzsche—as in his antithesis between the man of courage and the man of fear, and in his desperate fear of weakness. Rathenau imagined he could refute Marx, perhaps supplant him; Nietzsche remained a usually hidden presence in Rathenau's thought, a dangerous, seductive tyrant—the kind of discipleship that Nietzsche warned against.*

Rathenau experienced the primacy of economics—a primacy that grew throughout his life and that became overwhelming during the war and after Germany's defeat. Thus, in 1921, echoing Napoleon's admonition to the Germans that politics was fate, Rathenau declared, "The economy is our fate"—a phrase that has been oft-repeated.[11] Yet he wished that a revolution in consciousness would bring about *Das Reich der Seele*, a culture in which every human being would live an unfettered life in consonance with his own soul. As early as 1897, he wrote to Maximilian Harden: "Now capital dominates society; some day society will not possess but dominate capital."[12] He thought both the social and political conditions of imperial Germany dangerously deficient—one more reason that the country should need him. In 1907, he had published an essay on the political condition of the country, asking, "What cul-

---

* Nietzsche's omnipresence in the minds and feelings of German writers and readers remains an underappreciated and of course forever elusive subject. I found confirmation of my sense that in some of Weber's works, such as his magnificent "Science as Vocation," he struggled to come to terms with his own Nietzschean thoughts and impulses, in the remark that he made in February 1920, shortly before his death: "Today the integrity of an academic, especially of a philosopher today, can be measured by how he considers Marx and Nietzsche. Whoever does not admit that he could not accomplish massive parts of his own work without the work that these two did deceives himself and others. The world in which we live intellectually is a world largely formed by Marx and Nietzsche." Quoted in Wilhelm Hennis, *Max Webers Fragestellung. Studien zur Biographie des Werks* (Tübingen 1987), p. 167.

tural criteria justify the fact that Germany is being governed more absolutistically than almost all [other] civilized countries and more clerically than most of the Catholic countries. . . . We cannot maintain for ourselves a separate climate forever."[13]*

In the prewar years, Rathenau, though convinced that Germany was a world power, warned against the bellicose aspects of her foreign policies. He saw the danger of the Anglo-German naval rivalry, he grasped the horrors of a prospective war, and in 1913 he proposed a common economic market for all of Europe—in part to stave off the challenge from the United States. He emphasized that "the War God of our days is industrial power."[14] He was an intermittent critic and commentator—with vacillating views, sometimes writing in the manner of a *Realpolitiker* and at other times of an impractical idealist. To Lilly Deutsch, he once confessed he was a romantic: "Refined Jews often were romantics."[15]

There were occasions before 1914 when Rathenau seemed close to a ministerial post. Politics had its special magnetism for him: He wanted to be in the innermost circles where the great historic decisions were made, where *Geist* and *Wirklichkeit* presumably met. He was appalled by the relentless mediocrity of German leadership, just as Max Weber was, even as he made his occasional gestures of deference and opportunism toward the men of power. He knew that his intelligence, his experience, his perfect fluency in three languages far surpassed the abilities of other contenders for power. He also knew that his ambition—in a society that nurtured ambition—was

---

* In light of the still current debate about Germany's putative *Sonderweg*, it is remarkable that neither those who accept nor those who deny the existence of a *Sonderweg* pay sufficient attention to the opinions of representative figures from the Wilhelmine period, who readily acknowledged Germany's different path: Rathenau is but one example who regretted the political nonage of the German *Bürgertum* and the resultant absence of effective and responsible leadership. There was an intellectual elite that shared these misgivings, forcefully expressed by Max Weber, that attacked the structurally determined incompetence of Germany's political leadership.

thwarted by his Jewishness, by his being a second-class citizen barred from high office. Vanity, wounded pride, and the patriot's desire for public service propelled him forward.*

The Great War gave Rathenau the chance to realize some of his ambitions—at great cost to himself. He had an inkling of what a modern war would be like; until the last moment, he warned against Germany's allowing the weaker Austria to drag her into a world war. After the die had been cast, Rathenau wanted to serve, but his views remained characteristically ambivalent and vacillating. He never felt the "holy" joy that lifted so many German hearts in August 1914; a patriot yes, but someone who felt that the war made no sense, that it was clearly different from 1813 or 1866 or 1870. Mostly he thought that a catastrophe had overwhelmed Europe, the end of which none could foresee. But he also instantly recognized the precariousness of the German condition, and in the first days of August he warned the military that in a long war the Allies could throttle the German economy. The generals, however, were mesmerized by memories of the lightning victories of the past and oblivious of the part that the economy played in a war. They had yet to translate into modern terms the old adage that an army marched on its belly. Still, Rathenau's warning was heeded. Within days, the war minister decreed the creation within his ministry of a war raw material section, with Rathenau as its head, and with a chief official of AEG, Wichard von Moellendorff, as his aide. (Moellendorff, whose work and career have yet to be fully explored, was also a close friend of Fritz Haber.)

Rathenau's office came to control the supply and distribution of essential raw materials; he also created the so-called

---

* Rathenau's contemporaries were aware of his ambitions. Einstein has been quoted as saying: "If one had offered Rathenau the post of Pope, he would have accepted the designation. Technically, he would probably not have done it so badly." The comment says as much about Einstein's harsh wit as about Rathenau's ambition. *Walther Rathenau-Gesamtausgabe*, vol. 2, ed. Hans Dieter Hellige and Ernst Schulin (Munich, 1977), p. 874.

Kriegsgesellschaften (wartime enterprises), private companies, publicly controlled, charged with the production of specific goods. For Rathenau it was a time of translating vague prewar thoughts into harsh, wartime reality. The war proved an engine of modernization. He encountered intense opposition to his schemes: the military remained skeptical, and his fellow industrialists resented the diminution of their autonomous powers and the threat to the free-market economy in which they had prospered. Before the war, Rathenau, dreamy Jew, pretentious intellectual, had been ridiculed; now Rathenau, the economic czar who, some alleged, was favoring his own AEG, was vilified. His fellow industrialists were right in sensing that for Rathenau these innovations were no mere wartime exigencies; he did see them as the first step toward some different, more rational economic order, one that his friend Moellendorff called *Gemeinwirtschaft* or Prussian Socialism. Kessler thought that Rathenau's work in 1914 "did as much towards protecting the frontiers of Germany and frustrating the meeting of Cossacks and Senegalese-Negroes under the Brandenburger Gate as the battle of Tannenberg or trench warfare in France"[16]—an unfortunate remark.

In April 1915 Rathenau suddenly resigned his position, possibly in disappointment at not receiving the ministerial post he had coveted. After his resignation, the military leaders remained silent about his work, maligning him behind his back. The recently discovered Rathenau material in Moscow included his letter to the war minister, complaining about the shabby silence surrounding his departure and the consequent rumors and innuendos that while in office he had favored industrial plants with which he had had connections. No wonder that in a private letter he wrote that the fact that as "a private citizen and a Jew [he] volunteered to serve the state" would forever be held against him, by those who considered the state their domain—and by Jews.[17]

A few months after his resignation, his father died, and Rathenau assumed the presidency of AEG, which derived large profits from ever-growing military orders, as did other leading companies. But no single activity satisfied him. Intermittently he felt great gloom about the outcome of the war and he resented his own enforced passivity. He thought that the conduct of the war confirmed his fear that the merely "Mechanical" ruled the world: "Like a flock of sheep, understanding nothing, we are driven into the Unknown."[18]

His views concerning the war alternated. In 1914, he had advocated an early peace, with the proposition that a Central European customs union should be established, with France as an eventual member, a program that rejected the then-prevailing views for annexations in Belgium and France. Some time later, he publicly supported the use of forced Belgian labor in German industry—an act that clearly violated international law. He continued to have close relations with the civilian and military leadership. Usually he counseled moderation—and candor. He warned Erich Ludendorff, Quarter-Master General by title, close to dictator in fact, whom he admired,* against unrestricted submarine warfare, and in July 1917 told him that German public opinion had been systematically misled. "The English way . . . of constantly pointing out to the nation the seriousness of the situation was better. We . . . emasculated opinion by three years of deception; at least thirty illusions had come into being." Rathenau had come to disagree with Ludendorff, who by the end of the war became one of Rathenau's most vocal enemies. In a private letter in the same month, he wrote: "We still do not know today what we are fighting for."[19] Of course, Rathenau was not alone in denouncing the soothing lies that German leaders were feeding their people.[20] In May 1917, in a letter to the economist Gustav von Schmoller, he re-

---

* As, of course, did Gustav Stresemann; it is odd that the two outstanding foreign ministers of the Weimar Republic, both pursuing conciliatory policies, should have been wartime admirers of Ludendorff who was anything but moderate; the reason may have been that both men admired power and Ludendorff, the non-noble who was the virtual head of army and state, was one of the few Germans at the top who exuded power and authority.

iterated the need for parliamentarization and added: "The people atones for its leaders. . . . And this atonement is just because the people put up with this leadership whatever it did. The war seems to me to be the world revolution against the remnants of autocracy and feudalism in Central and Eastern Europe on the one hand and against the mercantile nationalism of English origin on the other. The Revolution against Caesarism and Imperialism. . . . If we emerge safely from this war, it is more than we deserved."[21] At the same time, he joined moderate semi-political circles that the war had spawned, the *Deutsche Gesellschaft 1914* and the *Mittwochsgesellschaft*.

Rathenau also resumed his writing—with extraordinary energy and power. In 1917, he published *In Days to Come*, an intellectually demanding and politically provocative book. It was at once a radical critique of German society and politics and a prescriptive prophecy of a future society that would and should be more egalitarian, efficient, and soul-enhancing. The tone was by turns radical and romantic, practical and inspirational, its program progressive, with a tinge of "green," and unquestionably a denial of all that his fellow capitalists believed in. The style remained hortatory and often cloudy, which somewhat muted the radical note. There was nothing modest or conventional about the book, which began asserting, "This book treats of material things, but treats of them for the sake of their spirit. . . . This book strikes the very heart of dogmatic Socialism."[22] Having said that, he could argue for a radical egalitarianism, for a society in which the proletariat would be emancipated, for a kind of nondogmatic, non-Marxist semi-socialism. The experience of the wartime *Kriegsgesellschaften*, the state-imposed restrictions on the free market, informed his implicit repudiation of economic liberalism.

For all its ponderous ruminations and literary allusions, the book was an attack on the power of the Prussian nobility, whose austere ethos he admired and whose egotistical politics he abjured. He denounced the plutocracy in its ascendancy, whose vulgar opulence he detested. And he rejected "dogmatic" socialism for its Marxist orthodoxy and, above all, for its faith in historical materialism.

Rathenau regretted the political subservience, the *"Untertan-bewusstsein,"* so common in Germany; it had its charm and utility but essentially signified "a childlike obedience."[23] A monarchist, he advocated a *Volksstaat* (a term denoting progressive political reform much used during the war) in which the people would actively participate in the country's political life. Germany needed a vital parliamentary system: "The curious and not always gratifying parliamentary machinery is indispensable because it provides a source and a school for statesmen and politicians—or should do so."[24] By the time Rathenau's book appeared in 1917, the issue of parliamentary reform was the most divisive one in German politics.

Rathenau also urged that the power of unrestrained economic individualism be broken and that a drastic change in the tax structure should close the immense gap between the rich and the poor. Present-day wealth, he wrote, was based on inheritance or some form of monopoly and was incompatible with the requirements of a modern society. Class egoism and class power prevented the unpropertied from acquiring *Bildung*. By redistributing the material goods of society, the state would put an end to the proletariat as a dispossessed, enslaved class that had little or no hope for betterment for its children, a class the very existence of which spelled misery for the many and deprivation for society as a whole. The brilliantly educated Rathenau inveighed against the upper-class monopoly on education (*Bildungsmonopol*), "which robs the individual and defrauds the state."[25] By attaining *Bildung* and greater political responsibility in the context of a more egalitarian society, the proletariat would be emancipated—and somehow the drudgery of monotonous work would give way to the joyous satisfaction of creative work.

Here indeed was a revolutionary program in conservative guise. By compression, the radical provisions become more striking; in the book, they were embedded in ponderous dis-

cussions of spiritual considerations. The program had its contradictions: the extension of state power, especially regulatory
and taxing powers, demanded a greater bureaucracy—all this
in the name of greater freedom, spiritual emancipation, and
political maturity. In its essence, however, the book sketched a
semi-socialist utopia—similar to other reformist schemes that
were spawned during the Great War.

Rathenau's argument depended on his insistence that consciousness shaped life, not life consciousness. This facile refuta-
tion of Marxism reaffirmed a distinctly Germanic notion that
Geist could alter social reality. But his criticism of prevailing
inequality was unassailably correct, and his sense that a more
efficient and more satisfactory workplace was needed also
proved correct. He urged a different division of labor, whereby
manual workers and managers would alternate at the workplace, an impractical solution to the problem of monotony—a
problem that in the 1920s came to occupy great artists, as for
example Charlie Chaplin in *Modern Times*.

The book proved a huge and controversial success. By mid-
1918, it had sold 65,000 copies.[26] It received extensive and re-
spectful reviews—and had little, if any, effect on the public
thought of the day. In his strictures of the present, there was a
striking resemblance to Max Weber's wartime articles—which
had much greater effect. Neither Rathenau nor Weber acknowledged their affinity of views, but then, as one observer
noted, both men were rather jealous of their own originality.[27]

In 1918 he wrote yet another plea, *To Germany's Youth*. The
essay was intended as a plea to youth to realize the terrifying
tasks that awaited them. Once more he intoned the failures of
the imperial regime, the horrors of the war, the moral bankruptcy of a devastated Europe. The tone was shrill and cloy-
ingly mystical; the book was a confessional as well, alternating
between self-abasement and self-righteousness. His earlier
writings, he mentioned, had been mocked by established
thinkers and doers; only the young had sometimes understood him. Much of what he wrote was true—and probably

unpalatable to many Germans in the final phase of the war. He decried as "the most shameful and the most un-Germanic [thing] that has happened in this war . . . the reckless, shameless showering of self-praise. Nothing has so contributed to the decline of morals in the country, to the disdain for law, to the hypersensitivity of mood as this prolonged self-glorification." He warned as well, "We Germans lack the personal sense of independence; we tend to willed dependency."[28] Once again anticipating later themes, especially popular with the radical right of the 1920s, he insisted that Germans were a young people, to be rescued by the young. In his dithyrambic style Rathenau was resorting to *"reichsdeutsch"* rhetoric (just as Nietzsche had said of some of Wagner's extravaganza that he could never forgive him for becoming *"reichsdeutsch"*).

He alternated visions of the future with prescriptions for the moment; in doing the latter, he took risks. In late September 1918, Ludendorff panicked and demanded that the newly installed, liberal-moderate government of Prince Max von Baden—which he had imposed on the kaiser—should instantly ask President Woodrow Wilson for an armistice. In a public response Rathenau called instead for a *levée en masse* and for a transfer of most troops from the eastern to the western front. He thought Ludendorff's sudden reversal "the most catastrophic stupidity in all history."[29] Rathenau found no support from the military, and his proposal earned him the sobriquet *"Kriegsverlängerer,"* a war prolonger. In fact, at the very same time, he privately urged Prince Max's government to appeal directly to the American people, insisting that a free Germany should be treated fairly, and offering at the same time that Germany would ultimately renounce the Peace of Brest-Litovsk (which had embodied German annexationism at its most extreme) and cease all U-boat warfare. Rathenau, claiming that he had always opposed annexationism, proposed a course that was at once idealistic and pragmatic—hence in tune with what was assumed to be the American temper. Yet the plan was utterly unrealistic: as long as Wilhelm II remained on the throne, he would have opposed such a scheme and his presence would have made it risible in American eyes.[30]

When the terms of the proposed peace became public in May 1919, Rathenau insisted that the German government should demand a modification of its terms—or yield all power to the Allies, in effect saddling them with the responsibilities arising from a retroactive, voluntary, unconditional surrender. At these two decisive moments, of the armistice and the peace treaty, he demanded that Germans should accept incalculable sacrifices rather than submit to Allied injustices. In short, he urged non-assimilation rather than degradation. He called on a people whom he glorified as being courageous to act in conformity to his ideals—a stand perhaps analogous to his own refusal to convert to Christianity.

Ernst Troeltsch called the months between the armistice and the peace treaty "The Dreamland of the Armistice," a time of uncertainty, when everybody was free to indulge in hopes or fears. For Rathenau, it was a time for both. Days before the Revolution, he noted that economic interest groups and right-wing organizations had marshalled a "quantum of hatred against me. Gratitude for my organizational or intellectual work I have never expected; the degree of hostility which has taken its place has not likely been attached to anyone else in decades in Germany."[31] And still, he assumed that the new government would need and use him. After all, the old imperial barriers against Jews in government had been breached. Rathenau knew that economic issues now dominated all aspects of politics, and, in this realm, he combined vision, expertise, and superb international connections.

In the days after the November Revolution he tried to organize a broad union of liberal democrats (including Einstein and Gerhart Hauptmann) that was explicitly not a party; the effort floundered almost at once. He then became an early member of the progressive Democratic Party, but his projected candidacy for the National Assembly failed when the Silesian section of the party rebuffed him—an act with clear anti-Semitic overtones. When his name was suggested for the Reich presidency, the right in the National Assembly reacted with uproarious laughter. And when the first socialization commission was established—its task to select enterprises for nationalization— the Independent Socialists vetoed his membership. He was appointed to the second socialization commission, whose recommendations were aborted. To his immense disappointment, the new regime seemed determined to ignore him. In December 1918, he already feared that huge reparation demands and the attendant "economic destruction of Germany" would injure the world economy—Keynesian thoughts before Keynes.[32] Later he offered unsolicited advice to Matthias Erzberger, the finance minister, on how to pay for the immediate reparations that the Allies were demanding.

Rathenau had become everyone's favorite target. The Allied press denounced him as the despoiler of Belgium and distrusted him as someone who had called for a *levée-en-masse*. The German radical left was suspicious of him as well and for the same reason: he was vilified as someone who would have willingly allowed more people to be killed in a vain effort to stave off defeat. The left generally distrusted the great industrialist with his murky reformist ideas. Finally there was a public quarrel with Rudolf Wissell, the Socialist minister in charge of prospective nationalization. Wissell (whose closest associate was Moellendorff) attacked Rathenau's schemes as designed to convert the German economy into one gigantic AEG, while Rathenau, in turn, attacked Wissell for stealing his ideas and maligning him as well.[33]

Rathenau was caught in several crossfires. In November 1919, Ludendorff, in justifying his own wartime conduct, attacked Rathenau of whom he had once been so appreciative. As his weapon, Ludendorff used Rathenau's recent disclosure that, at the outbreak of the war, he had remarked to a friend: "The moment will never come when the kaiser and his knights on their white chargers ride victoriously through the Brandenburg Gate. On that day world history would have lost all meaning."[34] Rathenau had meant to express his dismay at Germany's leadership, but Ludendorff insinuated that Rathenau had never believed in a German victory. At a time when the stab-in-the-back lie had become a capital asset for reactionaries, Ludendorff's deliberate misinterpretation confirmed rightist prejudice: Rathenau lacked the necessary patriotic fervor. To the right wing, he was a defeatist and a Jew—presumably, therefore, a kind of traitor.

Rathenau sought to clear his name of all these charges. To disarm his critics from abroad and from the left, he denied having been a *Kriegsverlängerer*, he denied complicity in the illegal treatment of Belgium, and he insisted that all along he had favored an early, reasonable peace. At the same time, he tried to deal with the right that traduced him: he recalled his services as head of the raw material section, as a one-time adviser to Ludendorff, as a supporter of the German war effort. His efforts at self-exculpation were perforce contradictory—and given the passions of the time, it is unlikely that he could have persuaded any of his enemies.

In the months before the actual signing of the Treaty of Versailles, Rathenau (like Fritz Haber) feared that he might be placed on the Allies' list of war criminals and perhaps be extradited to appear before an Allied tribunal. This did not happen, but the mere possibility further lessened his chances for a government post. He gave intermittent advice to the successive governments in Berlin. Like many others, Rathenau was afraid that a revolutionary tide might overwhelm the new republic, and he supplied funds, personally or through the AEG, for some of the reactionary Free Corps. When political coups and assassinations continued to threaten the survival of the new regime, Rathenau understood the need for a loyal republican force that would protect public order.[35]

Denied the political responsibility he sought, he spoke out in various forums, wrote a series of articles, and discharged his multiple corporate responsibilities. In his utterances he used new accents: the ponderous philosophizing, the deliberate complexity of argument and diction, yielded to a style that was crisp and lucid—with flights to prophecy. He feared for what he even then called "the improvised Revolution," which lacked, he thought, the intellectual-historic foundation that the Enlightenment had given the French Revolution. Germany had experienced not a revolution but a collapse. The democracy that emerged had few friends; even in the western countries democracy had degenerated, because "plutocracy is a fact of western democracy and one that is not even regarded as uncongenial: it is not appropriate for Germany."[36] But the new republic was also in great danger of succumbing to a plutocratic regime. Rathenau's lifelong attack on the customs and privileges of the rich and powerful were often ridiculed as self-serving and hypocritical. This owner of a former royal palace (Freienwalde, designed by the great Prussian architect David Gilly), just outside Berlin, and of a grand villa in Berlin denounced luxury—and praised Prussian austerity. Rathenau saw the contradictoriness of his own existence as a Jew, a German patriot, a plutocrat, a great entrepreneur—and a critic of his own class and people.

In the eyes of his fellow industrialists, he committed a further sin: he recognized the power of the Bolshevik Revolution as the most important challenge to the already weakened western democracies, expressing as it did a contagious *ressentiment* against the bourgeoisie, a promise of egalitarianism, and, as a novelty, government by councils. He quickly distinguished between the revolution's performance and promise: the former being negligible, the latter formidable.

In September 1919 he wrote a pamphlet, "The New Society," which again contained a scathing account of prewar Germany, where material interests predominated and where the people remained in willed nonage, in Bismarckian *Unmündigkeit*. Once again he insisted that the greatest regenerative force was *Bildung*, not the prescribed education in elite schools for privileged youth, but *Bildung* communicated by a kind of individual and collective *noblesse oblige* to everyone, perhaps by voluntary means; *Bildung* meaning knowledge *cum* the self-confident will to fashion a life of spiritual meaning. He cited English examples, especially Toynbee Hall. This new concept of a superior *Bildung* available to the citizenry should be given absolute primacy in public discussion and policy. But he failed to give substance to the soaring idea.[37]

In another essay, he denounced the servility of the German *Grossbürgertum*, which for the sake of all manner of feudal advancement, of medals and titles, had abdicated its responsibilities: "This treason [*Verräterei*] has destroyed Germany, has destroyed the monarchy, and has made us contemptible in the eyes of all the world."[38]

He believed that the old economic order, which he had often criticized before the war, was now near bankruptcy, that one reason for the fragility of the republic was the *Bürgertum*'s wish to preserve itself as "the pillar of the status quo," and its resultant aloofness from the new republic. In 1920, he declared, "We stand at the grave of the mega-capitalistic epoch."[39] He sharpened his vision of the future economic order. Three principles would have to govern it: a radical revision of tax and inheritance laws, so that exclusion from *Bildung*, the "harshest consequence of the unequal division of goods," would be eliminated; the principle of co-determination in all economic life, just as in the nineteenth century an ever-widening suffrage introduced *Mitbestimmung* in the political realm; and finally a new *Produktionspolitik* in every branch of the national economy. He inveighed against unproductive labor—advertising and all other aspects of what we now call consumerism—but also against a command or coercive economy (*Zwangswirtschaft*). His goal was an organized economy, a morally responsible type of capitalism: "the organization of the German economy on a social basis," which would also ensure fraternal ligatures.[40]

His views were not out of tune with his times, and they strike a chord with ours. In the post-1918 period, the German air was full of demands for a revised capitalism, beginning with Oswald Spengler's *Preussentum und Sozialismus*, Moellendorff's plan for a *Gemeinwirtschaft*, and all manner of right- and left-wing anticapitalism. But Rathenau foresaw later developments and needs more clearly than many others: his was the vision of a more rationalized and yet, he hoped, more humane and more egalitarian order. (He also demanded a year's compulsory labor service for every man and woman.) He understood what we have once again come to call political economy: more, he understood the moral-psychological necessities as well. But Rathenau's hope that exhortation, the power of the word, could revolutionize reality was illusory. Some elements of what he proposed were implemented, in brutally distorted fashion, under National Socialism; others were realized in Ludwig Erhard's model of a "social free market economy."[41] It would be wrong to make any claims that Rathenau's ideas spawned later developments; in fact it is likely that his exhortations were quickly forgotten. It is, however, a tribute to his imaginative intelligence that he sensed the needs of the future.

In 1920, at long last, Rathenau's talents were called upon. Joseph Wirth, a young man of the left wing of the Center Party, had come to rely on Rathenau's advice in economic matters, so clearly superior to the risible knowledge of other cabinet members. Wirth, then only a minister himself, insisted that Rathenau be added to the German delegation at the Spa Conference, where the modalities of reparations were to be discussed with the Allies. Rathenau shone by his substantive competence and political moderation. His immediate aim was to persuade the Allies of German readiness to fulfill its obligations—and in that way to escape a threatened occupation of the Ruhr. It was in Spa that the other great German industrialist-expert, Hugo Stinnes, who favored a totally rejectionist line vis-à-vis the Allies, spoke of his rival Rathenau as having the "soul of an alien race" (*fremdrassige Seele*), a phrase that stuck in the coming months.[42]

Wirth, blessed with great rhetorical gifts, became chancellor in May 1921 and, despite strong opposition, appointed Rathenau to head the all-important Ministry of Reconstruction. In the same month, the Allies served the London ultimatum on Germany, specifying that total reparations would amount to 132 billion gold marks. The Germans (and Keynes) believed this a sum far beyond Germany's means to pay, and a burden on the world economy that would be hard, if not impossible, to bear. Wirth believed in a policy that would try to come to terms with the Allies and saw in Rathenau a perfect executor of such a policy.* Time was limited; by October 1921, Wirth resigned over the Allied partition of Upper Silesia, but he formed a new government, without Rathenau, probably because the Democratic Party had decided to leave it.

In January 1922, Wirth persuaded Rathenau to accept the Foreign Ministry. Rathenau understood that Germany faced calamity. The country was impoverished, divided, and defenseless, confronted by former enemies whose undeviating harshness was sustained by fear of German resurgence. In a major speech to the Reichstag in March 1922, he recounted what Germany had already accomplished in reparations and disarmament—to little avail, as far as the enemy nations were concerned. At home, the crisis deepened: an ever-worsening inflation threatened ruin to the once prosperous middle classes and to the *Bildungsbürgertum*. He feared for German science, for what was left of Germany's legacy of greatness. He argued against France's opposition to Germany's having even a limited internal security force, warning that one lived "in a time in

* Lord D'Abernon, Britain's ambassador to Weimar and sometimes dubbed its Lord High Protector, recalled, "Rathenau enjoyed immense prestige abroad; he was regarded, perhaps, as rather demoniacal than saintly. . . . There was no Teutonic obstinacy or dourness about him; if he assented, it was with grace; if he differed, it was with urbanity. . . . He had one dominant weakness, an egregious vanity—a determination, if he could not rule in heaven, to shine on earth." Viscount D'Abernon, *Versailles to Rapallo, 1920–1922: The Diary of an Ambassador* (Garden City, N.Y., 1929), pp. 42–43.

which barely controlled destructive powers stir beneath the surface."[43]

The Wirth-Rathenau program was simple and inescapable: to abandon the policy of futile obduracy and to persuade the Allies that the Germans were ready to meet the onerous obligations imposed on them—within their much disputed capacity to pay. The need for an international loan was urgent; Allied efforts to dictate German fiscal policy had to be resisted for obvious domestic political reasons. Germany was already in the grips of a terrifying inflation, with the value of the mark sinking and the economic condition of its middle class in jeopardy. Rathenau, though he was bitter about the Allies' harsh, unreasonable demands, pursued "fulfillment policy" as the only means of preventing what he most feared: an Allied occupation of the Ruhr and additional efforts at fomenting separatism in southern and western parts of Germany—in short, the very disintegration of the Reich. But he apparently was beginning to doubt whether his policy of reluctant accommodation could preserve a viable German economy.[44]

A fulfillment policy, Rathenau once explained to the cabinet, would not constitute an unconditional "yes" to Allied demands; at a later and more propitious time, it should produce some modification, even an occasional "no."[45] Despite the massive changes that defeat and the Russian Revolution had brought about, his basic views remained relatively stable: he still hoped for a reconciliation with France, though this had been made immeasurably harder by the rise to power of Raymond Poincaré, who embodied French intransigence. In Poincaré Rathenau had an uncompromising, rigid foe. Still, he hoped to pursue a policy of rapprochement with the West, knowing better than most that economic realities dictated some form of cooperation. He also had a prescient sense that only some genuine form of European unity could compete with the rapidly expanding American economy. Finally he believed that he could initiate western cooperation functionally by negotiating for joint efforts to provide economic assistance to an impoverished Soviet Union.

None of this appealed to nationalists at home, let alone to the radical right, who saw Rathenau as the very personification of Jewish power and betrayal. Many Germans, traumatized by defeat and ever-worsening financial conditions, objected to any gesture of accommodation or any move of reasonableness. Some groups favored a rapprochement with the Soviet Union, a common front against the hated West. The secret translation of sentiment into hard policy could be found in General von Seeckt's successful effort to have the Reichswehr cooperate with the Red Army, which he thought was one means of evading the Versailles Treaty. A recent biography of Joseph Wirth asserts that Wirth knew of Seeckt's extensive ties with the Soviet Army and favored the collusion, keeping Ebert and all the other members of the government—probably including Rathenau—in the dark over this political scheming.[46]

Rathenau was at once an obvious choice and a strange one for foreign minister, obvious because his financial expertise was unsurpassed, as were his connections in Allied countries (a dubious asset in the eyes of diehard nationalists), and because in the winter of 1921, when he had held no office at all, he had advised the Wirth government, occasionally even participating in its formal meetings. But he was also radically different from his predecessors in that ministry, which had a special nimbus: he was not a career diplomat but a man from the world of economics (*Wirtschaftsmensch*), an intellectual—and a Jew. The Foreign Ministry itself was divided—and in so far as it was at all sympathetic to any form of reconciliation, its officers were split between pro-westerners and pro-easterners.

His term in office is best remembered for what happened at the Genoa Conference of May 1922: the Treaty of Rapallo between Germany and the Soviet Union. Actually the treaty was an improvisation, and it seemed to disrupt Rathenau's hope of reconciliation with the West; personal pique (an apparent snub from Lloyd George wounded Rathenau) and practical considerations combined. Some members of the German delegation feared, or pretended to fear, that the Allies might reach an agreement with the Soviet Union without Germany's participation, leaving the ominous question of German reparations to the Soviet Union unresolved. The treaty, unexpectedly arranged, removed the threat of possible Soviet demands for reparations and established normal German-Soviet diplomatic relations. A direct tie between Berlin and Moscow had thus been established (some such arrangement had been envisioned just before the opening of the Genoa Conference, but Rathenau had rejected it).[47] The treaty had few practical consequences, but it lives on as a distant symbol of German unpredictability and of some irrepressible inclination on its part to find special ties to the East. It also validated Lenin's expectation of 1920 "that Germany would be forced to ally herself with Russia."[48] This was hardly the legacy that Rathenau would have wished for.

Conflicts and paradoxes haunted Rathenau to the very end. The Treaty of Rapallo was his most dramatic achievement, but it did not in any way make up for the failure of the Genoa conference to resolve the most critical economic issues. Practical man that he was, with a strong affinity for the old Europe, he would have preferred a course that would have led to cooperation with the West. His *Erfüllungspolitik* aimed at obtaining financial concessions through political reconciliation. Still, he did not return from Genoa with empty hands. Perhaps he even felt some satisfaction at having mystified the world, at having regained—from Bismarck's old office—some measure of independence for German diplomacy.

Rathenau reached the pinnacle of power at a most unpropitious time. After decades of wishing for office, his chance came when an internally divided, politically seething country faced resolute adversaries, when every nation was threatened by unprecedented economic difficulties. There probably were no German alternatives to reluctant accommodation with the

Versailles terms, but Rathenau proved to be the wrong man at the wrong time. To embittered Germans his policy of accommodation in order to avoid still worse hardships (such as further Allied occupations) was anathema. Nationalists, who favored sullen obstructionism, found Rathenau an easy target of abuse; they were people who reveled in irresponsibility. The time was wrong as well: Germany was not ready for the fulfillment policy. It had to go through the devastating experience of France's intransigence—made palpable in the occupation of the Ruhr and an unprecedented inflation—before Gustav Stresemann, whose nationalist credentials were impeccable, could successfully conduct a policy that Rathenau had begun.* Rathenau had to deal with the irreconcilable Poincaré, while Stresemann could work with the more flexible, open Aristide Briand, a true European. Throughout his time in office, Rathenau was caught between the irreconcilables at home and abroad— forces, of course, that tended to reinforce each other.

RATHENAU had often been warned that he would have to pay for political prominence with his life; for years, he had thought of himself as a uniquely misunderstood and hated person. In the beginning of Weimar, political assassinations were a common instrument of the extreme right; in April 1921, Matthias Erzberger was murdered. Rathenau's mother was terrified at her son's assumption of office, and Einstein had urged him to desist: a Jew should not aspire to such prominence—the

---

* The extreme right detested Stresemann as well. For both men they invented jingles carrying death threats, a mockery of German delight in rhyme:

> Knallt ab den Walther Rathenau
> Die gottverdammte Judensau

> Kill off Walther Rathenau
> The goddamned Jewish sow

> Stresemann
> Verwese Mann

> Stresemann
> Putrefying man

revenge would be frightful.* Rathenau understood these warnings but ignored them.

After his return from Genoa, public attacks on him redoubled; Karl Helfferich, leader of the German Nationalists, in a major speech in the Reichstag, accused him of treason. Chancellor Wirth told him that a Catholic priest, breaking the confidentiality of the confessional, had warned that Rathenau was marked for murder, and Wirth begged him to accept rudimentary measures of security. Rathenau hesitated and refused.

It was his final choice. The *Zweckmensch* would have accepted Wirth's pleas, but the *Mutmensch* wanted to face death unafraid. Rathenau had long had premonitions of danger; shortly before his death, he told Lord D'Abernon that "he is sure to be assassinated."[49] Perhaps he had a secret wish for martyrdom, a hope for grandeur in death.[50] He often invoked the metaphor from *Phaedrus*: "I often wished the chariot would shatter when the hostile horses stormed upon one another, lay into each other's bit, and lamed each other's foreleg."

* Einstein often referred to Rathenau, whose life and fate affected him. In 1932, Einstein was asked for and refused to give a definition of "the spirit of the Jewish tradition." Instead he recalled "a phrase that Rathenau once uttered in conversation with me: 'When a Jew says that for his own pleasure he is going off to a hunt, then he lies.'" Einstein to Arnold Herrmann, April 13, 1932, Einstein Archives, Institute for Advanced Study, Princeton. In 1935, Einstein wrote that Rathenau's life also described "the drama of the German-Jewish upper stratum, which, however, in the case of less perceptive and less sensitive people played itself out in a less drastic form." Einstein to Alfred Kerr, July 20, 1935, *Gedächtnisausstellung zum 100. Geburtstag von Albert Einstein* (Berlin, 1979), p. 114. In 1943, Einstein described Rathenau rather well: "His affective allegiances were contradictory. He felt himself a Jew, was internationally minded and was at the same time—as incidentally were quite a few talented Jewish intellectuals of that generation—in love with Prussianism, its Junkers and its military forms. . . . He was far removed from the narrow-minded militaristic attitude of almost all German intellectuals. . . . Still, he was strangely enough dependent on the recognition of men inwardly much inferior to him in all human qualities. Despite this curious kind of dependency, he took pleasure in poking fun at events and persons. Such improvisations were often true works of art in their droll simplicity." Einstein probably felt an affinity with this man of wit and subtle malice. Albert Einstein, *Über den Frieden. Weltordnung oder Weltuntergang?*, ed. Otto Nathan and Heinz Norden (Zurich 1976), p. 72.

On June 24, 1922, as Rathenau was being driven in an open car to his office, another car, with five young murderers, most of them war veterans, forced his car to the curb, and the killers fired shots at close range and threw a hand grenade into his car. Rathenau died within minutes. His death was the climax of his life's conflicts and contradictions and a symbol of his nation's enraged divisions. Many people rejoiced at the murder; probably a greater number grieved and were frightened. Rathenau might have felt an affinity for the blond, blue-eyed fanatics who out of nationalist passion murdered him. For German workers, millions of whom marched in disciplined processions through the streets of Germany's cities to mourn him, proclaiming their outrage and their loyalty to the republic, he would have had a distant intellectual sympathy. The ceremonies attendant upon his death were a rare moment of public decorum for the republic.*

His death, a confirmation of earlier apprehensions, shocked reasonable leaders into realizing just how fragile the improvised Weimar Republic really was. At the funeral ceremony in the Reichstag, Chancellor Wirth uttered prophetic words: "The enemy stands on the right," and that enemy remained unappeased. In the name of some kind of national regeneration a patriot of great achievement and commitment had been struck down. Rathenau's murder was not an act of individual derangement but an anticipation of a great national upsurge, a yearning for revenge, an "image of that horror."**

* There were many eulogies, none more empathetic and politically incisive than that of his close friend Ernst Troeltsch. Days after the murder, Troeltsch, acknowledging Rathenau's complex personality and his patriotic idealism, blamed the murder on the old established classes who had used "their always repudiated and yet always incited and supported Catilinarians [conspirators against the Roman Republic] to cut him down, the first blood sacrifice out of the ranks of the highest and most intelligent stratum, the most brilliant among all the victims which ... the terrible Peace of Versailles and the Counter-Revolution with its use of anti-Semitic demagogy have imposed upon us." Ernst Troeltsch, *Deutscher Geist und Westeuropa*, ed. Hans Baron (Tübingen 1925), p. 264.

** Days after the murder, Troeltsch wrote that it presumably was part of a

All his life, Rathenau, so successful in the world around him, sought to divine ways for attaining a radically better future. There was much that was prophetic in his thought—and in his career and death. The self-conscious, second-class citizen, the Jew who yearned to be what he knew the world denied him, a Jew *and* a fully accepted German, had risen to unprecedented preeminence: for a fleeting moment, he had been his nation's most visible leader. His life and his career exemplified the aspirations and partial, embattled success of German Jewry; his murder expressed the country's raging passions and divisions and confirmed the debility of Weimar against which he had struggled. In a sense, his death was a rehearsal of "Days to Come," a portent of the future degradation of Germany, which ultimately consumed his own people. But the struggle for Germany's soul, as Walther Rathenau would have put it, remained in doubt. The immediate response to his murder was a spontaneous affirmation of Weimar, an affirmation to which a new generation, especially of young Socialists, dedicated their lives. Rathenau's life and visions can still instruct, as can his ever-compelling hope that his country might yet learn to nurture talents for leadership—in politics and in every branch of what that lonely man hoped would become a more fraternal life.

---

planned right-wing coup against the republic and "the work of the large organizations, richly endowed with money. . . . Precisely this man, the last pillar of our standing and credit had to be annihilated by the murder-organization of German Fascists." "Gefährlichste Zeiten," *Der Kunstwart*, 35, no. 11, July 7, 1922, pp. 291–296.

A recent study, based on new evidence that the Soviet Army captured in Germany during World War II and brought to a Moscow archive, places the Rathenau murder in the context of a strategic conspiracy by the notorious right-wing O.C. (Organization Consul): to provoke the left by a series of assassinations into an uprising, which would provide the occasion for a showdown with the Reichswehr and its right-wing allies that would in turn result in an authoritarian dictatorship. The target, then, was the republic itself. Anti-Semitic considerations were secondary but useful as a means of disguising the true purpose and sponsors of the murder. Martin Sabrow, *Der Rathenau Mord. Rekonstruktion einer Verschwörung gegen die Republik von Weimar* (Munich 1995).

PART TWO

The Great War and Consequent Terrors

Historians and the Great War:
Private Experience and
Public Explication

❖❖

In 1992 I accepted an invitation to give the second Isaiah Berlin Lecture at Oxford University. I first met Sir Isaiah in June 1942, when I chauffeured my father, a physician, to attend Mrs. Chaim Weizmann at a hotel in the Catskills. While my father examined his patient, I was placed in another room, where I found myself in the presence of this absolutely astounding Englishman from the British Embassy, with a mind so dazzling and deep that I was quite overwhelmed.

I mention this meeting with two extraordinary men because Sir Isaiah himself, in his portrait of Chaim Weizmann, liberatingly acknowledges what it means to have known, to have been in the presence of, greatness. In the encounter of some historians with the first calamity of our century, the Great War, from which all other calamities sprang, I believe intimations of greatness can also be found.

❖❖

THERE IS A NOBLE tradition of historians who have borne witness to the great upheavals of their times. Thucydides left us an account of a war in which he was a general, a war whose deep causes and contingent events he grasped with an unsurpassed perspicacity. No one has rivaled his analysis of how wars reveal the nature of polities, of leaders, of men, how

money and morale are equal factors in determining the outcome, how great moments can be explicated by their psychological roots. With his account of the Peloponnesian War he
intended to give posterity "a possession forever"—and he did.

Thucydides had anticipated this great war, sensing that
Athenian power and imperial sway inspired overwhelming
fear. But the catastrophes of our time began with the First
World War, a war that hardly anyone had anticipated—or, to
put it differently, the kind of war it became defied anything
that had ever been imagined. At most, people thought that the
existing imperial and Continental rivalries might result in a
short war, such as the Franco-Prussian War of 1870. The lessons of the American Civil War or of the Russo-Japanese War
were discounted, even in military circles.

A number of questions occur to me. How did historians respond to the totally unanticipated destruction that swept
across Europe? How did they experience it in their own lives,
and how did they explicate it to themselves? Could they, living
so close to it and under the constant pressure of patriotic
propaganda, attain a different perspective, muster some kind
of historical detachment? Is it conceivable that the war did not
alter their assumptions, that it did not affect their views of
human nature and of the historical process? Would it not have
brought them closer to new ways of understanding old processes? Did their experience affect their work? Did the war
then affect the historians' craft, which in turn would have its
effect on national cultures? I am mindful of what C. V. Wedgwood wrote in the midst of the Second World War: "The historian has much to answer for. History—that is, written history—has made and unmade States, given courage to the
oppressed and undermined the oppressor, has justified aggression and overridden law."[1] Here I would like to concentrate on
a few historians, who left records and who did matter, and I
shall limit myself almost entirely to the Great War.

I believe—these are the simple premises of my efforts—that
present and past are indissoluble, that life and work are hard

to separate even if the connections may remain obscure and partly unconscious. These are commonplaces that have replaced the older notions of a J. B. Bury, who believed in history as science, or a Fustel de Coulanges, who said—in genuine modesty, I believe—"It is not I speaking, but history speaking through me." The reckless subjectivity that has invaded our field in some areas might make one regret the passing of the older austerity, exemplified in Leopold von Ranke's wish to "expunge the self," but I believe that only totalitarian societies can extinguish the self. In all other situations, historians are unlikely to escape their own times or their own complicated selves.

Let me also acknowledge my own proximity to the topic— which with that great gift of the unconscious I came to realize only after I had chosen it. I grew up in Germany, in the shadow of the First World War; there were continuous reminders of it at home and on the streets, where every day one encountered mutilated men. I was born precisely at the midpoint between the two wars, and in life and work I have always been mindful of that first gripping horror. In the 1960s I began writing about the war, having involved myself in what was called the Fritz Fischer debate, the renewed German controversy about the degree of German responsibility for the outbreak of the war.[2] At the time I gradually became aware that I saw the Vietnam War and the Great War in some kind of reciprocal light; it was a useful and quite specific experience in how past and present interact.

IN December 1905, after the Boer and Russo-Japanese wars, the Belgian historian Henri Pirenne wrote to a friend: "Do you really believe in the possibility of a war? For me it is impossible to have the least fear in that regard."[3] I believe that before July 1914 most Europeans felt that way. Certainly, much of the academic elite lived a relatively privileged life, devoted to their studies and their careers, confident that they would always constitute an international community, at once collaborative and competitive; that frontiers would always be open; that intellectual and scientific progress would continue without disturbing the habitual course of life. Historians shared this comfortable outlook, which very much included the implicit belief in permanence; the very people whose work dealt with the great upheavals of the past believed that their world would remain predictably unchanged. There were exceptions, of course: among them were the pessimists, like Henry Adams; the radicals, like Charles Beard and Alphonse Aulard; and R. H. Tawney, who once said what Mr. Dooley had said before him—that his task was not so much to comfort the afflicted as to afflict the comfortable (actually, Tawney did both, which I find altogether admirable). But surely the collective and unconscious dream of most scholars was to bequeath the rhythm of life they had inherited: a life that encompassed study at home and abroad, work and career, family, and leisurely trips to foreign treasures.

To put it another way, most of these ideal types, if I may use a Weberian term ironically, were steeped in the classics and in the great literature of Europe. It was their patrimony. As E. L. Woodward remembered: "I was twenty-four when the war broke out. Hitherto without knowing it, I had lived too much in and with my books."[4] As a consequence, before 1914, many historians had cut themselves off from life, and had become more and more parochial and specialized. As Friedrich Meinecke remarked, "To express it crudely, history began to taste of the laboratory"—a humanist's characteristically condescending remark.[5] With some exceptions—such as Johan Huizinga—historians shielded themselves from the great apprehensions of artists and writers, who in the years before 1914 did sense the shakiness and hypocrisy of the established, repressive order. From its very beginnings modernism, in all its various forms, struggled to express the intuition that bourgeois appearances were but masks for ugly, opaque reality, and that the world was far more chaotic, far more disordered and disfigured than convention would have it. Artists, especially German artists, did have an intuition of some coming cataclysm, an intuition much sharper than mere cultural pessimism, that nostalgic longing for redemption. I believe that Modris Eksteins was right to say that "in early German expressionism there was a motif of violence—in theme, in form, in color—which was more intense than that to be found in either cubism or futurism."[6]

At first the war that broke out in August 1914 was seen as an adventure, an interlude, not as an end to customary life. By now it is a commonplace to speak of the German exultation of August 1914, of the instant transformation of something brutal into something spiritual. Even Hermann Hesse could write as late as December 1914, "I find that, on the whole, the moral impact of the war has been very positive. For many people, it was good to be shaken up out of that silly capitalist peace, and also for Germany. I think genuine artists will value a nation more highly if its menfolk have confronted death and experienced life in the POW camps."[7] For many, August 1914 was a judgment, a moral-psychological judgment on the pre-1914 world. Redemption by sacrifice was a common theme—one that had a special appeal to much of the cultural elite. There were other responses as well. In his *Memoirs of War* Marc Bloch wrote of those first days of mobilization in Paris: "The sadness that was buried in our hearts showed only in the red and swollen eyes of many women."[8] In some ways Marc Bloch was an unlikely soldier of the first hour: he was twenty-eight, an intellectual of the upper classes; already a historian, he became an astute observer of the war, seen and felt at first hand. Even in that first memoir he wrote as a witness to history. We know that his experience as a *poilu* informed his life: he volunteered again in the Second World War, and his sharp, relentless analysis of France's defeat in 1940 is a historian's masterpiece. Already endangered as a Jew, he joined the Resistance and eventually suffered martyrdom after torture at the hands of the Germans—all that is well known. Of the chain of horrors he was witness and victim at once.

I have found only a few records of the private experiences of historians in the Great War. But those I found tell of experiences and feelings that the silent multitudes might have recognized; they include representative as well as particular themes, authentic voices, and accounts that transcend the individual.

Most of the voices were French or British—and even between them there were differences. The French tended to see the war as a historical duty, once more a defense of *la patrie*. Among British historians, there was unease at seeing England enter the war, apprehension about its likely horror, and uncertainty about its justness. Young liberals had opposed the Boer War, and G. M. Trevelyan and E. L. Woodward expressed their doubts and scruples about the new conflict: was the violation of Belgian neutrality truly the cause of Britain's entry? Or, as Woodward, whom the war haunted to the very end of his life, recalled at a later time: "Was not England enmeshed in the same political selfishness as Germany, less crudely and boastfully, but caught up in the same predatory social system?"[9]

The German side was different: I found no record of a German Bloch or Tawney, of men established in the historical profession who found themselves in the trenches. The giants were too old and the masters-to-be too young. In an autobiographical fragment, Gerhard Ritter, the leading historian of the post-1945 period, simply recorded his service in Russia in a half-sentence. I have come across hardly any expressions of unease or apprehension at the beginning of the war. Some of the most renowned scholars—I think of Ulrich von Wilamowitz-Moellendorff or Dietrich Schaefer—led the chauvinist chorus, celebrating the attacks on France as the hereditary decadent enemy or on Britain as trying to throttle a blameless rival. If unease developed, it was often expressed in what might be called defensive aggressiveness. Some historians became leading Pan-Germans; others, following Max Weber, demanded internal reform in order to preserve a national unity that alone could secure some form of victory. There were pacifists, like Ludwig Quidde and Friedrich Wilhelm Foerster, but they had no following. For the Allies, or rather for Allied historians, the war itself was the great event; for the Germans, the beginning and the end, the sight of victory and the shattering defeat, were the decisive moments of emotion or changed consciousness.

The donning of a uniform, the implicit subordination to authority, the belief that there was nobility or at least necessity in this service—these were characteristic Continental responses; the virtues of the military life had been inculcated in most of the young. The uniform symbolized patriotic manliness. Englishmen and Americans were less used to this life—not that the martial spirit was unknown to them, but they preferred to celebrate it vicariously, as moments of the past.

But for all the historian-soldiers, including those who because of age volunteered for noncombat service, there were particular encounters or discoveries that I believe left an indelible mark on them. There was, first of all, the encounter with the self, with the unknowable about oneself in otherwise unimaginable situations. Consider Tawney, that gentle Christian spirit, who in 1916 wrote:

> In crossing no-man's land we must have lost many more men than I realized then. . . . Most men, I suppose, have a paleolithic savage somewhere in them, a beast that occasionally shouts to be given a chance of showing his joyful cunning in destruction. I have anyway. . . . Every man I fired at dropped, except one. I was puzzled and angry. . . . Not that I wanted to hurt him or anyone else. It was missing I hated. That's the beastliest thing in war, the damnable frivolity. One's like a merry, mischievous ape tearing up the image of God.[10]

To discover oneself in mortal danger; to watch hundreds die; to fear but also to risk death; to observe and experience in oneself and others the raw emotions, the aggression and the fear, compassion and unreflective decency: who could undergo all this and not be shaken? Survival was a matter of chance—and that, too, is a morally fraught experience.

There was another encounter that I believe was critical and universal: the encounter with men of other classes and regions, the sudden breaking out of a sheltered class existence. Let me cite Tawney again, for he was one of the most trenchant and honest of observers, in style not unlike George Orwell. Of the attack he wrote: "'If it's all like this it's a cake-walk,' said a little man beside me, the kindest and bravest of friends, whom no weariness could discourage or danger daunt, a bricklayer by trade, but one who could turn his hand to anything, the man whom of all others I would choose to have beside me at a pinch; but he is dead."[11] I say this experience was quite common: few felt it as deeply as Tawney or Marc Bloch, and perhaps some men, immune to it, remained sealed off, but I believe the wholeness of the bricklayer was one of the formative discoveries for historians, as it was for others in a class-divided society.

Let me turn to one of the very great historian-observers of the war, Élie Halévy, who was forty-four years old when the war broke out. He was already an established philosopher-historian, already famous for his history of the English people, a work born of his desire, as he put it in a letter in 1911, "to decipher the most indecipherable people, the most moral, the least familial, the most mobile, the most adaptable, the frankest and the most hypocritical."[12] Halévy is the one historian I have read who, having always thought of Thucydides as his master, saw the war as one of Peloponnesian magnitude, a war with such deep causes that it could last for decades. He had always hated war; but when it came, and when he learned that after the first battles there were already fifty thousand wounded, he volunteered for hospital service as an orderly, spending most of his time in Albertville in the Savoie. It was, he wrote, "the work of a domestic but useful, and the conversation of the trooper is saner in these times than correspondence with intellectuals."[13] Or as he put it in December 1914: "In wartime, if pacifist eloquence sounds false, martial eloquence sounds falser still. At the present time, only one writer satisfies me and that is Joffre [who had issued the order of the day that began the battle of the Marne]. The rest is, or should be, silence."[14]

But the rest was not silence. In fact, the din of propaganda, the ever-tightening web of mendacity troubled some of those who had been trained to seek and interpret evidence in search of some approximation of truth. Marc Bloch noted the spread of false rumors, the pervasiveness of what shortly after the war in a celebrated essay he called "fausses nouvelles."[15] At that time of great uncertainty, people were unusually vulnerable to insinuations, fears, thoughts of treason; censorship and ceaseless propaganda, concealing the truth, formed the elements of this atmosphere. Throughout the war Halévy recorded his fear of the steady growth of the state's authority over all aspects of life. Would the state surrender in peace what it had gained in war?

Again it was Tawney who saw the emergence of yet another untruth, one caused by the cleavage between home and the front. He began an article in 1916: "It is very nice to be home again. Yet am I at home?" He was sickened by the English public image of the fighting man, sickened by how civilians who had remained civilians needed to glorify those who had become soldiers:

> Yet between you and us there hangs a veil. It is mainly of your own unconscious creation. . . . You have chosen, I say, to make an image, because you do not like, or cannot bear, the truth. . . . Of the first material reality of war, from which everything else takes its colour, the endless and loathsome physical exhaustion, you say little, for it would spoil the piquancy, the verve, of the picture. Of your soldiers' internal life, the constant collision of contradictory moral standards, the liability of the soul to be crushed by mechanical monotony, the difficulty of keeping hold of

sources of refreshment, the sensation of taking a profitless part in a game played by monkeys and organised by lunatics, you realise, I think, nothing.[16]

Tawney's was a righteous, desperate anger, a sense of division burdened perhaps by some kind of foreboding, however unconscious: this false image will poison the postwar world as well; it will breed cynical disbelief. Tawney suggests a moral dilemma which even now besets us: how to talk dispassionately of the war without glorifying it, and yet have the honesty to be awed by the often unwilled heroism of the men in their misery.

I do believe that often the historian speaks not only for himself—even if his impressions have a more permanent bearing on his own life than may be true of others. Thus Marc Bloch sums up his first five months as a *poilu*: "a life at once barbarous, violent, often colorful, also often of a dreary monotony combined with bits of comedy and grim tragedy. In five months in the field, who would not have amassed a rich harvest of experiences?"[17] All historical facts, he later wrote, were psychological facts.[18] He saw men of all classes and regions and dialects turn into common soldiers; he came to live the camaraderie which he recognized as the source of courage. But Bloch came to know more than men; he sketched the villages and churches he saw all around him. As he put it: "It is undeniable that especially for a city-dweller the year spent in the blue-horizon uniform furnished the occasion to penetrate the intimacy of nature and fields much more than the earlier fleeting vacations ever allowed him."[19] All of Bloch's later work reflects this deep attachment to the soil, to the fields and villages, to the rural origins of France. He sought to re-create the earlier life of the French people; he was attuned to its tonality, aware of its spiritual and material forms. Clearly, Bloch's time as a soldier and an officer informed the rest of his life.

For many, the war in its endless, senseless suffering was a radicalizing experience. On the one hand, the war enabled the discovery of the common man—that virtue, courage, decency were not the property of any one class or faith. On the other, the war also exposed the inferiority of superiors, their incompetence and moral indifference. As Woodward wrote later: "Looking back at my own angry reflections on our commanders, I can see that I was a considerable prig, intellectually intolerant and affected by half-realized class jealousy." But more than his dislike of "military arrogance," he saw the "lowness of professional competence." He went on: "No one doubted their personal courage, their discipline, their coolness in difficult moments, their powers of endurance. Their trouble was lack of imagination and 'free intelligence.'" He concluded that "the victorious generals nearly destroyed European civilization by the methods which they employed to save it."[20] What he called their "mental illiteracy" was not merely a personal failing: a whole society had conspired to breed it. And in his not disinterested epic of the war, *The World Crisis*, Winston Churchill tried to echo the sentiments of desperately war-weary soldiers: "As in the shades of a November evening, I for the first time led a platoon of Grenadiers across the sopping fields which gave access to our trenches. . . . The conviction came into my mind with absolute assurance that the simple soldiers and their regimental officers, armed with their cause, would by their virtues in the end retrieve the mistakes and ignorances of Staffs and Cabinets, of Admirals, Generals and politicians—including, no doubt, many of my own."[21] The French and British desire in the Second World War to minimize human losses at the front—a desire that took radically different forms in the two countries—had its clear roots in the abdication of reason, humanity, and correctly perceived national interest in the First World War.

"Armed with their cause," Churchill wrote—but what was their cause, as perceived by historians? I don't think they believed themselves to be fighting for democracy and civilization, as Allied propaganda claimed with increasing self-righteousness; they were increasingly suspicious that Allied

war aims traduced the patriotic clamor. Among British historians, as with Marc Bloch and others, there was simply the stolid
sense that a German victory would signify an intolerable future. Most of these men had once cherished German scholarship and had admired a country that in so many ways had
been full of promise, with its astounding creativity in the sciences and its legacy of music and the arts. In truth, Germany
had been a country of thinkers and poets. But the old bonds
snapped in October 1914, when ninety-three of Germany's
leading artists, scholars, and scientists signed the Manifesto of
the 93, defiantly addressed "to the Kulturwelt," proclaiming
German innocence, insisting on the absolute identity of German culture and German militarism, defending Germany's invasion of Belgium, and denying all allegations of atrocities.
The manifesto, addressed to erstwhile peers and friends, was
instantly circulated in the West—and it was perceived as something like a second, a moral, declaration of war. This egregious
statement, an example of autistic arrogance, was perhaps the
first major declaration that intellectuals in our century signed;
it was intended to be an expression of freedom but actually
bespoke a deep subservience. Perhaps the antagonism between German and Allied intellectuals and scholars was inevitable; many who signed the manifesto may have hoped to
prevent such an estrangement—but achieved precisely the
opposite. Intellectuals in the outside world, including Americans like Nicholas Murray Butler, felt betrayed and violated:
their German colleagues had traduced truth and abandoned
even the most minimal standards of objectivity.[22] One more
ideal destroyed—and in the first few weeks of the war. Even so
reserved and independent a patriot as Élie Halévy was appalled at the manifesto and thought of publishing a list of
Germans who had not signed it, but abandoned that notion
when he realized that it would either provoke or compromise
them. In time, the Allied claims of righteousness probably
caught up with German bombast, as the servants of God and
the guardians of morality everywhere joined in choruses of

chauvinism. But it was fear of a victorious, arrogant Germany that made historians, with doubts and scruples that did them honor, continue to serve and believe in their cause—this fear and, above all, their commitment to fellow soldiers and to country.

When the Great War finally ended, there was little rejoicing among Allied historians. Relief and apprehension were the dominant emotions. There was no spiritual armistice after November 1918. Few believed that the lights that had gone out in August 1914 would be relit; few shared the benign optimism of G. P. Gooch, a fervent believer in the League of Nations, who wrote: "If we want to create a new world order, for which ten million young people gave their lives, then we must try to remove the causes, spiritual no less than material, out of which the greatest tragedy of history grew."[23] Some historians who had long labored for the national self-determination of Czechs, Poles, and South Slavs—I think here of R. W. Seton-Watson— found hope and satisfaction in the breakup of the old empires; many considered it a limited liberal triumph bought at an unimaginable cost. But I think G. M. Trevelyan caught the true, bleak note that most men and women felt: "We are at present no better than a company of antediluvians, who have survived the fire-deluge, sitting dazed among the ruins of the world we knew. . . . It is curiously different living before the war and after it. The certainty of permanence has gone."[24]

There is a bit of upper-class nostalgia in Trevelyan's remark, but he expressed a portentous change of mood that affected many Europeans. The sense of permanence *was* gone and so was the comforting idea of progress that had been the premise of so much historical writing and intellectual endeavor before 1914. For many in the pre-1914 world, the ideas of permanence and progress were happily assimilated.

As Felix Gilbert recalled in his memoirs: "Too young to fight in the war, but old enough to have to decide about my future course before the world had again settled into a stable pattern, I felt—and many of my contemporaries shared this feeling—

that we belonged to a special generation, different from the ones that preceded and followed mine. Skeptical about the values of the past, we were also skeptical about the likelihood of stability in the future."[25] It was a fragile, fearful, disenchanted world that emerged from the catastrophe; and in a myriad of ways, that war cast its shadow over the next two decades. Not a country anywhere was, in the oft-quoted words of Lloyd George's promise, "fit for heroes"—and the sense of disappointment may have heightened for some the attraction of Bolshevism, of that self-proclaimed egalitarian society that had supplanted Russian autocracy. Are we perhaps particularly attuned to this mood today? Do not our young feel skeptical about the values of the past and uncertain about the stability of the future—despite the hope that a young, transatlantically educated American president brings to the world?*

I have said little about German historians—but then, as I have said, there were few who recorded their immediate impressions at the front. At home, the larger number were uncritical supporters of the war; many, indeed, were propagandists who vilified Allied greed and hypocrisy and clamored for German hegemony in Europe. There were warning voices as well; the most insistent and penetrating of them, of course, was Max Weber's.

At the outbreak of the war, the fifty-year-old Weber was full of passionate ambivalence. In August 1914 he wrote in a letter: "*Regardless* of eventual success, this war is great and wonderful." But from the very beginning he also feared that Germany's "insane" and "frivolous" foreign policy since 1895 had weakened the country's ability to fight a war that he thought necessary in order to establish Germany's position as a great power. In October 1914 he wrote to the sociologist Ferdinand Toennies about "the hundreds of thousands who are bleeding because of the appalling incompetence of our diplomacy." He

---

* I made this remark in December 1992, a month after Bill Clinton's election; it was an appropriate remark to make in Oxford at that time. Six years later, it makes for melancholy reading.

himself sought service and for a year became a director of a military hospital. Thirsting for responsibility, he was incredulous that the country's rulers would not entrust him with political office: "Must one be an ass or a hustler to be acceptable to officialdom?"[26] He had realistic notions about a postwar order in which Germany would be in a stronger position. While he half-foresaw the war's outcome—though in less drastic terms—still he was devastated by Germany's collapse; at the moment of defeat he was reluctant to condemn the country's rulers, even though from 1917 on he had a sense of the potential power of outraged reaction. His realism grasped German folly and its deeper causes; his patriotism enjoined an excessive silence. In the calculus of a nation's power one should include its capacity for self-criticism, for collective reasoned indignation. In this century, silence, however noble the motives, has often been a calamity, most especially in Germany.

Friedrich Meinecke also attacked Pan-German madness. After the sudden collapse of the German war effort, these moderates faced a terrifying choice: to speak their minds, at the risk of giving comfort to radicals at home and vengeful Allies abroad, or to conceal their feelings about multiple betrayal. By their concealment or silence they left the task of exposing or unmasking the callous folly of the ancien régime's glorification of war to radical artists like George Grosz, whose vitriolic portraits affronted the old established classes. After 1918, the Germans carried on the war with unabated bitterness, among themselves and against their former enemies.

In private letters even the conservative Gerhard Ritter, while speaking in January 1919 of the unchained beast—meaning the German revolutionaries, whom it would be hard to capture again—acknowledged that perhaps not all had been right in the conduct of German policy before and during the war.[27] Ernst Troeltsch, the great liberal theologian, wrote on the day of the armistice: "At least the killing is over, the illusion dispelled, the old system collapsed under its sin." And in late October 1918, Friedrich Meinecke wrote that he, like everyone else, would wish for an honorable death, adding: "A frightful, dark existence awaits us under all circumstances! And as much as my hatred for the bestial greed of our enemies smolders in me, equally hot is my anger and outrage about the German power politicians, who through their arrogance and stupidity have driven us into this abyss."[28] But by and large German historians shrank back from criticizing the sins of the old system, the arrogance and stupidity of German leadership—in part because they remained attached to the old order. Defeat turned German nationalism, so triumphant in the beginning, lachrymose and resentful; at the same time, like other German academics, most historians became intransigent—and thus abetted the Allied reluctance to readmit them to the international community.

Defeat and the humiliation of Versailles embittered German historians and heightened their nationalist identification. In his biography of Luther, Gerhard Ritter celebrated the fact that Germany was not a Western nation; in his spectacular biography of Frederick II, the *stupor mundi* of the Hohenstauffen, the Jewish nationalist Ernst Kantorowicz, later an exile in Oxford and Princeton, glorified the Caesar-like hero—an implicit rebuke to the democratic pygmies of the time? There were, to be sure, moderates, exceptions who sought some form of intellectual reconciliation. Here I think of Weber, Meinecke, or the now-forgotten liberal Catholic historian Franz Schnabel. For a great historian like Otto Hintze, the war signified the need for a change in perspective; he abandoned the narrow, political, Prussian-centered studies of his prewar days and became a German comparatist. Curiously, even disturbingly, the thematic broadening toward social history in Germany came first under the National Socialists. But in Weimar there were, of course, the dissidents, the best known of them being Eckhart Kehr, who wanted to lay bare the domestic and social reasons for Germany's most fateful prewar decision, the building of a high-seas fleet. For these and other affronts to nation and profession he was treated as an outcast by the academic establishment. Kehr and his few peers became polemical in turn. Tolerance, openness, acceptance of controversy—these were not characteristics of German academic life. To use Sir Isaiah Berlin's term, a "counter-enlightenment" mentality pervaded much of German intellectual life—both before and, with noble exceptions, even more so after the war.

The post-Versailles era was characterized by regression, the German example constituting an extreme case. Many historians retreated to monographic work, finger exercises of the historical spirit. In the wake of the notorious war-guilt clause of the Versailles Treaty, prominent historians in all the former belligerent countries sought to establish responsibility, using as principal sources diplomatic reports, prudently selected by scholars who were not always free of official supervision. It was a futile effort, since the conclusions were often prescribed from the beginning.

I want to touch briefly on some of the exceptions to this dreary retreat, exceptions that suggest that the war also stimulated new directions in historical thought. In the 1920s the Belgian historian Henri Pirenne, now much neglected, was a revered and preeminent figure; in 1916, having already lost a son at the front, he led the resistance to German demands that the University of Ghent be reopened, with Flemish to replace French as its official language. The Germans, recognizing Pirenne's central role, arrested and deported him to Germany— though he was given sufficient freedom to write a book. (How splendid it would be to have a collection of the great books written in captivity!) He started to work on a history of Europe, beginning with the barbarian invasions. At the same time, he was a shrewd observer of his fellow prisoners and of the land that held him captive. He was bemused by his British comrades, who in captivity celebrated the anniversary of Waterloo, and he was appalled by what he saw of Germany, a country in which he, too, had studied and which he had admired above all others. In his *Souvenirs de Captivité en Allemagne* he drew a devastating picture of the German professoriate, of its servility, its glorification of the noose around its neck (as long as the noose had the requisite number of decorations). He thought the old German virtues were being bankrupted by the war; he depicted a country in hysteria, with racist thought rampant.[29] At roughly the same time, a French officer, also in captivity, intuited the crippling conflicts in German wartime leadership: Charles de Gaulle, sensing the conflict between civilian and military leadership, rightly entitled his now-forgotten book *La Discorde chez l'ennemi*.

Admired for his work in economic history, Pirenne became a hero of the guild after the war. He presided over the first postwar international historical congress, which was held in Brussels in 1923. Ten years earlier, the congress had met in London, with Germans the single largest delegation. At Pirenne's own insistence, Germans were not invited to Brussels. Pirenne had returned all his German honors and broken all ties with a country that had once been exceptionally close to him. Others, of course, did the same. And yet in his presidential address, Pirenne, regretting the nationalist excesses committed during the war, called for a break with traditional national history: only a comparative approach could simultaneously remove racial and national blinkers and discover the originality and individuality of each nation. The occasion lent the appeal a special importance, and Pirenne was pleased to see among his listeners both Marc Bloch and Lucien Febvre.

Febvre and Bloch had first petitioned Pirenne in 1921 to preside over the founding of a new, self-consciously *Allied* journal that would be dedicated to social and economic history, fields they thought to be in a sorry state in France. The impulse was historiographic *and* political: before 1914, the Germans published such a journal, *Vierteljahrschrift für Sozial- und Wirtschaftsgeschichte*; it had been suspended during the war, but even if it were to be restarted, "we could not with any tranquillity resume our collaboration as before 1914." Febvre and Bloch thought Pirenne the only possible editor: they genuinely admired him and were aware that the new journal needed an older scholar of his prestige. (How much these friendships across generations enrich our private and professional lives!) They also thought Belgium an ideal location, considering the Allies' common sacrifices in battle and those "unforgettable days [when] one could feel stir . . . the soul of a people who had that fortune: in a decisive hour to find its historian." Pirenne was also their only possible mentor; Febvre and Bloch were hard on their elders, their own "sad" masters, and felt they should be left out of this new enterprise: "Titles and positions don't always provide talent—in any case, they don't necessarily suggest . . . that sort of spiritual headiness [allégresse] which is youth."[30] Like Pirenne, they also wanted to scuttle all cooperation with Germans, at least for a while. On that issue the enterprise floundered: American money was needed, and Waldo Leland of the American Council of Learned Societies insisted that German participation was an absolutely essential condition for obtaining American funds. American support for European integration, for promoting German recovery, has a distinguished history.

In 1928 in Oslo, at the Sixth International Congress of Historical Sciences, Marc Bloch pleaded again for a new type of history, a comparative approach. Finally, in 1929, Febvre and Bloch started a purely French forum, the *Annales*, which aimed once more at what historians have often called for and rarely attained: a truly comprehensive view of the past, in which many elements, from economic geography to cultural milieu, would be studied in their connectedness. It was in *Annales* in 1933 that Bloch hailed Georges Lefebvre's work *La grande peur* of 1789 as a monumental study of a nation's hallucinatory experience. Bloch, with his understanding of "fausses nouvelles," saw the great virtue of precise psychological studies of political events; he saw Lefebvre's work for what we now know it to be: a study of *mentalité* before the fashion. On balance it must be said that only a few fulfilled the hopes of *Annales*; contemporary Annalistes often seem more interested in deconstructing method than in reconstructing the past.

By 1923, the great Dutch historian Johan Huizinga, in acknowledged spiritual affinity with Jacob Burckhardt, was already practicing a supranational history, which was, I believe, also suffused with the experience of the war. He wrote *The Waning of the Middle Ages* during the war, at a time of private and public grief. In that book I detect a special sadness at the violence with which an age ended, an emphasis on the destructive passions. "Now in the records of all periods misfortune has left more traces than happiness. Great evils form the groundwork of history."[31] Like Burckhardt, Huizinga was an engaged, apprehensive observer of his own times; the materialism, the spiritual emptiness, the technological command of life—all these appalled him, as did the rising tide of racial hatred in the 1930s. He was a European before his time: in an open letter to Julien Benda in December 1933 he pleaded for a common Europe of many nations and customs, whose members would not be subordinated to some monster authority, but joined in free association. "The nationalist bitterness which [now] has driven noble minds to insanity will in the end serve the European idea. The fever will subside. The great errors have as yet always been overcome."[32] But first that very national rage assaulted his country; he, too, became a leader in resisting German demands, supporting his colleagues at Leiden University who in the fall of 1940 refused to dismiss Jewish faculty members: "If we should be called upon to defend our university and the freedom of learning in the Netherlands, then we must muster everything we can: our goods, our freedom, and even our lives."[33] The German conquerors, recognizing an unbending enemy, deported the seventy-year-old to a German camp, where he gave courage to his fellow inmates by giving a deeply moving, carefully modulated lecture on the liberation of Leiden from Spanish tyranny.

In 1929, Élie Halévy delivered the Rhodes Lectures in Oxford, a series entitled, "The World Crisis, 1914–1918"—to my mind, the best analysis of the war, its origins and meaning. He saw the folly of the political-diplomatic inquiries into the origins of war: "Pills to cure an earthquake."[34] It was an apt metaphor: the war was the result of long repressed subterranean forces, the collision of violent stirrings within and among nations, the internal forces that pushed toward revolution, whether socialist or nationalist, and those that set the great powers against one another. He understood the interplay of domestic and external forces, and he also recognized what James Joll later called "the Unspoken Assumptions" of the great leaders. Perhaps he was the first to gain a proper detachment from the catastrophe, helped by the glow of the Locarno spirit. His broader interpretation has become the conventional view; the study of war, that great horror, was much neglected, and it is perhaps only now that Sir Michael Howard and John Keegan have rescued and deepened this field.

In the aftermath of the war, especially in France, two *idées-forces* emerged, at least as goals in our profession. The war had been a lesson in the costs of national insularity; hence the plea for a comparative history transcending that narrow perspective. Related, too, was the greater emphasis on social history in the broadest context; and did not the totality of the war experience demonstrate the artificiality of studying the past in discrete compartments, let alone in exclusive concentration on political events? Historians from Eileen Power to Richard Southern have depicted the past in these more comprehensive, grander terms, not weighted down with discourse about the text but steeped in the voices of the past. The memory of the war simultaneously obstructed and demanded new directions in historical writing.

The war and the peace that followed gave America a new prominence, and historians reflected the new position. Once the United States entered the war, the government and universities commissioned historians to prepare texts that would explain America's mission. Here, too, academics assisted in the mobilization of men's minds; but even so great a dissenter from academic conformity as Charles Beard, who in 1917 resigned his post at Columbia, believed that "a victory for the

German Imperial Government would plunge all of us into the black night of military barbarism."[35] More lasting were the efforts of American historians to determine the causes of the Great War. A European as against a narrowly nationalist perspective came more easily to American historians, as witness the work of Sidney B. Fay and Bernadotte Schmitt. Already in 1922 Charles Beard had written: "The study of European affairs is no academic exercise for Americans; it runs to the roots of our national destiny."[36] In the aftermath of the war, American historians became equals in the international community of scholars.

For much of the postwar period, the best American historians also responded to the imperatives of immediate experience, whether one thinks of William L. Langer, who had been a soldier in what he called America's great adventure and became a pioneer in what we now call international history, of Richard Hofstadter, whose works responded to the grave economic and moral crises of the Great Depression, or of C. Vann Woodward, whose writings reflect the experience of racial injustice and try to understand the anguished and embittered life of the defeated South.

I am in danger of talking of peaks where valleys were the norm. After the war, most historians returned to the cloistered insularity of earlier work, shunning the great themes of the past and the terrible challenges of the present. On the other hand, most Western historians resisted the great temptations of the time, bolshevism and fascism. Work was a comfortable shield; some months after Hitler's rise to power, Meinecke wrote to a colleague: "In one's work one sometimes forgets . . . everything else and behaves as if one lived outside time. You are right. We defeated ones, to the extent we are bourgeois, are all on the same tossing raft in a stormy sea and we should learn to get along with one another."[37] But German historians were not so much getting along with each other as they were being gradually complicitous with the new totalitarian regime or, as in the case of the Austrian historian Heinrich von Srbik, becoming demonstratively pro-Nazi. In the West, the legacy of the war divided historians. To some, appeasement seemed the appropriate lesson; to others, the need for rearmament and resistance to aggression. At the outbreak of the Second World War, Bloch confessed to Lucien Febvre: "In 1919–1920 and after we allowed the greatest stupidities to happen without protesting or protesting too little. . . . We sold our souls for our repose, for our intellectual work, we ignored that after four years of horror men wanted to live truly. We were wrong."[38] As Bloch himself insisted in his magnificent reckoning of France's defeat in 1940, the rot that flowed from national indifference poisoned the country, and the stupefied incompetence at the top reflected the lassitude, the conflicts, the loss of morale at the bottom, especially the bourgeois bottom. His book was a final tribute to the centrality of morale, of mentality.

Earlier generations in this century experienced disaster; some of us are left with what Henry James has called "the imagination of disaster"—a further incentive, perhaps, to explicate the past for the benefit of the present. Yet I fear that for many historians today the links between life and work have been much loosened; the great vogue of theory with all its abstractness can easily overwhelm experience in all its recalcitrant complexity.

But even in our narrow guild there is greatness that passes from generation to generation. During the phony war in early 1940, Marc Bloch, again in the field, began to write "The History of French Society in the Structure of European Civilization"—a work he did not live to finish. The dedication read: "To the memory of Henri Pirenne, who, at the time his country was fighting beside mine for justice and civilization, wrote in captivity a history of Europe."[39] In 1986, Bronislaw Geremek, the Polish historian of the marginal classes in medieval France, and also an imperiled leader of Solidarność, wrote an *hommage* to Marc Bloch, which—he being detained by Polish authorities—had to be read for him in Paris. Geremek ended by saying, "I do not believe I am being unfaithful to [Bloch's] thought in saying that after all 'on peut mourir pour Danzig.'"[40] The phrase had multiple meanings. Bloch had chosen to fight for Danzig, to resist Nazi aggression, and to die for his beliefs. Geremek had chosen a life in which to go to prison for the cause of freedom, "to die for Danzig"—Gdansk, the birthplace of Solidarność—had become reality. Perhaps the worst calamities in our part of the world are over, but the triad of Pirenne, Bloch, and Geremek remains an inspiration. Historians do have a civic responsibility and we do live by freedom.

Isaiah Berlin himself has borne witness to the calamities of our century. More: with moral force and wisdom he has explicated the great intellectual-spiritual traditions of modern Europe, examining most closely those that sustain and those that endanger liberty. He has validated for our time the virtue of history and the centrality of ideas in history. His work has given substance to a fleeting remark of Ranke's that "the important point is rather that human freedom makes its appearance everywhere, and that the greatest attraction of history lies in the fact that it deals with the scenes of this freedom."[41] By recalling such thoughts we are reminded that Clio has always attracted diverse master servants, few in number but great in spirit, and their works do become "possessions forever."

Chaim Weizmann and
Liberal Nationalism

❖❖

I first met Dr. Weizmann in June 1942, when I drove my physician-father to attend Mrs. Weizmann in the mountains north of New York City. The next day—one of the darkest days of the war—Dr. Weizmann took me on a walk. Tobruk had just fallen and the Germans were at the gates of Alexandria, even as they had conquered most of the Caucasus. He talked of the immediate danger to Palestine, but, he added, if that danger were to pass, as he thought it would, then on the morrow of an Allied victory, a Jewish homeland would become a reality; he spoke of how the country would be settled, how a desert would be transformed, and, pointing out the flowers along the path, spoke of the Negev and how it would be made to bloom. I have never forgotten that moment. I felt that I was in the presence of a great man with a great, transcending cause.

In March 1994 I gave the Annual Chaim Weizmann Lecture in the Humanities at the Weizmann Institute in Rehovot. I revised this lecture in the winter of 1997, in the weeks following the death of Sir Isaiah Berlin; I had first met him in Dr. Weizmann's company in 1942. Sir Isaiah's last thoughts on Israel, his political testament, published on the day of his death, breathes the spirit of Chaim Weizmann, the man he so brilliantly understood and remembered: "Since both sides begin with a claim of total possession of Palestine as their historical right; and since neither claim can be accepted within the realms of realism or without grave injustice: it is plain that compromise, i.e. partition, is the only correct solution, along Oslo lines—for supporting which Rabin was assassinated by a

Jewish bigot. Ideally what we are calling for is a relationship of good neighbors, but given the number of bigoted, terrorist chauvinists on both sides, this is impracticable. The solution must lie somewhat along the lines of reluctant toleration, for fear of far worse."

❖❖

MUCH HAS BEEN written about Chaim Weizmann and his achievement—by no one more movingly than Isaiah Berlin. Here, I want to explore the historical context of Weizmann's life's work. Weizmann once said to Berlin that "miracles do happen, but one has to work very hard for them."[1] This thought encapsulates the achievements of his own life. Much about his accomplishments remains inexplicable, even mysterious, but I would like to point out some elements in the spirit of the time that facilitated his work, some characteristics that Weizmann embodied and that called forth a special response in what we once with tacit pride called the West.

Why was it that in the years before and after the Balfour Declaration so many people were receptive to Weizmann's vision of a Jewish homeland, of something that had not existed for two thousand years, a home in which the best qualities of a people could be nurtured, in which men and women would make a barren land fruitful, unfettered at last from ancient hatreds and oppressions that had left such deep wounds and insecurities? At the time of Weizmann's birth in 1874, a seemingly triumphant and assimilated Disraeli said to young Montefiore: "You and I belong to a race that can do everything but fail." Weizmann believed, as some had believed before him, that the Jews in the Diaspora were born to the deepest kind of vulnerability, that only with a move to a realm of their own, which at the same time recalled the very essence of their spiritual experience, could they summon forth the qualities that in hostile climes had been stunted, deformed, or appropriated by host and hostile nations.

Weizmann was at home in the hospitable misery of East European Jewry. He was born near Pinsk, the third of fifteen children to parents who already had Zionist sympathies. He knew the inner warmth of the cold Pale. He grew up amidst a people that had no doubt about its identity, which flowed from a shared faith and language, from ancient and unquestioned traditions, and was forever reinforced by hostility and persecution. He was not yet seven years old when the murder of Tsar Alexander II in 1881 unleashed ever greater and officially sanctioned cruelty to Jews and thus ended the hope for a reformist, Westernizing Russia. Zionism had already taken roots in Russia and Eastern Europe, where Jewish life was preserved by outside dictate and sustained by internal cohesion and tradition. A new practical imperative was now added, made visible by the mass exodus of Jews to England and the United States. And even in those Anglo-Saxon havens, the tensions between the poor new immigrants and the established if ever struggling assimilationists was becoming a familiar story.

Already as a young man Weizmann lived in both worlds—in the familiar world of Pinsk and in the western world, in Germany, Switzerland, and, ultimately, England. The deepest truth about Weizmann's life was that his tie to his own people in the Pale was unbreakable, however great the distance between them. Culturally and intellectually he moved far from them; he succeeded in the western and gentile world beyond what most of his compatriots could even imagine, but his heart remained with them and his life was dedicated to them. As a very young man he read the classics of the West and the great works of Russian literature. He mastered the principal languages that would make possible his entrée into the West, where he could easily have become a rich and respected scientist. His talents drove him to the natural sciences, the one field in that late nineteenth-century era of astounding progress in which Jews were allowed to compete and flourish, and he was no stranger to the rewards of affluence. But neither the temptation of a life in the laboratory, to which he was devoted, nor the

frequent tribulations that his own people inflicted on him, deterred him from his commitment to the cause of Zionism. In a
celebrated letter to one of his teachers, the eleven-year-old
Weizmann already evoked Zionism: "For why should we look
to the Kings of Europe for compassion that they should take
pity upon us and give us a resting place? In vain! All have decided: *The Jew must die*, but England will nevertheless have
mercy upon us. In conclusion, to Zion!—Jews—to Zion! let
us go."[2]

Weizmann spent a life defining and, as much as any one
man could, realizing the child's dream. Weizmann's dream reflected the thought of his mentor, the Russian Jewish writer
Ahad Ha'am (Asher Ginzberg), one of the earliest champions
of a Jewish national revival.[3] Ahad Ha'am's vision was of an
inner rebirth, a spiritual transformation of Jewry. Weizmann's
dream was liberation and emancipation, the achievement of
rights that other groups and nations claimed for themselves: a
home, in Zion, where men and women could start a new life
among equals, a life close to the soil, a life both free of the
threats and constraints of the impoverished ghetto and free
of assimilationist subservience that he, like Theodor Herzl,
thought was "slavishness within freedom." Weizmann considered Karl Marx a traitor to his people, but he shared one thing
with him, a hatred of servility, and both of them sought to liberate people from it. Some measure of servility, conscious or
unconscious, remained the ineluctable fate of even the most
prominent or prosperous Jews of the West. In his later work,
Weizmann needed the help of assimilationist Jews, even of the
many Jews who were frightened and ashamed of this prophet
who insisted on speaking of and for a Jewish nation, while they
often rather ostentatiously embraced the nationalism of the
countries they lived and hoped to prosper in.

Already as a student, Weizmann uneasily divided his time
between scientific studies and Zionist commitment. In 1901, he
helped to found the Democratic Faction within the Zionist
movement, in loyal opposition to its leader Herzl, who hoped

to gain a Jewish homeland with the help of some great poten-
tate, to achieve Zionist goals by diplomatic means. Weizmann
objected that Herzl's approach neglected the all-important cultural renaissance of the Jewish people, the need for a synthesis
between Zionism and Europe's great artistic and scientific
achievements. In 1903, in a long letter to Herzl, a kind of credo,
he sketched his hope for this cultural synthesis, his fear of the
Orthodox (of the religious party, the *Mizrahi*) whose aim "to
weave religion into Zionism" would lead to "the suppression
of spiritual freedom." At earlier Zionist congresses, he had battled and ridiculed the narrow-mindedness of the rabbis. He
also worried that the best of Russian Jewish youth was in thrall
to Social Democracy, to the Bund, imprisoned in Russia for
their political faith, and growing up in a revolutionary, vio-
lently anti-Zionist world. The Democratic Faction was to "form
the connecting link between the older and the younger generation."[4] His rejection of the Bund and his later, uncompromising
denunciation of Bolshevism arose from his sense that these sys-
tems would bring forth new forms of coercion, new temptations for Jews seeking some form of assimilation. From the beginning, his belief in liberal and nonviolent principles set him
apart from and opposed to illiberal and nondemocratic factions within Zionism.

One of his earliest projects was the creation of a Jewish university, ideally to be located in Palestine, even before further
Jewish settlement there. Free, secular, practical, and classical
education was a prerequisite for freedom. In 1904, he became
coeditor with Martin Buber and Berthold Feiwel of a periodi-
cal, *Der Jude. Revue der Jüdischen Moderne*, another effort in
which he hoped to link the disparate worlds of self-conscious
Jewry and of modern thought, to build "a golden bridge . . . on
which the intellectuals of Europe will meet with our Jews"; he
wanted to bring "the ghetto to Europe and Europe to the
ghetto."[5] That combination—ghetto and Europe—he himself
embodied, devotion to the good of the former and to the promise of the latter.

Weizmann was not a political theorist or philosopher; his premises were simple, acquired, I think, as "self-evident truths": men and women should live in legally circumscribed freedom, they should be autonomous citizens, and their talents should no longer be inhibited but coaxed into achievement. He was a liberal by temperament and even more by experience, and all his life he showed that respect for civilized life, for truth and openness, for tolerance and nonviolence, which mark the liberal spirit. His was an intuitive version of a liberalism that Judith Shklar has defined as having "only one overriding aim: to secure the political conditions that are necessary for the exercise of political freedom," and that is dedicated to the protection of all, especially the weakest, against the supreme evil that "is cruelty and the fear it inspires, and the very fear of fear itself."[6] For Weizmann this was no textbook dictum—it was the immediate lesson of the ghetto and of Jewish history. East European Jewry had begun the great trek westward, to freedom; Weizmann wanted to "nationalize the emigration stream," to find ways to settle some of these Jews in a Jewish homeland, in Palestine.[7] But such a homeland had yet to be created.

In order to achieve a Jewish home embodying freedom and tolerance, Weizmann did not always practice liberal virtues. In common parlance, he used people; he has been called charming, seductive, secretive, and conniving—all as part of his work for the miracle. Devotion to cause merged with personal ambition; cause and self served each other. Surely that is a common characteristic of great leaders and remains a mysterious ingredient in a revolutionary life.

The eleven-year-old thought that the kings of Europe would show no compassion for Jews—more likely they would show hostility. And the young Weizmann saw that even as Jews in the West were gaining wealth and some forms of power, their ascendancy accelerated the spread of a new, often racial anti-Semitism. The Dreyfus affair had been the original stimulus for

Theodor Herzl's crusade; Weizmann's Zionism sprang from a deep faith in the need for a Jewish renaissance, but he also believed, or so he told Richard Crossman decades later, that every gentile carried the bacillus of anti-Semitism in him. I think he assumed a historic antagonism between Jew and gentile, to which Jews contributed their share, and he hoped that when Jews were truly free and in a home of their own, that antagonism would be attenuated, perhaps disappear. Subtly, and therefore successfully, Weizmann intimidated moral Christians by recalling their legacy of historic animosity to Jews and the consequent injustices.

The eleven-year-old had written of England; the thirty-year-old, deep in the Zionist movement, went to settle there, as a chemist at Manchester and a Zionist everywhere. Fortuitously it was the year of Herzl's death. In 1904, Weizmann had no fixed position as a Zionist, no office or formal following, and yet, as he wrote his fiancée in 1904, "I have assumed the role . . . of self-styled diplomat of . . . Russian Zionists to the British Government." A year earlier, after his first visit to England, he had written: "I brought the impression away from London that we can accomplish a great deal there. We can win over influential circles; we must manifest our desire for Palestine with deeds rather than shallow phrases. We must place our political activities—I simply call it propaganda—in the hands of first-rate men who will win over the sympathies of Europe."[8]

"To win over the sympathies of Europe": that was the road to success, and none grasped this better than Weizmann. How was it possible to win the sympathy of Europe and the United States? What was it in England and the United States in particular that found Weizmann and his cause congenial and demanding of support? I believe that in the decade before the Great War a new kind of practical, reformist liberalism sprang up—a liberalism that to varying extents recognized the need for change, often through the interventionist state which (to quote Walter Lippmann) should end drift and attain mastery.

That liberalism carried with it a strong emancipatory impulse, favorable to the rights of women, supportive of oppressed groups or nationalities.

In our own time we have seen the horrors of aggressive nationalism, of frenzied violence masquerading as something noble, and thus we tend to forget the force of benign national sentiment. As Isaiah Berlin once put it, "Nationalism is an inflamed condition of national consciousness which can be, and has on occasion been, tolerant and peaceful."[9] Liberal nationalists aimed at emancipating their people from foreign or imperial dominion so that they could live in a state in which traditional civic freedoms would be anchored in constitutionally defined institutions. They would be free to cultivate their own language and ethos, to create their own civil society. Thomas Masaryk, father of the Czechoslovak Republic, did not think that the Czechs were superior to other nations nor did he harbor aggressive designs against them. He believed in the rights of minorities. Such ideals were strong in the early years of the century; they also inspired some of the great liberators of Europe's colonies, and most recently, they inspired the leaders of Solidarność and Václav Havel.

In the United States in the years before the Great War, such emancipatory impulses were particularly strong, especially among the very men who formed a bridge between Weizmann and Woodrow Wilson, namely Louis Brandeis and Felix Frankfurter, both of whom believed that the United States had a unique mission to serve as an exemplar to other nations, to help bring freedom to the world. As yet it was an innocent faith. Brandeis and Frankfurter were part of the Progressive movement in America, which was "determined to remedy the . . . social ills of industrial society." As the American historian Richard Hofstadter has written, "They asserted—and they were the first in our history to do so with real practical success—the idea that government cannot be viewed merely as a cold and negative policing agency, but that it has a wide and pervasive responsibility for the welfare of its citizens, and for the poor and powerless among them. For this, Progressivism must be understood as a major episode in the history of the American conscience."[10] That conscience also favored the national self-determination of peoples, and it proved receptive to Zionist hopes.

For most liberals at the time, science was an unquestioned good, the fullest expression of human reason and human genius, an obvious instrument of human progress. The scientist was held in the highest esteem; he was the selfless servant of discovery. Perhaps only scientists themselves knew how much ordinary human ambition and even greed inspired their work. In Manchester and beyond, Weizmann's great achievements in practical chemistry were matters of passionate concern for him and they also earned him some financial independence. More: science helped to establish his authority, it facilitated his reception in gentile circles, and it constituted an inalienable realm of work, an assured refuge, when he was repudiated by events or his own people. Also, it enhanced his friendships; at one critical moment in his life, in 1931, it was his scientist friend Richard Willstätter who eased his way back to the laboratory.

During Weizmann's decade in Manchester before the Great War, he encountered success and failure both in chemistry and in Zionism; he experimented with various ways of producing synthetic rubber—at a time when natural rubber was becoming scarcer and dearer. As his research progressed, he took out patents and made his own agreements with chemical firms. His pursuit of fame and gain brought him into conflict with his Manchester patron and eventually cost him the much-coveted professorship in Manchester. The serenity that marked his later life was a triumph of temperament over hardships and disappointments. Still, Weizmann, a foreigner not yet proficient in the English language, made important friends; he was received with remarkable hospitality. All in all, the years in Manchester confirmed his expectations of English life and strengthened an Anglomania that resembled Isaiah Berlin's depiction of Felix Frankfurter's view:

> touching and enjoyable Anglomania—the childlike passion for England, English institutions, Englishmen—for all that was sane, refined, not shoddy, civilized, moderate, peaceful, the opposite of brutal, decent—for the liberal and constitutional traditions that before 1914 were so dear to the hearts and imaginations especially of those brought up in eastern or central Europe, more particularly to members of oppressed minorities, who felt the lack of them to an agonizing degree, and looked to England and sometimes to America—those great citadels of the opposite qualities—for all that ensured the dignity and liberty of human beings.[11]

For Weizmann, faith in England was a comforting and essential premise; when the tie with England broke, it nearly broke his spirit as well.

But for the moment he found sustenance for it: Manchester was a liberal city and in 1910 he became a British subject. In 1906 Weizmann met A. J. Balfour and Winston Churchill, as both were campaigning in Manchester at the time of the general election. Balfour was a Conservative by party affiliation but a liberal by inherited tradition, as were many of his party colleagues. From the first, he found Weizmann appealing, not surprisingly, since he was, as he put it himself, "untiringly interested in scientific development. . . . My business was with the groundwork of living beliefs; in particular with the goodness of that scientific knowledge whose recent developments had so profoundly moved mankind."[12] And even at this early date, Weizmann would have been able to convey his vision of a Jewish homeland with something of a scientific tinge: he did think of the future Palestine as a scientific laboratory, both in the literal sense of settlers transforming the land by scientific means, and in the figurative sense of Palestine as a human laboratory where under well-regulated conditions people would be able to better themselves. Unlike others in our century, Weizmann wished to create "the new man" not by decree but by creating conditions that would allow for self-cultivation. In his spontaneous faith in science, in progress, in human improvements, Weizmann was close to the prevailing liberal assumptions of Britain at that time, in which the contrary views of racism, degeneracy, or just plain bloody-mindedness in politics were still marginal.

It has been said that in those years Weizmann was more successful in appealing to English gentiles than to fellow Jews. David Ben-Gurion once called him "the greatest Jewish emissary to the Gentile world," and J. L. Talmon wrote, "The Jewish people have never had a more impressive and persuasive apostle unto the Gentiles than Weizmann." Among Jews, particularly among wealthy assimilated Jews, he usually encountered fear and rejection, fear—put simply—that once Jews were declared to constitute a nation they themselves would be charged with "double loyalties." As we will see, Weizmann could be scathing in his views of such "eminent" Jews. But among the gentiles he found a hearing, especially among Protestant Englishmen who perhaps more than other people retained an attachment to the biblical tradition even in a secular age. In his essay on Weizmann, Norman Angell wrote: "Now, to a very much greater extent than the British themselves often realize, their own culture, particularly on the ethical side, is also Jewish. The only religious literature which has deeply affected the common people of England, the only literature to which they turn in moments of the deepest sorrow and the deepest joy, and in the hour of death, is Jewish literature."[13]

Weizmann could also appeal to the English romantic imagination, to their fascination with the East, to their sense that returning to Jerusalem might be a noble venture. More, they had in certain circumstances demonstrated an enthusiasm for the downtrodden, the persecuted, or the oppressed of other nations. After all, some Englishmen had died for Greek independence and many celebrated Garibaldi in their midst; Gladstone had written, in "Bulgarian Horrors," a powerful indictment of Turkish misrule at a time when national interest demanded Britain's support of Turkey against Russia. About freedom, let alone independence, within their own empire they tended to be more reticent, and the claims of the Irish, geographically closest to them and very much on the political agenda, divided British politics. Of David Lloyd George's support for Zionism, it was said that it came easy to the Welshman; as he himself once said of the Welsh to a Jewish audience: "It is an ancient race, not as old as yours, and although I am very proud of it, I am not going to compare it with yours . . . but all I know is that up to the present it is the small races that have been chosen for great things."[14] And, we should note, Balfour was a Scot.

In the prewar period, most English liberal nationalists accepted the notion that at least the British Empire was a civilizing enterprise. The Boer War, however, had split the intellectual class. Americans were opposed to other peoples' imperialism, though divided about their own, which broke upon the world with full force in the Spanish-American War of 1898. That the tacit or unquestioned acceptance of imperialism depended on a presumption of racial inequalities is obvious, and racism was on the rise in Europe and America.

Weizmann knew, of course, that baser instincts or forces were also favoring Zionism. Ever since the 1890s, England had received more East European Jews than any other country in Europe. To many English, therefore, a Jewish homeland would be a happier alternative to a continued absorption of countless more Jews into their own country. Anti-Semites of the more virulent stripe welcomed the assertion that Jews were a separate nation—it confirmed their sense of the repugnant otherness of Jews. Finally, Weizmann knew that because gentiles feared an ever greater Jewish power in the markets and the press of the world, they often thought that a pro-Zionist policy could win over Jewish support in general.

The outbreak of war in 1914 stunned Weizmann, who was vacationing in Switzerland and hurried back to England. He grasped instantly that the war would transform world politics—one way or another. His sympathies were entirely on the Allied side. In October 1914 he wrote, "With Prussia's victory all Jewish hopes—including the Zionist—must fall. . . . I conceive this war as the struggle between Siegfried and Moses." And Moses had withstood "worse things than 17-inch guns." Instantly and consonant with his liberal beliefs and rational considerations, he pinned his hopes on the Allies: "It is in the interest of peoples now fighting for the small nationalities to secure for the Jewish nation the right of existence. Now is the time when the peoples of Great Britain, France and America will understand us. . . . The moral force of our claims will prove irresistible; the political conditions will be favorable to the realisation of our ideal."[15]

Weizmann was a supreme realist—or his ideals would have remained noble words. He understood that the British empire had not been created in a fit of absentmindedness but in relentless pursuit of British self-interest, however transfigured. The British then, as the citizens of some great powers today, believed that their interests corresponded to some great universal ideal. Weizmann flattered that presumption: a Jewish homeland in Palestine under British protection would serve British interests and would constitute an act of universal atonement. Palestine would become a bastion for the empire, and a defense for the Suez Canal, an "Asiatic Belgium in the hands of the Jews."[16]

During the Great War, Weizmann assumed the mantle of a statesman; he possessed what decades later Václav Havel called "the power of the powerless." His was the power of a moral presence, and yet he was a pragmatist, sworn to the success of his cause. In September 1914 he met C. P. Scott, editor of the *Manchester Guardian*, and probably Britain's greatest journalist. Of Scott, it was said that he "was a great Liberal with whom nationalism was a tradition and a passion."[17] Weizmann and Scott became friends; Scott believed in him and his cause, and introduced him to Lloyd George, then chancellor of the exchequer, and to other men of power.

Weizmann believed that a common destiny linked a benevolent Britain and Zionism. He had acquired a formidable, even intimidating moral authority, and he knew how to wield it. "Weizmann was not only a dexterous and resourceful advocate—flexible, sure-footed, highly sensitive to atmosphere, and with an unerring instinct for timing; he possessed in a high degree the power to kindle the imagination and to impart to others some of his own mystical faith in the destiny of his people and the significance of its survival."[18] As Richard Crossman remembered, "No man knew better than he the art of using the conscience and ambition of British politicians (including, perhaps, the author of this book) in the interests of the Jewish state."[19]

Weizmann had made friends with and pro-Zionists of some of Britain's great leaders, but no manner of ingenious persuasion would have prevailed but for this invocation of British self-interest; he kept insisting that after the defeat of Turkey and the assumption of British control over Palestine, a Jewish presence there would serve British interests. Meanwhile and immediately he served British interests at home. He had developed a new method for obtaining acetone, a vital ingredient in the manufacturing of heavy artillery, especially for the Royal Navy. The British government asked him to organize the production of acetone according to his technique. Weizmann threw himself into this new assignment in London, which enhanced his standing with the British establishment and added stature to his unofficial standing in the Zionist world.[20] Thus the Great War, which saw the paroxysm of rapacious nationalism, proved as well to be the great historic chance for Weizmann and for Zionism.

By 1917, the Lloyd George government, itself but recently constituted, faced a desperate situation. The Germans had re-

sorted to their ultimate weapon, unrestricted submarine warfare, and British losses on the high seas imperiled British subsistence. It was not certain that the country could hold out until
American power could be thrown into the balance.

Meanwhile another battle had been going on for some time:
the competitive exploitation of national discontent behind
enemy lines. Germans encouraged rebellion not only in Ireland
but in all possible areas of the British and Russian empires. The
Allies, somewhat less cynically, sought to rally the national minorities within enemy lands, especially those of the Austro-
Hungarian Empire. The subversion of Arabs against their
Turkish rulers was an important, exotic enterprise—of great
potential importance to Zionists. Some British liberals—here I
think especially of R. W. Seton-Watson—had long studied and
championed the demands of the Czechs, the Poles, and the
South Slavs. For Britain now to champion their cause during
the war was expediency gilded by principle; the Americans
came to take up the cause out of missionary zeal and a tinge of
domestic political opportunism. Even as the Allies drew up
plans for their own aggrandizement, they promised liberation
to peoples outside their dominion. In many ways, the promise
of national self-determination, however noble in the abstract,
was to become the poisoned culmination of liberal hopes.

Already in peacetime, Weizmann had urged on leading British politicians the moral imperative of a Jewish homeland. I am
thinking of Balfour, Lloyd George, Churchill, Mark Sykes,
Robert Cecil and the great South African Jan Smuts. The war
lent urgency to his demand just as his own scientific-practical
talent in the service of British munition-making confirmed his
loyalty. He now persuaded some of these same leaders that
support of Zionism was to Britain's immediate and long-term
advantage: it would rally Jewish opinion in Europe and the
United States at a time when the Germans were making serious efforts to claim Zionism for themselves and to play a pro-
Jewish card in the parts of Eastern Europe they had newly conquered. Above all the British believed that support of Zionism

would wean American Jewry from its pro-German (because largely anti-Russian) stance.

Zionism needed help—in Europe and especially in America. In Europe let me cite but one example of the help received from that most admirable and principled of national liberators, Thomas Masaryk. Born in Slovakia, brought up in a Catholic, anti-Semitic milieu, he gradually became a champion of the Czech nation and of humanist philosophy. In 1899-1900 he was a lone voice in defense of Leopold Hilsner, a Bohemian Jew accused of the ritual murder of a girl and at first condemned to death. At the time, Masaryk was proclaimed a Zola in this Austro-Czech analogue of the Dreyfus affair. He was also an early supporter of Zionism, drawing inspiration, as of course Weizmann had himself, from Ahad Ha'am. In 1900 and subsequently he expressed his admiration for Ahad Ha'am's Zionism, for his efforts for a spiritual regeneration and an inner rebirth of Jewry. He thought this movement akin to his own hopes for a Czech national renaissance. Masaryk's views of Jewry were complicated, but after the Hilsner affair he was celebrated by Jews, especially in America.[21] And in his years of rising prominence, Masaryk supported Weizmann's diplomatic efforts, most importantly at the Paris Peace Conference. Both men admired—and possessed—character, and they felt "a great affinity" for each other.[22] When Weizmann became president of Israel, he recalled Masaryk's role as president and father of a new state, wishing, I think, that he might be able at least to approximate Masaryk's authority. It was not to be— but the sympathy and support of Europe's most admired national emancipator had bolstered and confirmed Weizmann's extraordinary position.

At the beginning of the war, Weizmann sought to establish Zionist leadership in America. Louis Brandeis, the great American progressive, had converted to Zionism after his experience as a mediator in a garment strike in which East European Jews were pitted against each other: in his view both sides were tough, spirited, impressive, and he thought such talents should be set free. He became the head of the Provisional Executive Committee for General Zionist Affairs in 1914. Brandeis saw in the idea of a Jewish homeland the possibilities of extending the progressive crusade for social justice. "Our main task must be to make fine men and women in Palestine, and it will be desirable to correct there, so far as possible, those distortions of character and mind which too much commercialism enforced by separation from the land many centuries, has entailed."[23] Thus did American liberals and progressives support Zionism, to the dismay of most rich and assimilated Jews. In America as elsewhere, Zionism often found powerful friends more easily among gentiles than among Jews—among whom there were many competing factions with conflicting aims. American Jews were dismayed by the upsurge of anti-Semitism during the war, making Brandeis all the more determined to support the Zionist cause. Both Brandeis and his younger but immensely resourceful colleague Felix Frankfurter did their best to gain President Wilson's support for a proposed British declaration in support of a Jewish homeland in Palestine.

The Balfour Declaration of November 1917 marked the triumph of Weizmann's early hopes. It was, in the words of a well-known diplomat-historian, Sir Charles Webster, "the greatest act of diplomatic statesmanship of the First World War."[24] Here was a British commitment, a charter for the homeland. Weizmann knew perfectly well just how much British self-interest had inspired the declaration. As a leading historian recently pointed out, "The British were . . . determined to retain control of Palestine, once they had conquered it . . . to strengthen their position in a region deemed vital to the defensive system of the entire Empire."[25] Weizmann assumed that there was and would remain an identity of interest between a powerful Britain and an emergent Jewish presence in Palestine, an identity of interest that would begin with a British protectorate over Palestine and ultimately promote Jewish statehood. He failed to foresee the decline of British power and self-

confidence—but then only in retrospect do we see that the
Great War desperately weakened the empire that had just endured its greatest trial. A country in decline, saddled with
doubts about its imperial mission and with stirrings of guilt
about the Versailles Treaty, would prove an uncertain protector of Zionism.

With the Balfour Declaration, Zionism—once a dream of
redemption, a fantasy of hope—became enmeshed in world
politics. That inescapable involvement was brought home
symbolically when within days of the declaration, the Bolshevik Revolution broke out. Weizmann understood the multiple
dangers instantly. He saw how radical Jews, long oppressed,
had risen to be among the top leaders of the Bolsheviks and he
feared that the very existence of Bolshevism would arouse still
greater anti-Semitism. Even a man so free of anti-Semitism as
Winston Churchill declared a short time later that Bolshevism
was but the rabble of East European ghettos. I doubt that anyone foresaw how Bolshevism would become this fatal double
source of anti-Semitism—arousing it abroad even as it gradually and cruelly practiced it at home.

When Zionism was thrust into world politics by the Balfour
Declaration, Weizmann inevitably but also by his own ambition arrogated to himself the role of international statesman,
even as he had created his earlier role in England. In doing so,
he thought of Camillo Cavour as a model,the Piedmontese patriot who by prudent diplomacy achieved Italian unification, a
goal that the great rouser of masses, the fiery Garibaldi, failed
to reach.[26] He also thought that Lincoln's spirit was of more
lasting importance than Napoleon's conquests. He knew the
Balfour Declaration was a mere beginning, an opening; much
more had to be achieved before intent could be turned into
reality, before the practical work in Palestine—which Weizmann thought the most urgent and continuing effort—could
be resumed. Then, as throughout his life, the obstacles were
great and the enemies legion. The most immediate opponent
was France, unwilling to allow Britain so important a presence

in the Middle East. The other opponent was Arab nationalism, which the English had also carefully nurtured in their efforts to defeat the Ottoman Empire. As early as June 1917 a leading British Zionist and one of Weizmann's closest, if critical, lieutenants, Harry Sacher, had written: "Even if all our political schemings turn out in the way we desire, the Arabs will remain our most tremendous problem. I don't want us in Palestine to deal with the Arabs as the Poles deal with the Jews and with the lesser excuse that belongs to a numerical minority. That kind of chauvinism might poison the whole of [the] Yishuv. . . . We must have a big constructive program to oppose the rifles and the machine guns of our jingoes."[27]

On his first trip to Palestine, in March 1918, as British troops advanced into the Ottoman-held Holy Land, Weizmann tried to reach out to the Arabs, via personal diplomacy, in his meeting, for example, with Emir Feisal. His efforts were unsuccessful, and gradually he came to see the Arabs as fanatical and untrustworthy. But they were on the ground, and quite soon they gained the support of British officialdom in Palestine—to Weizmann's chagrin.

Weizmann had always believed in an Allied victory and himself contributed to it. For a short moment, it seemed as if the Allied victory would also mark a great leap to a new liberal world order. The war had seen the suspension of liberalism in everyday practice, but intellectually liberals in England and America had fastened on a revolutionary idea: that the new nations and the old should in the future live in a new system that would provide collective security for all of them through a League of Nations. Thus would be banished the conditions that had led to the monstrous conflict. This had been Robert Cecil's idea, and he later thought that the League and Zionism were equally great achievements of his time and effort.[28] The League, enshrined by Woodrow Wilson in the great Jewish and Presbyterian word "Covenant," was indeed established at the Paris conference; it was to protect minorities, resolve conflicts, deter or defeat eventual aggressors. We all know the fate

of the League—a noble liberal hope that was instantly traduced by the other sections of the peace treaty that left the Germans seething, feeling they had been betrayed and gratui-
tously humiliated. John Maynard Keynes aroused the liberal
world to the disastrous economic consequences of the peace;
Weizmann's friend Jan Smuts, a great believer in the League,
saw the political consequences of the peace and regretted
them.[29] The new world order was a noble sham, but a sham
nevertheless, created and enfeebled by the United States. In the
end, liberalism itself was one of the permanent casualties of
the war.

At the Paris Peace Conference, where Zionist leaders made
their first diplomatic appearance as representatives of a nation
that did not yet exist, American support was critical, and Felix
Frankfurter marshalled all manner of forces to persuade President Wilson as well as other negotiators to accept the Zionist
aspirations. Weizmann himself had a long interview with President Wilson and was the most important voice at the Zionist
meeting with the Council of Ten at the Paris Peace Conference,
a meeting in which unexpectedly intra-Jewish disputes became
exposed. To some Americans, a British protectorate in Palestine smacked of yet greater imperialism, and hence aroused
skepticism. In the end, Wilson acquiesced to the Zionist
wishes, mindful, however, that Arab rights had to be protected
as well. The Paris Peace Conference did not settle the Middle
Eastern questions; that was to happen later in a treaty with
Turkey, the successor state to the Ottoman Empire.

After the peace conference, the collaboration between Weizmann and Brandeis broke down and conflicts ensued. There
were substantive disagreements and personal antipathies between two autocratic democrats. Brandeis thought that the
Balfour Declaration and the Allied victory should mark the
end of the political phase of Zionism; not so Weizmann.[30] Yet
the Brandeis-Frankfurter coalition, so clearly identified with a
liberal-progressive cause, had been invaluable, not least because the British had a strong, almost exaggerated, sense of

the power of American Jewry. The special tie between Frank-furter and Weizmann persisted, despite disagreements and suspicions.

In 1921, Weizmann became president of the World Zionist Organization; his constituency—what exactly was it?—was di-vided in various ways, making his often authoritarian leader-ship more critical and controversial. He had to deal with great, immediate tasks. The Allies had not yet accepted the idea of Britain's acquisition of a mandate over Palestine—the mandate system being the continuation of imperialism with a guilty conscience. This was finally achieved at an Allied conference in San Remo in 1920—and Weizmann exerted every possible means in order to have a reluctant France and an aggrieved Italy accept it. He had been shocked by the outbreak of Arab violence against Jews a few months earlier. But still more had to be done: The Council of the League of Nations had to accept the British Mandate, and Weizmann worked hard to bring the reluctant non-European powers in line.*

Finally, in July 1922 the League Council voted in favor of the British Mandate, which thus came into being *de jure* as well as *de facto*. Again, as with the Balfour Declaration, history added its own symbolic context. At the time, the various coincidences may not have been noticed, but 1922 was a year in which the enemies of liberalism scored ominous victories. A month be-fore the council vote, nationalist thugs assassinated Walther Rathenau, Germany's Jewish foreign minister. Many right-wing Germans thought of the murderers as idealists—further evidence of the fragility of the young Weimar democracy and of the virulent combination of German nationalism and anti-

---

* In a letter to Einstein of June 2, 1922, just after the League had postponed its scheduled meeting, Weizmann voiced his despondency and drew an extrava-gant picture of his enemies: "In the meantime all the shady characters of the world are at work against us. Rich servile Jews, dark fanatic Jewish obscuran-tists, in combination with the Vatican, with Arab assassins, English imperialist anti-Semitic reactionaries—in short, all the dogs are howling." Weizmann had a rich sense of drama. *The Letters and Papers of Chaim Weizmann*, vol. 11 (Jerusa-lem, 1977), p. 104.

Semitism. In October of that year Mussolini staged his march on Rome, and the great nemesis of liberal thought, fascism, achieved national power. Here was the triumph of frenzied irrationalism *cum* aggressive nationalism, fused into a pseudo-religious movement that attracted many followers. The murder of Rathenau and the rise of Mussolini prefigured the ultimate evil, National Socialism, which constituted the other great temptation of the century. Finally—almost too neatly—in October 1922, Lloyd George was forced to resign and thus was lost not only Weizmann's supporter but England's last liberal prime minister. In other words, the implementation of the Balfour Declaration occurred not at the height but in the after-glow of the great liberal era. The Jewish homeland, in so many ways the embodiment of liberal hopes, had to struggle to survive in an illiberal era. Britain's Tories had few compunctions in sacrificing the very democracies that Britain itself had helped to create.

In the 1920s, liberalism, defensive and uncertain, was overshadowed by the simpler and seemingly more promising ideologies of fascism, socialism, or communism. Liberal achievements had been great, most dramatically in the founding of the United States. In western countries, torture had been abolished, only to be brought back by Mussolini's mobs. Liberalism embodied a set of simple human values; its elitist bias also held that only mature and historic peoples were ready for full self-government, hence the condescending attitude toward most nonwhites. Weizmann shared this elitist attitude and moved most easily in an elitist world. With Balfour there was almost instant trust and mutual respect; with Ernest Bevin, at a later time, almost instant distance and enmity.

Weizmann had always insisted that Palestine would have to be built gradually, step by step and acre by acre; he hoped for organic growth under what he assumed would be a benevolent or at least a neutral British protectorate. The opening of the Hebrew University on Mount Scopus was a testimony to his spirit and success; he laid the cornerstone in July 1918, making clear that Hebrew would be the language of instruction—a quiet, revolutionary step. Two great scientists supported him at various critical moments: Paul Ehrlich in 1913 and Einstein in the early 1920s. Einstein was the principal speaker at the actual opening of the Hebrew University in 1923, a moving experience for him; afterward he became one of the most insistent critics of the university. And Weizmann had additional problems with it.[31]*

Even in the very first years of the mandate, Weizmann had to fight the local British authorities who increasingly favored Arab interests over Jewish claims: the British could feel compassion for the Arabs as underdogs, as a people who were being dispossessed; I suspect that there was as well the feeling that Jews were recalcitrant and grasping while Arabs were exotic and childishly pliable. Arab hostility mounted until it exploded in the terrible violence of 1929, the murders in Hebron and Safed, to which, Weizmann noted, the British reacted with "a mixture of indifference, inefficiency and hostility," and seemed to show greater understanding for the perpetrators of violence than for its victims.[32] Reluctant to confront the Arabs and sympathetic to their claims, the British retreated from the Balfour position and started on the road to appeasement. Weizmann, desperately disappointed, was made the scapegoat for their sins.

Weizmann was also caught in Jewish crossfires, in battles between impatient radical and pacific Jews. The greatest

---

* *And* with Einstein. Their relationship was at its closest in the mid-1920s; Einstein agreed to become a member of the Jewish Agency provided he did not have to travel or do more than lend his name and thus not disturb his necessary life as *Grübler*, as ruminator or thinker. But he understood the difficulties that Weizmann was having: "It can't be easy to be the Chosen of the chosen people. Palestine was really the great experience for me, as you prophesied it would be." In 1924, when Weizmann hoped Einstein would again go to the United States with him, Einstein declined, but was pleased that Weizmann had such "success in America in the conversion of the Jewish Great-Goyims [Gross-Gojims]." Einstein to Weizmann, October 27, 1923, and February 29, 1924, Weizmann Archives, Rehovot.

challenge came from an erstwhile ally, the fiery Vladimir
(Ze'ev) Jabotinsky, whose Revisionist Zionism in the 1920s was
militant and close to illiberal. He had followers who became
radical, violent nationalists. On the other side was the most
celebrated Jew of the time, Albert Einstein. In 1929, after and
because of the Arab attacks on Jewish settlements, Einstein
warned Weizmann of "nationalism à la prussienne," by which
he meant nationalism relying on force:

> If we do not find the path to honest cooperation and hon-
> est negotiations with the Arabs, then we have learned
> nothing from our 2000 years of suffering, and we deserve
> the fate that will befall us. Above all, we should be careful
> not to rely too heavily on the English. For if we don't get
> to a real cooperation with the leading Arabs, then the En-
> glish will drop us, if not officially, then *de facto*. And they
> will lament our debacle with traditional, pious glances to-
> ward heaven with assurances of their innocence, and
> without lifting a finger for us.[33]

Einstein's prophetic taunt mocked Weizmann's faith in the
British. Einstein, the man who had said of himself in the same
year, and with genuine astonishment, that he had become "the
saint of the Jews" was also capable of inflicting exquisite
wounds. Weizmann, in response, expounded his views, which
were somewhere between Zionist extremism and the irenic
Einstein, and in vain he also pleaded with Einstein to cease his
injurious attacks on the Zionists. All these conflicts took their
toll on Weizmann's health and contributed to his forced resignation from the Zionist presidency in 1931.

It was an excruciating time for Weizmann. Weeks before his
resignation, he expressed his disappointments and apprehensions in a letter to his friend, Gisela Warburg:

> Perhaps I was too far ahead of the other Zionists. . . . I can-
> not get intoxicated on phrases and forget even temporar-
> ily that the Jewish misery increases from day to day, but

that Palestine is a small, difficult, ungrateful country; that 650,000 Arabs live there who do not want to let us in, and the number of Arabs increases every day. . . . However, the Jews, who are unfortunately scoured by all the furies, do not understand the slow tempo. It is difficult to preach reason and patience to the tormented. . . . What we, however, suffer is only a small part of what shakes the whole world now, a kind of illusionism which assumes different forms in different countries—Hitler, Mussolini, Stalin— almost the same, all of it.[34]

How few observers of the day understood the threat of this unholy trinity—two years before Hitler's coming to power!

With the advent of Hitler in 1933, Weizmann's lifelong concern about German anti-Semitism was tragically vindicated. As a nineteen-year-old he had responded to his German-Jewish schoolmaster's assurances that Germans would shed their anti-Semitism once they had realized how much Jews were contributing to German life: "*Herr Doktor*, if a man has a piece of something in his eye, he doesn't want to know whether it's a piece of mud or a piece of gold. He just wants to get it out."[35] Whatever his critical views of German Jewry may have been, he now led the efforts to facilitate Jewish emigration from Germany. He was hoping to attract some of the best German scientists, Jewish or not, to Palestine. He reached out to men like Fritz Haber, who had converted, and to Richard Willstätter, who had not. Among scientists, none was as important as Einstein, who continued his intermittent criticism of the Hebrew University and eventually withdrew his name from it. For a while Weizmann endured his—not unjustified— remonstrances, but in the end he wearied and in April 1938 he wrote to him that while five million Jews were in danger and "a war of annihilation" was forecast, the Jewish elites of wealth and intelligence tended to sit idly by. The Jewish people deserved better than that.[36] He gave up on Einstein, at least for a time, and, no stranger to vituperation, wrote to a friend,

"Einstein seems to be acquiring the psychology of a *prima donna* who is beginning to lose her voice."[37]

Weizmann realized the terrible plight that had befallen European Jewry and in 1936 declared before the Peel Commission that for the six million Jews in East Central Europe "the world is divided into places where they cannot live and places where they may not enter."[38] By now the enfeebled English, face to face with a resurgent violent Germany, huddled under the umbrella of appeasement and hoped not to weaken their position in the Middle East as well. The years of Arab attacks and the British White Paper of 1939, which all but throttled further Jewish settlements in Palestine, saw Weizmann's lifelong hopes for British support and decency betrayed.

In the Second World War, Weizmann, already a sick man, once more volunteered his scientific service to the Allied cause. The British spurned his offer. Still, in its darkest days, he saw in Churchill's leadership and Britain's gallant resistance a confirmation of his earlier hopes—only to have these dashed again at the end of the war and at the hands of a Labour government.

Hitler's defeat brought to light the devastation that had all but destroyed European Jewry. For Weizmann this was the moment when the moral claim seemed overwhelming: the National Home must now be realized, a moral reparation for unimaginable crimes, for sins of German commission and British omission. Coincidental was the instant concern to rescue the remnant of European Jewry, the barely living survivors, the displaced persons, as they were called—and displaced they were in every sense. In May 1945 Weizmann demanded of Churchill the immediate revocation of the White Paper, which had virtually barred Jewish emigration. "Open the gates of Palestine" was a powerful cry in the civilized world. The new Labour government, radical at home, in bewildered retreat abroad, rejected all such pleas. The Labour Party, pro-Zionist in opposition, betrayed the promises it had made in earlier times.

The lines hardened. In November 1945, the Jewish underground, desperate, resorted to violence in Palestine, their action sanctioned by David Ben-Gurion. Weizmann, not consulted, "was stunned and a heavy depression descended upon him."[39] He warned the Yishuv against violence, as he continued his huge efforts to mobilize world and especially American opinion against defiant Britain. In the summer of 1946, the Irgun, under the leadership of Menachem Begin, turned from violence to terrorism against the British, who within days retaliated with draconian measures. Weizmann acknowledged the horror: Palestine is "not merely a police state: it is the worst form of military dictatorship. . . . Something has definitely snapped in the relationship between Jews and British in Palestine . . . and what has been destroyed is so deep, so vital, and of such moral significance, that it cannot be restored by projects, resolutions, and kind words."[40] Detesting violence, Weizmann now saw it in every quarter: Jews, British, and Arabs were caught in a spiral of violence, and he was made the scapegoat for British sins. He thought Jewish terrorism an offense against practical reason and moral principle; he had a premonition that it "represented a grave danger to the whole future of the Jewish State."[41]

Betrayed by the British government, pushed aside by his own people, in fragile health, Weizmann battled still to redeem Jewish rights by peaceful means. Persuasion and political action still mattered; by 1947 the United Nations had to determine the future of Palestine; by November of that year, a resolution for the establishment of a Jewish state in a partitioned Palestine passed—with borders that Weizmann successfully insisted had to include the Negev. But hostile reluctance in the West persisted, and in the early months of 1948 the United Nations nearly reversed itself. A sick Weizmann came to New York to marshal support, and, with the help of liberal New Dealers, once again headed by the tireless Felix Frankfurter, persuaded President Truman to stick to earlier promises and to recognize instantly the state of Israel. In May 1948, Weizmann's vision was realized, but the vision had yet to be defended.

Weizmann was no pacifist—he was much too much of a realist for that. As he himself wrote: "Independence is never given to a people; it has to be earned; and having been earned, it has to be defended."[42] And still he saw in violence and terrorism the negation of Jewish hopes. In April 1947, in a letter to a Revisionist friend, he wrote of the terrorists: "They have chosen the revolver and the bomb as salvation in the present . . . and I confess I doubt whether the Messiah will arrive at the sound of high explosives"—a phrase he repeated in his memoirs.[43] He knew his people and he hoped that a haven of their own would bring about a moral renaissance, that the National Home would have a grandeur worthy of the ancient past. But he was a man without illusions; he knew that the Jews were not immune to the temptations of power that had ensnared all other peoples.* He knew that the new state of Israel, whose leaders needed and neglected him, was not safe. He begged his friends "not to permit the destruction of the thing we have labored over for years."[44] He had led the way to independence. No one else could have done as much.

LET me conclude with two observations. These days my discipline and our culture like to deny the historic importance of individuals. It is an odd conclusion to reach at the end of a century that has had some terrifying and a few benign examples of people who by themselves shaped world history. But ours is an age of denigration. Tocqueville taught us that an un-

---

* A year after the Six Day War, the distinguished Israeli historian J. L. Talmon wrote: "I am not enough of a chauvinist to believe that the Jews are exempt from the snares and perversions which lie in wait for all mankind. . . . For an Israel which lost its old bearings—Jewish, liberal, and idealistic—would become repulsively similar to the arch persecutors of the Jews." "Israel among the Nations: Reflections on Jewish Statehood," *The City College Papers*, no. 9, 1968.

willingness to recognize great individuals is often found in democratic societies, and Thomas Carlyle lamented that in his day people "account" for great men by saying, "He was the creature of the Time, . . . the Time called him forth, the Time did everything, he nothing—but what we the little critic could have done too! This seems to me but melancholy work."[45] I side with Isaiah Berlin, who believed "that if great men—heroes—have ever existed, and more particularly if individuals can in any sense be said to be the authors of revolutions that permanently and deeply alter many human lives—then Chaim Weizmann was . . . a man of this order."[46]

Of course there is an interplay, a deep ineffable connection between a great person and the surrounding culture. I would say that Weizmann was of his time and yet, in his roots and in his vision, outside it. The only power he had was that of moral persuasion: he knew how to evoke, even compel, consent, and when in the tragedies of his later life he sensed a growing dissonance between himself and his times, he began to retreat into himself and to his haven in Rehovot. But his life is proof again that individuals do matter, that greatness does exist, and that the denial of greatness traduces experience and diminishes our collective lives.

In our century a host of new states were founded and old ones fundamentally transformed. Some of these had the exacting fortune to have been led to nationhood or independence by great persons, founding fathers. I think of Masaryk and Paderewski, Gandhi and Weizmann. They were philosophers and scientists, musicians and poets, political beings by necessity and by some special calling. All of them pitted the human spirit against power and authority, but none had to overcome greater obstacles than Chaim Weizmann. None, I believe, was more appealing, freer, more dedicated to the improvement of his people. In Dr. Weizmann's formal reception room I was happy to see the bust of George Washington. Great fathers are a treasure, but they leave a demanding legacy. They may prove burdensome and at later times and under changed conditions seemingly irrelevant. And still, a founding father leaves an inestimable gift to a nation's sense of identity. Chaim Weizmann, however, belonged to a still wider world: he was in harmony with what was best in our century, and it was that harmony that empowered great labors to work a miracle.

◆◆◆◆◆◆◆◆◆◆◆◆◆ **7** ◆◆◆◆◆◆◆◆◆◆◆◆◆

Freedom and Its Discontents:
The Travails of
the New Germany

◆◆

The two Germanies were formally united in 1990, and the old West Germany has been investing roughly 10 billion deutschmark (DM) annually to rebuild the *Länder* of the old German Democratic Republic. The infrastructure there has been dramatically modernized, and some of the new *Länder*, Saxony and Thuringia, for example, may develop into the most advanced economic regions of Germany or Europe. Modernization means a loss of jobs, and material disparities between the two parts remain: unemployment is significantly higher in the East, wages are lower than in the West.

More serious still are the persistent moral and psychological consequences of unification, the principal concern of this article. Many East Germans continue to think of themselves as second-class citizens in the new country; they do not feel at home there. They resent the incessant reminders of West German superiority that they encounter, and on the other side of the divide, West Germans regret what they regard as ungrateful self-pity among Easterners.

A successor party to the old Communist Party in East Germany continues to attract between twenty and twenty-five percent of eastern votes, mostly among the older generation which feels that their lives have been retroactively devalued. Germans are divided about the true nature of the party. In the fall of 1998, the Bundestag elected a Social Democrat from the former East, Wolfgang Thierse, as its president, and he memorably defined the earlier experience of his fellow citizens in the East: "A real, decent life in a false, indecent system."

The urban landscape is being transformed. The center of Berlin, the new capital, is Europe's biggest construction site. The inner landscape remains perturbed; the several German pasts continue to divide the present. Most Germans assume that it will take a full generation until the country has truly grown together. Until then, the politically unified Germany remains divided—in unprecedented freedom.

❖❖

IN 1983 THE PRESIDENT of the Federal Republic, Richard von Weizsäcker, published a collection of essays entitled, *German History Has Not Stopped*. Even he could not have predicted the pace of progress since then. And as the process of unification has unfolded, one can see the drama of German history continue as well. The economic consequences of unity are apparent; the moral and psychological consequences are harder to grasp and may prove longer lasting.

While the two states of postwar Germany existed, Germans could believe in the unity of their nation, of a people with a common language, a common past, even a common fate. Now unified within one state, the deep divisions among Germans are more visible. No doubt there is truth in Freud's words about "the narcissism of small differences" that divides neighborhoods and family members, and yet in 1989 there was an expectation that Germans would understand Germans. In the first flush of enthusiasm, people forgot the estrangements that had grown so strong over forty years, as West Germans came to regard the French or the Tuscans or the Dutch as closer to them, perhaps more attractive, than the East Germans. For their part, East Germans lived with a prescribed if gradually attenuated hostility to the Federal Republic, and with an unprescribed envy and resentment of its freedom and prosperity, witnessed nightly on their television screens.

Visitors to East Germany sensed the estrangement. I did, on repeated visits. And in the Federal Republic, for all the ritualistic invocations of German solidarity, for all the many individuals who genuinely cared about their fellow Germans in the East, one sensed an enormous, unacknowledged indifference to them. Sudden commonality, sudden huge demands, did not instantly transform indifference to openhearted solicitude.

Both Germanies gained greater, if sharply different, kinds of freedom after unification, and with freedom came new uncertainties and discontents. In the East it was freedom from the knock at the door, freedom to travel, release from a regimented, intimidating, false existence, freedom to examine one's life. But almost immediately 17 million East Germans discovered that freedom also meant freedom to face an uncertain future, freedom to lose a job, to lose support nets, however inadequate they may have been.

For forty years, most East Germans had accommodated to life in a world of public lies and private doubts. Totalitarian regimes mobilize people into passive participation in politics. After twelve years of Nazi rule and forty years of Communist rule, they may have survived psychologically by practicing denial, by wishing not to see. After 1989 avoiding reality became impossible, given the economic dislocations of transforming a dysfunctional, decaying command economy into a market economy—as if there was but one type of market economy. The closing of state-run enterprises led to mounting unemployment. Moreover, economic affairs were only part of what had been prescribed under the old command economy. So much of life had been lived in the public realm. So much of it had been ordered from above or came by inherited routine. Suddenly East Germans, released from public control, had to learn to make their own choices, think their own thoughts, find their own truths. They were indeed privatized at a time when the associational life of a civil society was being but slowly introduced.

Market economies presuppose legal structures, a system of private and public law—a legal code that has to be taught, learned, and gradually assimilated. But the art of evasion also flourishes in market economies, as the 1980s so vividly illustrate. Western enthusiasts for the free market in the former G.D.R. often ignored the social costs of the transformation. Worse, the abrupt introduction of new forms of economic life also created what sociologists and Marxists have long identified with modern capitalism: alienation, anomie, insecurity. For the East Germans, the move from the rigid world of Communist rule to the demands of a mobile society was hard. The very notion of planning for a market economy had an ironic ring to it. A new dependency developed. Much of life in the new eastern *Länder* of the united Germany came to be organized by Westerners who were practiced in taking decisions, in making things work, and in assessing the risks of the market, who had the skills and the funds to take charge. East Germans had been taught to live and work by plans that bore little relation to reality; they had learned to suffer and endure but not to take responsibility or to live by trial and error.

East Germans hoped that the end of Communism would bring instant rehabilitation as well as instant improvement in their living standard. But soon they began to think they were being "colonized"—a commonly used word that was infuriating to Western ears. Defeated, humiliated, more object than subject, many East Germans expressed their disappointment in terms of self-pity and resentment. Was there no end to their being victimized? In the early years of their occupation, the Russians had dismantled and taken what was left of German industrial plants in their zone; a current estimate is that the Russians extracted some 54 billion DM in reparations. All this took place while the Western zones occupied by the Americans, British, and French—later to be the Federal Republic— received Marshall Plan aid. Of course the balance sheet is far more complicated: West Germany also benefited from a huge influx of Germans expelled by Poland and Czechoslovakia and of refugees from the Soviet zone; on the other hand, Bonn did make restitution payments to Israel and gradually gave support to the G.D.R. But East Germans believed, with some justification, that they had paid disproportionately for Hitler's war.

After 1990 both East and West Germans had to consider their separate and joint pasts. Former G.D.R. citizens had to address questions that have beset other countries at other times in the twentieth century: questions of collaboration and collusion, of culpability and trustworthiness. Which of them were so compromised that they could no longer be teachers or judges, civil servants or plant managers, professors or members of renowned academies? Who was to make these judgments, and on what basis?

West Germans, hardly at peace with their own past, seemed ready to make their judgments about Easterners. From the moment of unification I was concerned that the West Germans would be far more cheerfully, self-righteously assiduous in punishing suspected collaborators with the Communist regime than their forebears had been in dealing with the servants of the Nazi regime. The very popularity of that regime had made de-Nazification difficult. Even now, West Germans with an undetected, compromised past continue to flourish. In 1993 a prominent West German physician was forced to resign from a major post in an international organization because it was revealed that he had participated in the Nazis' euthanasia program.

The Nazi past divides West Germans still, as shown by the controversy surrounding President Reagan's visit to Bitburg in 1985, by the so-called historians' debate, and by the decades it has taken to document the complicity of the German army in the atrocities on the Eastern front. To this day many Germans, in and out of uniform, choose to believe in the *Wehrmacht*'s innocence. National Socialism never needed a wall; there was never a threat of a mass exodus. By comparison, over two million East Germans voted against the Communist dictatorship with their feet. Under the Nazis an indeterminate number of

Germans had gone into "inner emigration," tried to remain insulated, to purchase peace at the price of silence. West Germans who were confounded by this past—and divided among
themselves about it—were now called upon to judge fellow
Germans who had lived for a further forty years under a totalitarian regime initially held in place by foreign bayonets.

Most East Germans knew that their leaders, piously mouth-
ing slogans of peace, had believed in violence and had no
mercy. What they could not have known, because the tape was
released only in 1993, was that in 1982 Erich Mielke, head of
the Stasi, the state security police, had told his closest colleagues that to save the lives of millions one might have to kill
a bandit: "All this drivel about not executing and no death sentences, all crap, comrades."

The tone does remind one of Nazi evil. Party leaders ordered
alleged enemies of the regime to be tortured, incarcerated, or
shot; they organized espionage and initiated or facilitated international terrorism. In the post-Stalinist era East German
leaders, like leaders throughout the Soviet bloc, sought to replace torture with other kinds of intimidation, including the
abomination of psychiatric wards for political opponents.
These same leaders after 1970, and especially in the 1980s, gar-
nered official recognition by other states. Chancellor Helmut
Kohl received them in Bonn; Franz Josef Strauss visited them
and arranged for the G.D.R. to receive a billion deutschmark
credit. West German Social Democrats collaborated with functionaries of the East German Communist Party to hammer out
a joint paper defining areas of agreement and disagreement.
Until his death the former East German leader, Erich Honecker, was free in Chile, and only a few frontier guards are in
prison, while tens of thousands of teachers and other East German civil servants have been suspended or dismissed.

As the Communist regime crumbled, East Germans, left in
their crowded, drab, decaying dwellings, saw pictures of how
the *nomenklatura* had lived in insulated comfort and read about
the perquisites those party regulars had enjoyed, from special

medical care to Swiss bank accounts. Had they really not noticed before that the much-touted egalitarianism of their socialist state had been traduced daily, visibly and invisibly? The
apparatchiks had their own Volvos, their children had privileged access to education, and all of them could shop in the
Intershops, where Western goods could be bought for Western currency. The revelations of the extent of these special
benefits (petty by Western standards) enraged many East Germans. They felt betrayed. They remembered the leaders' endless invocations that, unlike the rapacious capitalist West, the
G.D.R. was an egalitarian society where austerity and sacrifice provided a psychological guarantee of a better future. But
they must have had at least an inkling that their leaders had
not practiced the virtues of delayed gratification that they
preached.

The resultant outburst sprang from what I think was an ambivalence about deprivation. They minded it, of course, but
they may have felt that austerity was virtuous—in old Germanic terms, ennobling. To have stark proof that their leaders
had mocked this notion was offensive. In this largely Lutheran
country, was this a distant echo of Martin Luther's attacks on
a Roman hierarchy that preached poverty but lived in corrupt
luxury?

The East Germans were made to realize something far
worse. Their insidious, malevolent regime had managed to en-
trap vast numbers of them in collusion and corruption. The
state security police had organized an unprecedented web of
surveillance. In its final days, the Stasi consisted of 97,000 full-
time employees—with perhaps as many as 140,000 unofficial
collaborators, most of whom had acknowledged their commitment in writing. (Only the higher ranks of society, such as professors or members of elite academies, were allowed to regis-
ter their agreement orally). In addition, membership in the
Communist Party rose to two million, people who were particularly vulnerable to Stasi demands. All this machinery for 17
million Germans! The Gestapo, helped by countless voluntary

informers, at the end of the Nazi regime had only 32,000 members for 80 million Germans. The Stasi files—nearly 100 miles of them—offered poisonous proof of a poisoned society.

The Stasi were the eyes and ears of a regime that was deeply distrustful of its own people. Born of distrust, the Stasi became an agent of distrust. In a world without laws or enforceable rights, a person searches for the like-minded, for another person to talk to, if need be in some outside place where surveillance is more difficult. West German observers thought that East Germans managed to have closer, more trusting relationships than they. Some East Germans probably did have a particular affinity for trust and friendship. They invested in them as rare human goods at a time of moral scarcity. Imagine then the shock, the retroactive dissolution of trust, when one discovered that one's friend had been an informer; husbands had informed on their wives, wives on husbands, parents on children, friends on friends. As more information is divulged, the web of suspicion spreads ever wider.

During the 1970s, when the East German regime gradually replaced physical terror with calculated intimidation, the Stasi, like other secret police, learned to play with fiendish aptitude on people's vulnerabilities, operating an ever more elaborate system of carrots and sticks. The rewards for being an unofficial collaborator varied, such as advancement in a career or travel to the West. The sticks were formidable, often involving the punishment of children for the alleged sins of their parents, or more lethally, efforts to bring about "personal destabilization," including undermining marriages—a whole array of Iago-like villainies aimed at destroying trust among friends and potential critics of the regime.

Stasi revelations have threatened some of the most promising political careers in the new *Länder* of the united Germany. Two examples may suffice: Lothar de Mazière, the first vice chancellor of the unified Germany, resigned when it was said that he had had Stasi contacts; and in the early 1990s insinuations continued to be made against the then only Social Democratic minister president in the new *Länder*, Manfred Stolpe of Brandenburg. Stolpe had worked in and with the Protestant churches in the G.D.R. and had helped them to help victims of the regime. He had regular contacts with the Stasi—how else to aid people entrapped by them? Knowledgeable defenders of Stolpe, and of others similarly accused, insist that any responsible person who tried to help people who had fallen afoul of the regime had to deal with the Stasi. But critics claim that even to talk to a Stasi official was to take the first step on a slippery slope. Others, myself included, might argue that in a tyrannical system only absolute immobility can protect one from the dangers of that slope.

Once upon a time the Stasi oppressed a people. Its legacy has been to demoralize them and perhaps to deprive them of some of the good political leaders they might have had. Opposition to the G.D.R. regime was feeble compared to that elsewhere in the Soviet bloc. After the one great outburst of June 17, 1953, when East German workers took to the streets to defy their ever more demanding and repressive regime and were crushed by Soviet tanks, there was apparent conformity. Not in East Germany were there the repeated uprisings or the great alliance of workers and intellectuals as in Poland's Solidarność, or in the Hungarian rebellion of 1956, or in the Czechoslovak spring of 1968. It has often been said that Germans are somewhat untutored in civic courage. They have the word for that quality, *Zivilcourage*, but not the all-essential practice. Albert Hirschman once wrote of moral resources, including civic spirit and trust: "These are resources whose supply may well increase rather than decrease through use. . . . Like the ability to speak a foreign language or to play the piano, these moral resources are likely to become depleted and to atrophy if not used."

The Ulbricht-Honecker regime, mixing German traditions with Soviet models, had time to promote a separate cultural life in the G.D.R. They wanted to create athletes of the spirit, writers and artists who could dazzle the outside world and satisfy at least some aspirations of their own people. As the East German molecular biologist and admirable citizen-thinker Jens Reich makes clear in his book, the regime sought to implicate the entire intelligentsia—technicians as well as poets—and to a devastating degree it was successful. For many reasons the *samizdat* literature that flourished in Poland, Czechoslovakia, and Russia hardly existed in the G.D.R. In the early years of the regime, writers like Robert Havemann were imprisoned, and gifted irritants like Wolf Biermann were expelled. The action against Biermann prompted East German writers to protest for the first time. But by and large the limits of state tolerance for dissent were rarely, if ever, tested.

Gradually the demands for socialist realism were relaxed. Other kinds of art were allowed. The novelist Christa Wolf was able to depict life in the G.D.R. with some degree of candor. Writers jousted with censors, and parodists ventured the occasional mischief, as when the writer Heiner Müller said, "We are the most progressive state ever: 95 percent of the people are against it. Such a thing has never happened before," or when he sang, "The Stasi is my Eckermann." Now come the revelations that some of these writers, too, were once part of the Stasi net. In the late 1950s and early 1960s Christa Wolf was an unofficial informant, unbeknownst even to her husband. Decades later she described at length how she too came under Stasi surveillance. As the most prominent of East German writers, she has been denounced and defended. She illustrates how easy it was under that regime to move from being accomplice and perpetrator to victim, and how difficult it is to judge the conduct of people enmeshed in a system with so many visible and invisible tentacles.

There is still great controversy about the conduct of East German authors and the intelligentsia. Some West German critics express outrage, and there is a danger that in time the work of these writers might be altogether forgotten. This would be a distortion and a loss. Some of them were guarded witnesses to life under dreadful conditions. Now, in the unified Germany, West Germans who were spared anything like these terrors have assumed a leading role in decision-making, in dismissals and recruitments throughout the eastern *Länder*. Their work is officially subsumed under the term *Abwicklung*. This sanitized bureaucratic term, once used by the Nazis, suggests legal procedures or business liquidations. It bespeaks distance and condescension; it is unattuned to tact or compassion.

The question of judgment is inherently difficult. In the case of many of the accusations against former East German citizens, one must ask, how reliable are the Stasi files, and how often were they slanted by inferiors trying to curry favor with their superiors? Finally, as Jens Reich has implicitly warned, the Stasi could easily become a scapegoat for the G.D.R. regime. The greater villains were the party and state functionaries; the Stasi were not autonomous villains, and some of their collaborators may have had mixed or honorable motives. Only the clearest picture of life in the G.D.R. can help to render humane judgments. There may be good reason to sympathize with those West Germans of an impeccable past who say of all these leaks and revelations, "Enough." This "enough" has been much heard in the countries of Eastern Europe.

IN the years to come Germans of both East and West will continue to find it difficult to deal with the history of the forty years of the G.D.R. and F.R.G., two entities that lasted almost as long as the Reich created by Bismarck. Polemical, divisive arguments have already begun about who supported whom and when, who promoted unification and who opposed it. Right-wing Germans or newborn nationalists are already accusing the old Federal Republic's left of national neglect, of having slighted the goal of national unity, of having collaborated with the Communist Party, or of having been "soft" on East German criminals or collaborators. In time, after the calumnies and the memories are extinguished or transformed, later generations may "bracket out" the G.D.R.'s history—as Germans call such a deletion—while finding that it remains

hard to expunge the Nazi past. As former President Weizsäcker has remarked, the G.D.R. neither started a war nor
committed genocide. It may gradually fade from historical
consciousness, be dismissed as a Soviet satellite, an alien excrescence of something called the Cold War. The West Germans' earlier indifference to the G.D.R. will facilitate so con-
venient a lapse of memory. But the G.D.R. in all its ambiguity
needs to be remembered and in some way integrated into the
history of Germany and Europe in our century.

It is the beginnings of the G.D.R. that are most likely to be
forgotten, the time immediately after the war when in the Soviet zone of occupation a so-called socialist state was gradually
established, expropriating the large estate owners and nation-
alizing what was left of German industry there. In the baggage
train of the conquering Red Army arrived Moscow-trained
German Communists—many of whom had been tortured in
Nazi camps—determined to forge a union between socialists
and Communists and create what they called a great antifascist
bloc, a bulwark against a revived German fascist-type nationalism. True socialists, remembering how at the end of the
Weimar Republic Communists had in fact aided the rise of
Nazism, defied Communist pleas and demands; men like Gustav Dahrendorf and Kurt Schumacher never had any doubts
about the true nature of Communism. A few socialists in the
Soviet zone believed that the Communist Party was genuinely
antifascist, that it would radically purge all former Nazis and
would recruit its own cadre, mostly of young, untrained people from the unpropertied classes. The claim that the German
Democratic Republic, formally established in 1949, would become the first socialist state in German history, that by its extrusion of Nazis and dismantling of capitalism it was cleansing
German soil of Nazi poison, that out of devastation it was
building up an egalitarian society—all this had a certain appeal, particularly for writers and intellectuals. Bertolt Brecht,
long the lyricist of a proletarian culture, happily left his American exile, with its capitalist culture and McCarthyite hysteria,

to win honors and his own theater in East Berlin. Lesser writers followed. Thomas Mann accepted an honor from the new state—though he decided to settle in Switzerland, spiritually equidistant from both Germanies. In the G.D.R., as elsewhere at the time, Communists had the inestimable advantage of claiming to be the vanguard of a new culture; judge us by some distant future, they said, not by the bleak present. Intellectuals, once committed to the faith, found it hard to break with it, to confess to themselves their error.

In the last few years an old German word, adapted from a Norwegian term used by Ibsen, has reappeared over and over again in books and articles. Although there is no English or French analogue, *Lebenslüge* roughly means the lie that is life-giving, the lie that is essential to a particular life, the lie that a person or a people may know to be false but without which a person or state would perish. The G.D.R. was saddled with one *Lebenslüge* from the start: the fundamental insistence that the Soviet Union was at once liberator and fraternal master and model. The East Germans sensed the travesty of truth. They knew that the Red Army had raped and looted. They knew that the Soviets had despoiled their country, and they sensed as well that their German rulers, at least in the beginning, were servile instruments of Soviet masters. One of the many East German witticisms—the one commodity in which they out-performed the West Germans—insisted that the Russians were indeed brothers with whom one had indissoluble fraternal bonds: friends one chooses, brothers are unalterably inflicted. Gradually the antifascist principle, the G.D.R.'s sole threadbare claim to legitimacy, lost its credibility as well: to call the Berlin Wall the great antifascist wall was too grim an absurdity.

The Soviets and the G.D.R.'s rulers needed each other. For the former, East Germany was the frontier state against the West, the most important defense post with the greatest arsenal of weapons. For the rulers of the G.D.R., the Soviet presence constituted the ultimate reserve army against their own people. For contrast, when the Federal Republic, its own legitimacy accepted by its people, tied itself to the West, the attachments enhanced security and prosperity and corresponded to the wishes of most of its people. In the 1980s the East German regime, encouraged by the Federal Republic's ever more enterprising *Ostpolitik*, sought to gain some greater room for maneuver, some independence from Moscow. Characteristically, Honecker's greatest moment of independence came at the end, when he banned Soviet publications carrying Gorbachev's liberalizing message. To the last, Honecker remained a German Leninist—German in the tinge of sentimentality in his inhumanity. He and his closest advisers, most of them ardent believers in the powers of repression, ignored younger members of the *nomenklatura* who understood the need for reform in East Germany. Their day came too late. The G.D.R. was founded on deception, on various *Lebenslügen*, and its end was hastened by the self-deception of its aged leaders.

The G.D.R. leaves an ambiguous legacy, as does the Federal Republic; the difference is that the institutions of the latter, far from ending, are in the process of adapting to different conditions. The old political culture of the Federal Republic is being tested and, in part, measured by Eastern ideals. In the historic rivalry between Communism and social democracy, the former by its very collapse has ironically scored a major triumph. For many people, especially on the political right, rejoice in confounding Communism and socialism, interpreting the dismal failure of the one as irredeemably discrediting the other as well. Thus it is doubtful whether the historic task of democratic socialism, to correct the most grievous, ruthless qualities of what Jacques Delors once called "*capitalisme sauvage*," will ever be totally completed.

The G.D.R. is dead, and some East Germans already have their nostalgic moments. Disappointed in the present, prompted by a selective memory, they ask: "Was everything wrong in the last forty years?" And they tend to erase from memory the hopelessness of the old regime and remember that at some level of subsistence, however drab and uniform, even ordinary citizens could count on the essentials of life: housing, however wretched, food, however meager, medical care, however inferior and indifferent. They remember that in the old G.D.R. there was no crime, no drugs, no pornography. The Communist rulers of the G.D.R. could have echoed President Nixon's boast: "We have taken crime off the streets"; the government had assumed a monopoly on crime.

Citizens remember the much vaunted *Kinderkrippen*, a grandiose term for child-care centers to which working parents could send their children. The memory of the *Kinderkrippen* evokes the G.D.R.'s traditional concern for family life, for women's rights, including the nontraditional right of abortion, for social welfare—all this in contrast to the cold life in unified Germany, where the cash nexus rules all. These *Kinderkrippen* have become a kind of symbol for the better side of G.D.R. life. People forget that these benefits were palliatives for deeper pain. The *Kinderkrippen* were the decorous part of a controlled society that violated the home it pretended to protect.

On some deep psychological level the unified Germany is more divided than before; the physical wall has been internalized. Where once had been the untroubled hope that at some future date the division of the country, unnaturally maintained, would be healed, there are now painful inequalities of power, wealth, experience, and assertiveness. The living standard of East Germans is still much lower than that of West Germans; wages are lower and unemployment is at least three times higher. Economic inequalities heighten psychic discontent: East Germans are given to self-pity, West Germans to unspoken arrogance and exasperation. Some West Germans themselves complain of Western self-righteousness. Both sides deserve understanding. There are many Germans who demand solidarity not in words but in deeds, but their pleas are lost on pusillanimous politicians who, in confusion, think mostly of the next election.

In March 1993 the Bonn parliament finally approved a solidarity pact that brought some predictability into the economic

picture. It provided for new taxes to fund specified payments
to the new *Länder*. Approximately seven percent of GNP will
be transferred to the East over the next decade—roughly one
trillion DM. In July 1993 even the European Community
agreed, reluctantly, to provide 27.5 billion DM over the next
six years to the new *Länder* out of its regional assistance funds.
The strains are clear: Germany as a whole is in a deep recession, with continued negative growth; according to many observers, it is the most serious recession since the founding of
the Federal Republic. Hence the great unease pervading both
parts of Germany. Still, the solidarity pact affords real chances
for the new *Länder*, as Kurt Biedenkopf, minister president of
Saxony, made clear in a speech to the Saxon parliament—a
candid speech that exemplified the possibilities of democratic
leadership.

The old Federal Republic has also gained greater freedom in
1989, but a very different kind of freedom from the East Germans'. Unification has fulfilled the old national dream and attenuated—even on some level removed—Germany's dependency on its Western allies. From the beginning, the Federal
Republic needed Allied protection, most clearly in the ever
vulnerable western part of Berlin. For forty years this dependency dictated the parameters of choice. Now questions about
German national interest and purpose reemerge in full force.
In the ongoing debate there are some who demand greater
German assertiveness, who have grown tired of being held
hostage to the memory of the Nazi past. That sentiment is so
strong that Jürgen Habermas warned against yet another *Lebenslüge* for Germany, the *Lebenslüge*, as he put it, "of us being
a normal nation." How understandable the wish of so many
Germans to be liberated of the burden of the past, to "relativize" Nazi crimes, to seek a retrospective moral equality. How
understandable, and probably how unattainable.

It is one of the tragic ironies of the 1989 revolutions that they
coincided with deepening crises in the West. The newly liberated countries reached out for a market economy at a time of

worldwide recession. They sought to embrace democracy when the democratic countries had plunged into scandals of corruption and a general paralysis of leadership. They looked to Europe just as the hopes of Europe 1992 faded in a post-Maastricht malaise and when the term "democratic deficit" seemed to have resonance beyond the internal arrangements of the European Community.

Germany's unanticipated unification, with its staggering demands, came at a time when the old Federal Republic was already experiencing mutually reinforcing pressures. The West German economy—in the past the guarantor of West German democracy—was slowing down. The capitalist world was not at its most dynamic, or at what Joseph Schumpeter defined at its most destructively creative, when East Germans clamored for a free market and the many gurus of the market economy urged instant transformation. West Germans, including leading politicians, were not immune to the greed and corruption of the Reaganite 1980s. Faith in the political system was shaken. Put differently, the twin miracles of Bonn's beginnings, the economic miracle and the political miracle, the emergence after the devastation of the Nazi years of unprecedented political leadership, had come to an end. Germany faces its gravest crisis since the end of World War II.

A new and ultra-right-wing Republican Party has scored some victories. It is doubtful that the massive increase in asylum seekers between 1987 and 1992—an increase of some 800 percent—is solely or even primarily responsible for the dissatisfaction that this party exploits. People in all parts of Germany feel an imbalance between the economic and moral requirements of the newly unified state and their political response. There has hardly been a time in which the political classes were held in such low esteem—as is true in the rest of Europe. The present uncertainties prompted Marion Countess Dönhoff, Helmut Schmidt, and a few like-minded citizens to issue a manifesto in November 1992 entitled, "Because The Country Must Change." Or consider Jens Reich's fears of

future unrest "when I observe our dance around the golden
calf called property, prosperity, consumerism ... which we
hold sacrosanct. Even now I see the coming disgust and the
helpless failure of the putative victors. Late socialism clung to
the illusion of eternal growth and progress. We should not succumb to it under a different guise."

Eruptions of xenophobic violence, killings of Turkish
women and children, horrify the world; hundreds of skinheads
are supported by thousands of nationalist, perhaps even neo-
Nazi, sympathizers. Yet millions of Germans organize silent
marches to protest this ugliness, a demonstrative solidarity
never before seen in Germany. To some, the very silence of
these marches, however impressive in themselves, is disturbing. Germans need speech, thought, and moral authority,
charged questions about asylum seekers and fiscal measures
that will grapple with the needed transfer payments to the
east. All these require public argument. Over and over again in
his last years as chancellor, Helmut Kohl was admonished to
"tell the truth."

In all parts of Germany there is a palpable deficit of trust—
trust in leaders, trust in almost all aspects of life. The English
philosopher John Dunn has spoken of trust as the core element
of democracy. And while trust is in short supply in all countries, its steady decline in Germany is alarming. Degrees of
trust cannot be quantified, unlike the interest rates of the
Bundesbank, yet the two are linked. The deutschmark remains
the symbol and instrument of Germany's economic stability,
and the unarticulated incantation could be "In the deutschmark we trust." In a decade or so, that same deutschmark, or
rather its successor, the euro, will—by the painful transfer of
some thousand billion DM—transform the new *Länder*, especially Saxony, into the most modern region of Europe. But the
moral-psychological recovery and unity will take much longer.

I say this with a certain sadness, sadness that the promise of
1989, or what I thought of as Germany's second chance in this
century, has been trapped in pain and disappointment. Once

again Germany's history did not have to be like this; there was nothing inevitable about it. More truth, better leadership, and greater tolerance would have made a difference. Even now some pessimists see a political system without leadership, a repeat of Weimar. Optimists see the possibility of rejuvenation and reciprocal learning, of which there has been too little.

To seek freedom in defiance of the state is not part of the German political tradition, as it is of the English, Dutch, French, and American traditions. And yet twice in the last half century Germans defied a tyrannical state: on July 20, 1944, a few Germans tried to overthrow Hitler—they failed, and the two Germanies have had a difficult time assimilating or celebrating their memory; and in the fall of 1989, hundreds of thousands of East Germans successfully defied their regime— at a time, admittedly, when neighboring countries had already thrown off the Communist yoke, but nonetheless a momentous achievement in German history. Their leaders have already sunk into oblivion, and the memory of those great days has faded. People refer to these events as *die Wende*, the turn, transforming what had been dramatic and heroic into something prosaic and bureaucratic. For all the subsequent disappointments we should celebrate not merely the collapse of the Berlin Wall, but the men and women who by their demand for a better and freer life made that collapse one of the great moments in their history and ours.

The revolutions of 1989—however darkened in the meantime by the return of barbarism in many parts of the world— have given us an opportunity to live in trust and truth, to validate the hopes of Václav Havel.

◆◆◆◆◆◆◆◆◆◆◆◆◆ **8** ◆◆◆◆◆◆◆◆◆◆◆◆◆

The Past Distorted:
The Goldhagen Controversy

◆◆

In the early autumn of 1996, at the invitation of *Foreign Affairs*, I wrote an essay on Daniel J. Goldhagen's *Hitler's Willing Execution-ers: Ordinary Germans and the Holocaust*. The essay, which appeared in the November-December 1996 issue, was entitled: "The Gold-hagen Controversy: One Nation, One People, One Theory?" Mr. Goldhagen's response appeared in the next issue of *Foreign Affairs*. I have made minor stylistic and no substantive changes in my essay.

After I wrote this essay, a work of remarkable distinction ap-peared: Saul Friedländer's *Nazi Germany and the Jews*, Volume 1, *The Years of Persecution, 1933–1939*. In my review for the *New York Times* in February 1997 I mentioned the care with which Friedländer de-lineated the context of the horror, adding, "A great merit of this book is its implicit moral judgment on so much culpability, complic-ity, and cowardice among not only Germans but also those not yet under the German heel."

◆◆

HOLOCAUST LITERATURE abounds, as survivors seek to bear witness and historians try to understand. So far the very mag-nitude of the satanic murder has inspired a kind of awed reti-cence about pronouncing overarching explanations. Now a thirty-seven-year-old political scientist from Harvard claims: "Explaining why the Holocaust occurred requires a radical re-vision of what has until now been written. This book is that revision." *Hitler's Willing Executioners: Ordinary Germans and the Holocaust*, published in the United States in April 1996 and in Germany four months later, became an international sensation, a bestseller on both sides of the Atlantic.

The book is a deliberate provocation—I consider this a neutral judgment. Provocations can shock people out of their settled, comfortable views; they can also be self-promoting attacks on earlier work and professional standards. Goldhagen's title is provocative and delivers his thesis: the executioners of Jews were willing murderers, who willingly chose to torment and kill their victims; they were ordinary Germans, not Nazi monsters, not specially trained or indoctrinated by party membership or ideology, but simply acting out of what Goldhagen calls the common German "eliminationist mind-set." And being "ordinary" Germans responding to a common "cognitive model" about Jews, their places could have been taken by millions of other ordinary Germans.

Goldhagen's book comes in two related parts: the explanatory model, or "the analytical framework," as he also calls it, and the empirical evidence. The parts are joined by a single intent: the indictment of a people. The duality of presentation marks the style as well. Goldhagen depicts horror and renders judgment in evocative and compelling phrases. He bolsters polemical certainty with concepts drawn from the social sciences, relying on the vaporous, dreary jargon of the worst of academic "discourse." Unintelligible diagrams distract, even as horrendous photographs confirm. "The book's intent is primarily explanatory and theoretical," he notes. Theory explains and, as there is a persistent mismatch between the powerful, unsparing description of Holocaust bestiality and simplistic theoretical explanation, theory triumphs. Astoundingly repetitive, the book has 125 pages of notes but, regrettably, no bibliography, which would have been a great convenience to other scholars.

To say it at once: the book has some merit, especially in the middle section, which depicts three specific aspects of the

Holocaust, and it has one overriding defect: it is in its essence unhistorical. It is unhistorical in positing that one (simplistically depicted) strain of the past, German anti-Semitism, explains processes that the author strips of their proper historical context; it is unhistorical in over and over again presenting suppositions as "incontestable" certainty. Sir Lewis Namier, a great English historian, once remarked that "the historical approach is intellectually humble; the aim is to comprehend situations, to study trends, to discover how things work: and the crowning attainment of historical study is a historical sense— an intuitive understanding of how things do not happen." Goldhagen's tone mocks humility, and he seems to lack any sense "of how things do not happen," of how complex human conduct and historical change really are.

Goldhagen begins with a disquisition of some hundred pages on what he believes is the peculiar character of German anti-Semitism, emphasizing medieval Christian hostility to Jews and concluding that in the largely secularized Germany of the nineteenth century this doctrinal hostility sharpened into a racial one, demonizing Jews as alien, as the enemy that needed to be eliminated. This version is of course dangerously close to the old cliché that a clear line of authoritarian, anti-Semitic thought runs from Luther to Hitler and was largely responsible for the triumph of Nazism.

Goldhagen draws on the rich literature about German anti-Semitism even as he dismisses it, distills what is useful for his thesis while ignoring whatever might contradict or complicate it, and then celebrates the originality of his own version. The result is a potpourri of half-truths and assertions, all meant to support his claim that German anti-Semitism was unique in its abiding wish to eliminate Jews, its "eliminationist mind-set." He suggests that one needs to look at Germans as anthropologists look at preliterate societies; they are not like "us," meaning Americans or Western Europeans.

He considers but dismisses the need to compare German anti-Semitism to other varieties, although we know that anti-

Semitism was endemic in the Western world. Some scholars, including George L. Mosse and Zeev Sternhell, have plausibly argued that before 1914 French anti-Semitism was more pervasive and more aggressive than German anti-Semitism (on the other hand, French defense of Jews was more vigorous than similar efforts in Germany). Or take a perhaps even more revealing comparison: a leading historian of Germany, James J. Sheehan, wrote in 1992 that "animosity towards Jews [in the pre-1914 era] was substantially stronger in Austria than in Germany," and estimated "that whereas Austrians made up less than 10 per cent of the population of Hitler's Reich, they were involved in half the crimes associated with the Holocaust." Goldhagen certainly knows that thousands of non-Germans were willing executioners, willing auxiliaries to the Holocaust. But their motivation or, indeed, their historical role, is of no interest to him.

Even in his discussion of German anti-Semitism he fails to make the necessary distinctions. There was a wide range of attitudes toward Jews, from those few who did indeed see them as the enemy and chief corrupters of their society—as "vermin" to be exterminated—to those men and women who welcomed Jews but regretted what they saw as Jewish "pushiness" or preeminence in some realms. Goldhagen takes remarks out of context and treats almost equally the ranting of the rabble-rouser and the private musings confined to a writer's diary. Everything is grist for his mill.*

* One example of Goldhagen's modus operandi is his only reference to Thomas Mann: "Thomas Mann, who had already long been an outstanding opponent of Nazism, could nevertheless find some common ground with the Nazis when it came to eliminating Jewish influence in Germany: '... it is no great misfortune ... that ... the Jewish presence in the judiciary has been ended.' The dominant cultural cognitive model of Jews and the eliminationist mind-set that it spawned was dominant in Germany." A note indicates that he takes the citation from an essay of mine in which I quoted passages from Mann's journal.

I consider Mann, married to Katia Pringsheim, the daughter of a prominent Jewish family, perhaps the best example of the ambiguity and complexity of German anti-Semitism, and I cited this passage, written in the early months of

A Goldhagen version of anti-Semitism in twentieth-century America might lump Eleanor Roosevelt's early remarks about "Jew-boys" in Franklin's law school class with Henry Ford's championing of the *Protocols of the Elders of Zion* or Father Coughlin's tirades. Only by summary judgment and indifference to nuance can Goldhagen contend that in the nineteenth century "German society . . . was *axiomatically* anti-Semitic." And hence, "It is thus *incontestable* that the fundamentals of Nazi anti-Semitism . . . had deep roots in Germany, was part of the cultural cognitive model of German society, and was integral to German political culture. . . . It is *incontestable* that this racial anti-Semitism which held the Jews to pose a mortal threat to Germany was pregnant with murder" (my emphasis). Incontestable? I would say unprovable and implausible.

The very Germany Goldhagen discusses was the country in which Jews had made the most extraordinary leaps to cultural and economic prominence. But Goldhagen omits this integral element of history. After emancipation and after legal equality was decreed in 1869, German Jews began their astounding ascendancy. Their achievements were the envy of Jews else-

---

the regime, precisely because of its fascinating vacillation of tone and meaning. The very next—indeed, inseparable—sentence, which Goldhagen omits, suggests Mann's own distaste at his thoughts, which he characterizes as "secret, disquieting, intense," but the passage concludes with his musing that the process of historical change, just recently initiated by the Nazis, had in it "nonetheless things that are revoltingly malevolent, base, un-German in the highest sense. But I am beginning to suspect that the process could well be of that kind that has two sides."

Another example: Goldhagen mentions the late Israeli scholar Uriel Tal's comment on liberal disappointment with Jews in the late nineteenth century but omits that Tal observed in the same context: "Political and racial anti-Semitism during this period [the Second Reich] failed to exert any appreciable public influence, and whatever effectiveness it had was limited to short intervals and restricted regions."

Such procedures from someone who can be so censorious of others! In 1989 Goldhagen reviewed an earlier thesis-driven book on the Holocaust, saying: "But it is itself an artful construction of half-truths, itself in the service of an ideology. And it is riddled with extraordinary factual errors which amount to a pattern of falsification and distortion."

where. It is perfectly true that any hope they had for complete acceptance remained unfulfilled. They knew that they were being treated as second-class citizens, and their very successes heightened their vulnerability. But this was a society at once dynamically expanding and severely weakened by internal strains; it seems odd to single out "eliminationist antisemitism" as the key social dynamic and say nothing of the still sharp antagonisms between Protestants and Catholics, or the intense class conflict that Germans called "the social question" and that weighed on them far more than "the Jewish question" did.

The salience of German anti-Semitism varied with the mood and condition of German politics. During the Great War these politics became radicalized, and by 1917, when hope for total victory turned to apprehension of defeat, an enraged right wing fastened on violent, chauvinist, anti-Semitic beliefs; for many other Germans defeat was the result of internal enemies, the Weimar Republic was a Jewish excrescence in German politics, and both Marxism and Bolshevism were Jewish machinations. But men and women on the left or liberal end of the German political spectrum rejected these delusions and defended the republic, in which Jews had achieved a certain political prominence. Of all this Goldhagen says very little; the Great War, during which both Jewish patriotism and German anti-Semitism flourished as never before, is mentioned in only one paragraph. This distorted view of German political culture is unconvincing in its simplicity.

Scholars have long debated whether Hitler's anti-Semitism was central to his electoral victories at the end of the Weimar years. It is generally accepted that the more the National Socialists tried to widen their appeal, the more they muted their anti-Semitic theme. In one of Hitler's key addresses in 1932, for example, he hardly alluded to Jews at all. Yet Goldhagen insists: "The centrality of antisemitism in the Party's world, program and rhetoric—if in a more avowedly elaborated and violent form—mirrored the sentiments of German culture."

Actually, it exposed the sentiments of only *some* Germans. In the last free elections in 1932, some 67 percent of the German electorate did not vote for Hitler, although there can be no doubt that even among these were groups that harbored suspicion and dislike of Jews. Perhaps many Germans had some measure of anti-Semitism in them but lacked the murderous intent that Goldhagen ascribes to National Socialism. Put bluntly: for Goldhagen, as for the National Socialists, *Hitler was Germany*.

But was anti-Semitism the sole or even the most important bond between Hitler and the Germans? Was it responsible for the failure of Germans to protest the first terrorist measures of the regime, the suppression of civil rights, the establishment of concentration camps in March 1933? The existence of the camps was made public specifically because they were intended to destroy political enemies and to intimidate potential opposition. From the very beginning the Nazis used every vicious means of humiliation and terror—in public sometimes, within the insulated realm of the camps always—against all opponents, real and imagined, German or German Jew, man or woman. They unleashed their pent-up savagery on Socialists and Communists (with the greatest brutality if they happened to be Jews as well). Men were beaten in these camps, and murdered—yet silence was pervasive among the Germans, who had begun to exult in their society's outward order and slowly returning prosperity and power. Would Goldhagen not acknowledge the likelihood of some link between Germans so sadistically falling upon their fellow Germans and their treatment of people whom they came to demonize—Jews and Slavs in particular?

The silence, and in some cases the easy acquiescence of the German elites, including those in churches, universities, and the civil service, have long been considered moral and civic failures of portentous importance. They saw their own freedoms threatened, their own principles violated; yet they showed, in Norbert Elias's phrase, "a lust for submission."

They met with silence the first extrusionary acts against Jews; only very few protested when colleagues were removed from their posts or lost their jobs, when friends were ostracized, when all Jews were made the target of steady abuse. One must remember that active protest against the National Socialist regime in the spring of 1933 would not have demanded martyrdom—far from it. The price for the exercise of decency rose only when the regime became stronger.

Goldhagen argues that the road to Auschwitz was straight, and he pays little heed to the improvisations and uncertainties of the regime's first five years. Yet policies during that period aimed at the extrusion, not the extermination, of Jews, at their isolation and impoverishment, so as to drive them out of the country. Goldhagen rightly emphasizes both the anti-Semitic propaganda of the time and the way Jews were already to some degree "fair game"; yet in Germany there were few acts of spontaneous violence against them, as compared to the explosion of sadistic anti-Semitism in Austria immediately following the *Anschluss*. Nevertheless, for Goldhagen it is in Germany that the "eliminationist" mind-set was most virulent.

Goldhagen rightly ponders the Germans' responses to the Reich pogrom in November 1938 known as *Kristallnacht*, with its burning of synagogues, smashing of Jewish property, and public arrest of some 30,000 male Jews who were then herded into concentration camps. He notes that while "the world reacted with moral revulsion and outrage, the German people failed to exhibit equivalent revulsion and outrage—and principled dissent from the anti-Semitic model that underlay the night's depredation—even though what had occurred was done in their name, in their midst, to defenseless people, and to *their* countrymen" (Goldhagen's emphasis). But Goldhagen has been at pains to demonstrate that Germans had never regarded Jews as their countrymen. He continues: "This, perhaps the most revealing day of the entire Nazi era, the day on which an opportunity presented itself for the German people to rise up in solidarity with their fellow citizens, was the day on

which the German people sealed the fate of the Jews by letting
the authorities know that they concurred in the unfolding
eliminationist enterprise, even if they objected, sometimes vo-
ciferously, to some of its measures." What a historical aberration! What chance was there for a people "to rise up" against
a firmly entrenched terrorist regime that, moreover, had just
scored the most extraordinary peaceful triumphs of incorpo-
rating Austria and emasculating Czechoslovakia—and all this
with the passive or even active support of the western democracies? The November horror occurred six weeks after the Munich conference and a month before the signing of a special
Franco-German friendship treaty. If Germans "concurred in
the unfolding eliminationist enterprise," why did the National
Socialist regime make such strenuous efforts to hide its later
crimes from them, to carry them out, as the famous phrase put
it, "in night and fog," to place the early extermination camps
outside the borders of the Reich? Was it afraid of phantoms?

Moreover, Goldhagen slights the acts of decency that did
occur, every act at the risk of horrible retribution. (In general,
these acts of decency and defiance have received too little attention, especially in Germany itself.)

American readers will soon be able to read German works in
translation that either supplement or balance Goldhagen's version of events. The diaries of Victor Klemperer, kept in secret
from 1933 to 1945 and only now published, have been a bestseller in Germany.* They record the sentiments and sufferings
of a Jewish professor married to a Christian; they offer a nuanced picture of both the Germans' brutality and callousness
toward Jews and their moments of decency and quiet help.
Wolfgang Sofsky's *The Order of Terror: The Concentration Camp*
is a major study that characterizes the camp as the emblematic
institution of the Nazi regime and insists "that the universe of
the concentration camp is unprecedented in its torture and de-

---

* In 1998, Random House published a translation of the first volume: *I Will
Bear Witness: A Diary of the Nazi Years, 1933–1941.*

struction," in its organized effort at degradation and murder. Goldhagen's one-sided remarks about the anti-Semitic attitudes and even murderous complicity with the regime of some of the heroic men who tried to kill Hitler in July 1944 receives more thorough and balanced attention in Joachim Fest's *Plotting Hitler's Death: The Story of the German Resistance*.

Less than half of this irksomely repetitive book deals with Goldhagen's own research into three specific aspects of the Holocaust: the murderous conduct of police battalions (the ordinary men of the title), the misnamed work camps that were way stations on the road to death, and the death marches at the end of the war. Goldhagen focuses on the perpetrators, particularly on their putative motives, and gives most terrifying, memorable accounts of their wanton cruelty. He reminds us that a very large number of Jews perished not in the gas chambers but by means of executions, planned starvation, and induced disease, always amidst unspeakable bestiality.

Goldhagen examines the lives and cruelties of the men of Police Battalion 101—a reconstruction made possible by the thorough record of a German prosecutorial investigation conducted after 1945. These men, most of them from the lower or lower-middle class in Hamburg, tended to be older than soldiers; most of them were family men and only a few of them were members of any Nazi organization. In 1992, Christopher R. Browning's *Ordinary Men: Reserve Police Battalion 101 and the Final Solution in Poland* was published, a meticulous study of precisely this same police battalion of 500 men, in which he examined their backgrounds and vicious deeds, their massacres of Jews—men, women, and children in Poland—just because they were Jews. The commander offered his men nonpunitive exemption from such horror as killing mothers and babies, but most men participated (as happened elsewhere), some with apparent sadistic satisfaction, some even though they had wives with them in Poland who knew and on occasion saw what their husbands did.

Goldhagen analyzes much of the same material but fiercely rejects Browning's account of the murderers' motives. Browning acknowledges the effect of the relentless Nazi propaganda against the Jews but wisely considers what other factors may have been responsible, including the fear of breaking ranks or acknowledging "weakness," and, in a few cases, considerations of career advancement. Goldhagen will have none of this. He insists on a monocausal explanation: anti-Semitic beliefs alone accounted for this behavior. Browning thinks that "the historian who attempts to 'explain' [this behavior] is indulging in a certain arrogance." True.*

Next Goldhagen analyzes some of the so-called work camps, in which Jews were treated as worse than slaves, whipped to perform such senseless tasks as carrying rocks from one end of the camp to the other and back again. They were meant to die at hard, purposeless labor; they were starved, beaten, and killed, caught in a hell ruled by dogs and the whims of all-powerful sadist-guards (not all of them German). Jews were destined for extermination in these work camps, even as the Reich suffered from a labor shortage that led it to exploit more than seven million foreign slave laborers. Goldhagen emphasizes the economic irrationality of this strategy, citing it as proof once again of the primacy of the German drive to exterminate Jews. True, but there were many other instances of both economic irrationality and cruelty to *non*-Jews that were just as injurious to German interests.

The book's most gripping chapter concerns the death marches that began in the winter of 1944 and spring of 1945, when Jews, separated from non-Jewish fellow prisoners, were hounded from camp to camp as the Allied armies closed in on

---

* In an extremely odd note, Goldhagen dismisses Browning, saying that the plausibility of "his explanation depends upon a person's own understanding of the cynicism of people. Scholars who believe that for a promotion or for a few marks, these Germans were willing to slaughter Jews by the thousands should also believe that for tenure at a university . . . virtually all their colleagues today, and they themselves, would mow down innocent people by the thousands."

Germany. Goldhagen concentrates on one hellish march in particular, the twenty-two-day trek from the Helmbrechts camp in Franconia to a place some 120 miles away, across the Czech border. The march "began and ended in slaughter." From the first, Jews were beaten, killed, or left to freeze, starve, and die under conditions far worse than the abominations that non-Jews suffered. All this in spite of the fact that Himmler had given orders—for his own opportunistic reasons—to cease killing Jews. The guards on this march disregarded the orally transmitted order and indulged in crazed sadism, women guards showing special cruelty. (When a few Germans tried to throw the prisoners scraps of bread, the guards brutally prevented such succor.) Goldhagen's passion finds its best expression in this and other accounts of harrowing horror. He recounts these scenes of utter inhumanity with admirable fortitude. But the ever-repeated judgment is of course less compelling: "These Germans . . . were voluntaristic actors. . . . Their trueness to meting out suffering and death was not an imposed behavior; it came from within, an expression of their innermost selves."

Reviewers have commented on the originality of his treatment of the death marches. Actually, Martin Gilbert's *Holocaust*—a book Goldhagen does not mention—gives an overview of the marches from accounts of the few survivors, focusing on the victims and not on the few known perpetrators.

All these acts of barbarism, these human enactments of the worst of Hieronymous Bosch's nightmares, were committed by Germans (and, Goldhagen notwithstanding, by non-Germans) who, according to Goldhagen, felt neither shame nor compunction. The Jew was the enemy, at once all-powerful and subhuman; the demonization had struck roots. Goldhagen wants to correct a perspective that focuses on "the desk murderers." The Holocaust was more than a bureaucratic operation; it was not the work of so many banal cogs in the wheels of evil. But while he rightly points to the thousands of individual tormentors and murderers, he tends to underplay the powerful role of the state apparatus that gave those murderers license, one that involved the collaborative efforts of the rulers of the Reich and their servants, officials in multiple ministries, party desk officers, the government, the army, the judiciary, and the medical establishment.

Goldhagen singles out those murderers who were "ordinary Germans" and who, he insists, were motivated solely by their "cognitive model" of the Jew. He then moves from specific and harrowing examples to a grotesque extrapolation: having examined the acts of some hundreds or perhaps even thousands of people, he insists that almost all Germans were moved by the same hatred, approved the killing, would have acted in like fashion if chance had so decreed. As he writes, "The institutions treated here . . . should permit the motivations of the perpetrators in those particular institutions to be uncovered, and also allow for generalizing both to the perpetrators as a group and to the second target group of this study, the German people." The leap from individual cases to the German people as a whole is unpersuasive, but necessary for his indictment of his "second target group."

Some fifty years ago, at the end of the war, this view of the uniqueness of German criminality was commonly held. It was once a comforting certainty that Germans and only Germans were capable of such organized atrocities—for which Goldhagen is the first to assign a single motive. But in time the interpretation of the Holocaust became more differentiated, less self-exculpatory; we also know more about atrocities today, whether in Cambodia, Biafra, or Bosnia.

Can one even try to explain the Holocaust (the horror of which for many, myself included, somehow eludes understanding) without regard to its historical context? Should one? The Inferno occurred at a given historical moment, at a time of mounting barbarism and moral indifference, which had returned to Europe in unimaginable force during the Great War, barely diminished in the interwar years, and reached an apogee during this second world war. National Socialism, we know, was at once Germany's most criminal and most popular regime, Hitler the century's most charismatic leader. The terror that he launched in Germany spread to conquered Europe: German troops of various formations extended the terror to Poland, Russia, Greece, everywhere. Thus villages were burned, hostages shot, and men, women, and children hounded, starved, separated, and killed—all that and everywhere. There were thousands of massacres in Poland, and 2.5 million Russian prisoners of war were deliberately starved to death. The links that connect this pervasive brutality to the systematic extermination of European Jewry cannot be found in specific documents or individual decisions, but can those links be doubted? Furthermore, scholars have now established that both Germans and non-Germans knew far more far earlier about the Holocaust and the atrocities in the east than was once assumed. But most of these people worried about their own predicaments and tried to preserve their complacent self-regard, their moral self-esteem, by choosing not to know or believe—a denial that has marked much of the world in our century. In brief the Holocaust took place in the long night of organized bestiality. That is its context.

Hitler's Willing Executioners and its reception in the United States aroused instant concern in Germany. The German media organized extensive discussions on the book; some of the talk was favorable, as were the first reviews in America, but much of it was critical, sometimes in an ad hominem way.* In early August, just before the German translation was published, *Die Zeit*, Germany's celebrated weekly, which had already given

---

* The first book about the book is a collection of critiques published in Germany, also with a provocative title: Julius H. Schoeps, ed., *Ein Volk von Mördern? Die Dokumentation zur Goldhagen—Kontroverse um die Rolle der Deutschen im Holocaust* [A people of murderers? Documentation concerning the Goldhagen controversy about the role of the Germans in the Holocaust] (Hamburg, 1996).

uncommon, perhaps unwarranted, attention to the book, allot-
ted Goldhagen exceptional space to respond to what he called
"The Failure of the Critics." In his response, Goldhagen attacked all his critics and rejected all their arguments—with
dazzling arrogance. He accused them not only of failing to answer central questions but even of failing to ask them: "If then
they are confronted with a book that delivers precisely these
answers, then they react in a rage that makes one think of people who want to silence someone because he touches on a long-
preserved taboo." But these scholarly critics include precisely
those liberal German historians who for decades have done the
most to analyze and document the nature and atrocities of
the Third Reich, who by meticulous research have established
the complicity of so many German individuals and institutions, including the churches and the Wehrmacht. Goldhagen
nowhere acknowledges the immense, courageous labors of
these German historians and writers, who have presented their
people with as stark and honest a portrait of their past as is
possible—and have done so to the irritation of many "ordinary
Germans" who would prefer not to be reminded of the uniqueness of that past.

Der Spiegel, which also extensively covered the Goldhagen
sensation, reports that the German edition (which I have not
seen), with a new introduction by the author, modifies or
mutes some of his more sweeping allegations. In his many in-
terviews he has taken pains to highlight the exculpation that
appears in a mere note at the back of the American edition,
where he writes that he did not mean "to imply that a timeless German character exists. The character structure and the
common cognitive models of Germans have developed and
evolved historically and, especially since the loss of the Second
World War, have changed dramatically." In his appearances
before German audiences, Goldhagen denied ever having had
the notion of collective guilt and seemed eager to attenuate
such sentences in the book as "Germany during the Nazi period was inhabited by a people animated by beliefs about Jews

that made them willing to become consenting mass murderers." His subject of course touched the deepest German questions of guilt and individual responsibility, and did so, apparently, in a fashion different from the book. It would seem that he tried to please his German audiences.*

Hitler's Willing Executioners was a bestseller in the United States, and it sold 80,000 copies in the first four weeks after its publication in Germany. Some Germans have remarked that whatever the book's flaws, it should be welcomed because it will reinvigorate the debate and stimulate new scholarship. *Der Spiegel* has made this same point, as has the distinguished American historian Gordon Craig. But the book also reinforces and reignites earlier prejudices: latent anti-German sentiment among Americans, especially Jews; and a sense among Germans that Jews have a special stake in commemorating the Holocaust, thereby keeping Germany a prisoner of its past. The book is now a major datum in German-American relations. Perhaps it could be viewed as an academic equivalent of the simplistic television miniseries "Holocaust," which also had an enormous impact.

The astounding reception of so polemical and pretentious a book can hardly be attributed solely to its topic or thesis. Shrill, simplistic explanations of monstrous crimes obviously command attention, but there is more at work here: the author's ceaseless boast of radical originality was endorsed on the book's jacket by two well-known scholars, both distinguished in fields other than German history—and between them praising Goldhagen's work as "phenomenal scholarship and absolute integrity . . . impeccable scholarship, a profound understanding of modern German history . . . obligatory reading."

---

* According to German press reports, he did so triumphantly. In my brief visit to Germany in early October 1996, I was told that his charm, telegenic presence, and conciliatory manner enthralled his public and bested his critics. German commentators remained puzzled, as I am, by the discrepancy between the public acclaim and the scholarly criticism, coming especially from the liberal side, and by the discrepancy between the writer's arrogance and the speaker's appealing modesty.

The American and German publishers touted the book with all the great promotional power at their command. Perhaps Gold-hagen's manipulated, public-relations-orchestrated success tells us more about the culture of the present than the book's substance tells us about the horrors of the past.

❖❖❖❖❖❖❖❖❖❖❖❖❖ **9** ❖❖❖❖❖❖❖❖❖❖❖❖❖

Lost Homelands: German-Polish Reconciliation

❖❖

This is the text of a lecture I delivered in Berlin on June 1, 1995, at a German-Polish gathering organized by Janusz Reiter, then Poland's ambassador to Germany, and the State Government of Schleswig-Holstein. A panel discussion followed the lecture, the panel consisting of Marion Countess Dönhoff, of the Hamburg newspaper *Die Zeit*; Konstanty Kalinowski, director of the National Museum in Poznan; Andrzej Milczanowski, Poland's minister of the interior; and Manfred Kanther, Germany's minister of the interior. Milczanowski and Kanther were born the same day, and, like all the others on the panel, had been uprooted from their native homes during the Second World War: they had experienced "lost homelands." The German participants had been dispossessed of homelands taken over by Poland, the Poles of homelands taken over by the Soviet Union.

❖❖

I MYSELF SHALL never forget my father's tears when the train pulled out of Breslau, when we left his hometown in September 1938. I had never seen paternal tears before; it was a singular outburst of feeling, grief at a shattered past, anxiety about an uncertain future. As a boy of twelve, I felt nothing but joy, for I was escaping the abominations of that time and place. And still: when a German interviewer several years ago asked me, "What comes to your mind when you hear the word

'*Heimat*'?" my instant, unreflected answer surprised me: "*Heimatlos*," or homeless. There are, after all, many ways of losing a homeland. One can be dispossessed of one's homeland while physically still at home, an experience suffered by millions in this century.

To have lost one's homeland has been a recurrent fate, and like war—indeed usually a consequence of war—it is an integral part of world history. In our century, more than 100 million people have lost their lives or their homelands in war. As a historian and unwitting witness I concern myself with this theme.

Expulsion and loss: in the beginning was the Word, and in the beginning was the primal pattern of expulsion, the expulsion from paradise. Banishment and expulsion are enduring historical features. And aren't the feelings of paradise lost, of innocence gone forever, the experience of every child as its early, all-protective world vanishes? We often see people regret the passing of a happily transfigured childhood; in our century perhaps childhood is also often negatively transfigured, seen as the source of trauma and transgression. Often people driven from their homelands—even like such children—live on falsely compressed memories, fastening most vehemently on what was good or what was bad.

Hatred, envy, fear, and lust for power—these all-too-human motives have made expulsion from the homeland a recurrent phenomenon in world history. The twentieth century has witnessed a prolonged, bloody repetition of this horror. In previous centuries in Europe, people deemed different were frequent victims of persecution and expulsion—one thinks of the Jews and, after the Reformation, of Christians of warring denominations. Later came the political and ideological persecutions; exile has been a salient, often honorable, fate, especially in German and Polish history. In the course of nineteenth-century industrialization, millions of people were uprooted from the land, forced to find new abodes in the growing slums of Europe's cities. Our own century has been even more cruel:

consider the Armenians and the Greeks, the Spaniards forced to flee their country at the end of the Civil War, the victims of the Second World War, the Jews, the Poles, the Russians—and the Germans who after 1933 became expellers and expellees by turns. There were as well millions of Muslims who fled India and Hindus who left Pakistan, the Palestinians, *pieds noirs* who had to abandon their Algerian homeland. Aggressive nationalism was responsible for many of these persecutions; in the Second World War, it was racial hatred and delirium that caused millions of deaths. Also, millions of so-called class enemies in the territories of the Soviet Union were deported or liquidated, and since 1989 we have witnessed the analogous tragedy of ethnic cleansing.

The ideas we associate with the Enlightenment—tolerance and the recognition of human dignity—were in our century vilified and violated by the National Socialists and brutally set aside by other regimes as well. And yet the principles of the Enlightenment remained alive. In the underground cellars of the French Resistance—where to a fictive German friend, Albert Camus wrote that he loved his country too much to be a nationalist—or, more recently, in the East European opposition to Communism, Enlightenment ideals lived on.

Lost homeland—what does that mean? First it means a loss of property and sustenance. But the human-psychic loss cuts much deeper. Homeland signifies security; it forms a person's unconscious sense of self or, as a modern discourse puts it, it forms a person's identity. In what we call *Heimat* is bound up one's deepest feelings of attachment, involving nature itself: memories of specific woods and meadows, of streams and shapes of buildings, smells and sounds, of everything one was once accustomed to. Most often we connect family memories with our homeland, the recollection of some special place at home or garden linked to parents or cherished friends. Often enough it is only after its loss that we come to feel, to realize how irretrievably precious homeland really is, the true value of all that was familiar. Homeland is like the air we breathe: we are aware of it only when it isn't there or is poisoned. After its loss, an image lingers in memory, springing to consciousness at unexpected moments. Language reveals the pain: we speak of homesickness, *Heimweh* or *mal du pays*, of heartache when we are far from home.

Heinrich Heine—the German Jewish poet in exile in Paris— was the classical poet of homesickness. He once observed: "It's an odd thing with patriotism, with true love of the fatherland. You can love your fatherland and reach the ripe old age of eighty and never be conscious of it, but then you have had to stay at home always. We recognize spring's inner essence first in winter, and the best poems about May are written around the stove. Love of freedom is a dungeon flower: only in prison does one feel freedom's worth. Thus, too, love for the German fatherland arises only at Germany's frontier, but most especially at the sight from abroad of Germany's misfortune."

The first time I chanced across these lines was November 8, 1992, a few hours before I was to speak at a memorial in New York for Willy Brandt. They fit Brandt perfectly, his love for his German homeland when in exile during the National Socialist years; an exile may loathe his country's tyrant and love the homeland all the more.

The very word *Heimat*—with its special Germanic ring— often invites sentimentality—and one must guard against it. There have been the frightful expulsions that often ended in death. I focus on the survivors who have endured loss but whose individual fates and feelings often differ greatly. How a person responds to this calamity depends not only on given historic circumstances but on personal character, on age and temperament. After all, loss can also mean gain, the sense that in a new life, while loyal to the best of the old, one should pluck from injustice a new determination to fight every new injustice, to become a truly committed citizen. I believe that Countess Dönhoff and her fellow panelists represent models of such admirable adaptation.

Others who have lost their homelands remain prisoners of the past, embittering their own lives with hatreds of those who expelled them. One might hope that after fifty years such feelings would recede, but we know that all too often they are encouraged and exploited for partisan purposes. They ritualize—indeed poison—the remembrance of the past, while obstructing life in the present. (We know that especially in postwar Germany expellees or their descendants have organized around a cult of *Heimat*, hoping to extract new political capital from old injustice.) Nor do I want here to deal with *Heimat* as kitsch, as media hype. The memory of homeland is a private matter; the question of how it was lost requires an understanding of past events, of context, and raises the question of how the wound was inflicted. And here, perhaps, historians can make a contribution.

Václav Havel has been the passionate interpreter of the longing "to live in the truth." The truth is that today's fixed and immutable borders must be understood as an injunction and a possibility for mutual understanding. Poles who try to recall, not repress, and even cultivate the memory of the German past in Silesia help to strengthen their new homeland. Germans who seek to promote a better, wider appreciation of Polish culture are doing the same. To acknowledge that injustice occurred, that a lost homeland is a grievous thing, is the prerequisite of formal reconciliation. There is also an internal healing, as when the memory of the lost old life is blended into a new one. Ultimately, only you yourself can lose your homeland, by trying to repress or falsify the memory of it. Or as Herbert Lüthy, splendid Swiss historian, once put it, we need to learn "to mourn without hating."

We know that the first victim in war is the truth, and so it was in Europe from August 1914 on. Instead of many struggles over truth, which after all is not an absolute, there were decreed lies, denials of reality. Lies and terror were intended to subject people to a new political nonage. Not until 1945 for

Western Europe and not until 1989 for the entire continent was the path to truth opened again. It is not easy for a people or for an individual to live in the truth; for Germans after 1945 it was especially hard.

In a recent memorable address before the German Bundestag, its president, Rita Süssmuth said: "What counts is . . . a truth that brings about reconciliation, [truth about] the memory of the monstrous crimes that in the past were committed by Germans and in Germany's name. To speak of that painful truth so often would perhaps not be necessary except for the attempt over and over again to relativize it," to assert, in other words, that Nazi crimes were somehow comparable to—no worse than—other historic crimes.

In the last fifty years West Germans had the opportunity to examine the past; for the Poles living under a Communist regime that was scarcely possible. All the more important was the address of the Polish bishops to their German counterparts in 1965, in which they acknowledged the terrible grievances on both sides, stretched out their hands "granting forgiveness and asking forgiveness." But the Polish regime itself decreed silence concerning the sufferings of the Polish people after 1945, about the forced resettlement of Poles from territory annexed by Russians. We must recognize the suffering endured by these people, too, when they were expelled from their homeland. The Polish poet Adam Zagajewski has given a masterly account of how Poles felt in 1944–45 when they were shipped westward like so much freight; people who ended up in Gliwice (in what had been Gleiwitz in German Silesia) still went on believing in Lwow, and for the older generation Lwow alone existed—they were strangers in a deserted city, at home only in a city they had been forced to abandon. Perhaps only now can we recognize the full measure of pain suffered by the tormented Polish people; therefore, perhaps, it is only now that Germans and Poles can fully grasp the misery that their fellow citizens suffered in the past. This is the human truth: the recognition that homelands were lost on both sides of the Oder-

Neisse border. Let me recall the speech by Wladyslaw Barto-szewski, Polish foreign minster, to the Bundestag: "Now that we are allowed to speak of the fate of the expelled from Vilna and Lemberg [Lwow], it is also easier to recognize the human dimension of the drama of those expelled from Breslau and Stettin. . . . We lament the individual fate and the [collective] suffering of innocent Germans afflicted by the consequences of war and who were deprived of their homeland."

Germany's final recognition of its border with Poland was a long time in coming, and one can only hope that the agreement the politicians signed has also taken firm root in the hearts of the citizens. Recognition both of fixed borders and of past in-justices is a precondition for reconciliation—a comparative ranking of past injustices would be a new evil. German crimes against Poles and Jews remain unparalleled in history. The war that Nazi Germany unleashed was the sole cause for the alli-ance between the Western Allies and the Soviet Union and it was the cause for the loss of homeland that millions of Ger-mans suffered at the end of the war.

Historical truth—a daring phrase—makes reconciliation possible and historical experience suggests that such reconcili-ation demands celebratory moments. Reconciliation between Germany and France—which in time helped German-Polish relations—had its symbolic moment in the Cathedral at Reims when DeGaulle and Adenauer worshipped together. Willy Brandt's kneeling at the gate of the Warsaw Ghetto was an equally unforgettable moment. The courageous speech of For-eign Minster Bartoszewski—himself an early prisoner in Auschwitz and an underground fighter against German occu-piers and helper of Polish Jews—was a new proof of reconcilia-tion, in both a substantial and symbolic sense. But reconcil-iation demands more than symbolic gestures: it demands daily efforts, and these, too, are taking place in many projects testify-ing to friendship between neighbors. Historians can contribute something here, too. German-Polish enmity has a long, long history, the final, horrible chapter of which was written by

Stalin. At the beginning of the Second World War, Hitler, Stalin, and their henchmen decided to eradicate the Polish elites. The German occupation killed five million Poles, including three million Polish Jews. After these losses, after the 1943 Warsaw Ghetto uprising and the Warsaw uprising in 1944, Poland suffered a new occupation, this time by the Red Army and its own satellite tyrants. Despite—and also because of—this reign of terror, new elites formed in Poland. Now, and only with the development of genuine German-Polish understanding, only with German commitment to support Polish interests in Europe (as the former Polish Prime Minister Tadeusz Mazowiecki recently urged in Weimar), only with German-Polish trust—only then can we say that Hitler and Stalin have finally been vanquished.

My first visit to Warsaw took place in June 1979—by chance, a few weeks after Pope John Paul II had first returned to his native country; one could tell that Poles of all faiths and none saw in him the true sovereign of their country. I had the good fortune on that occasion of meeting Bronislaw Geremek, distinguished historian, deeply engaged in the dissident movement in Poland, and Adam Michnik, journalist and editor of *Kritika*, an underground journal.* (I would have been pleased to accept Geremek's invitation to lecture at the Flying University, of which he was a program director.) In June 1980, I returned to Warsaw and reminded a well-known, prudently reformist Communist editor of Jean-Jacques Rousseau's comment in 1772 that the Polish people will one day once again astonish the world, and I asked him when this might occur. Unhesitatingly, he replied: "Not this month, not this year, but within this decade." Four weeks later, Solidarność was founded. Geremek and Michnik became principal advisors to Solidarność, cementing the close relations between dissident workers and dissident intellectuals. Both men were impris-

* Years later I discovered that *Kritika* in 1988 had published the speech I had given to the German Bundestag on June 17, 1987: I remain grateful for this honor.

oned after the introduction of martial law; both men were deeply involved in Poland's march to self-liberation. I treasure the Geremeks' friendship more than I can say. Solidarność was at once champion and model of liberation: with what courage and intelligence was the path from prison to the "round table" taken! How much all of us owe to those who steadfastly resisted all forms of tyranny. The United States deterred the Soviets; they defied them.

The rebuilding of postwar Germany has been a success as well. A stable democratic order has been established; a different political culture has taken root. The very mentality of its citizens has been changed. The dream of a "special path," a *Sonderweg* of sorts, for Germany, has been laid to rest, and the nationalistic sense of German superiority has been overcome. In the Germany of Bismarck and Wilhelm II, of the Weimar Republic and of Hitler, many Germans were proud of not being a part of the West. That too is gone. German efforts to come to grips with the past has been a considerable achievement. It has been an important achievement as compared to perhaps all other nations, my own included. It took some time till the confrontation with the past could really take hold. I recall a speech that the Social Democrat Ernst Reuter, then lord mayor of Berlin, delivered on the tenth anniversary of the annihilation of the Warsaw Ghetto: "As Germans we must . . . never forget the infamous deeds perpetrated in our name, the name of Germany. . . . When will our German people ever be able to wash themselves clean of this infamy—and will it ever be possible to bring those upon whom this was inflicted to the point not of forgetting but of forgiving?" I think Ernst Reuter would be pleased to see us gathered here today.

He, too, was dispossessed of country, figuratively and literally. In the early Nazi years, he twice experienced the horrors of the concentration camps. He then emigrated to Turkey where he built a new life for himself and his family, always hoping for the day when the fatherland he loved so would be freed of the Nazi pestilence. In the same speech in 1953 he called for "an inner rebirth of the intellectual, political and moral foundations of our entire economic, public and political life." That rebirth was achieved slowly and only in part. Today's Germany is firmly anchored in the West—hence beset by Western weaknesses. And still we fear a cold in Germany more than a fever elsewhere. People in Germany and outside are frightened when they hear of violent excesses and neo-Nazis in German life; we are revolted by pictures that remind us of an earlier time when terror reigned in Germany and the regime was jubilantly feted nevertheless. But what is called neo-Nazism has become a western, even a global phenomenon. To put it honestly: Hitler remains an abiding symbol for anti-democratic fanatics and psychopaths everywhere, the swastika an emblem for all the followers of the most brutal racism and xenophobic violence—precisely because it deeply offends decent people everywhere. It would be foolish to underestimate the power of this *ressentiment* in our world today.

Ours was a short century—I believe and hope—a century that began in 1914 and ended in 1989; I say this even though I know our hopes have been dimmed since 1989, our thoughts darkened by renewed deeds of violence. But we must see German-Polish reconciliation in its world-historical context: we live at a time when people almost everywhere recognize former injustice and when so many have the will to reach out for reconciliation. I am thinking here of Central and Eastern Europe, now liberated; of Russia, now facing up to the truth; of South Africa, Northern Ireland, many countries in Latin America, perhaps Israel and its Arab neighbors as well. We know that evil and crime are contagious, yet practical reason can be a model, too. Spain's transition from dictatorship to democracy, for example, had its beneficial influence on Poland's march to freedom. We need to search for context and connections. No country finds it easy to confess guilt. The United States finds it hard to deal with memories of Hiroshima and Vietnam; even after fifty years, it seems incredibly difficult for the Japanese to acknowledge their own enormous guilt. It is so much easier to recall one's own pain, to indulge in self-pity.

Reconciliation does not heal all old wounds, nor does it obliterate the memory of lost homelands. But as Countess Dönhoff put it so aptly in 1962: "Perhaps the highest form of love is to love without possessing." To build a home, while cherishing what was good in the old, has been the historic experience of so many people dispossessed and exiled.

I had the good fortune to come to the United States, a country that has always been a home for the homeless. The United States has been discovered and created by millions of people, seeking more or less voluntarily a new homeland. Their reasons were many: to flee religious or political oppression, to build a new life in "the land of unlimited opportunities," a term much used in the nineteenth century. (German emigrants during the Nazi period spoke wryly of the "land of unpaid opportunities"; life was hard even for those fortunate enough to have found refuge in the United States, which itself was still battling the effects of the Great Depression.) The country was proud of being a nation of immigrants, even as its elites were largely native-born. The old American dream of the "melting pot"—today wrongly disdained as an ideal—was realized only in part. Emigrants became Americans quite quickly—I think my early German experiences made me all the more keen to take seriously the responsibilities of citizenship.

The country was generous in its expectations: citizens should be loyal—and yet remain faithful to the language and some of the customs of their "old country." Buffalo and Chicago were and still are German *and* Polish cities, for example, where for generations both groups have lived together in generally amiable discord. That generosity to immigrants can be rewarding for the nation itself is nicely demonstrated by the fact that the former chairman of the Joint Chiefs of Staff, John Shalikashvili, was born in Warsaw, and the head of the CIA, John Deutch, in Brussels. Would that be possible in any other country?

There is a happy analogue of a country inviting people who had lost their homeland to settle in a new place—I am referring to French Protestants, the Huguenots, expelled from their own country by royal intolerance, and invited in the seventeenth century by Brandenburg-Prussia's Great Elector to start a new life here. The Huguenot achievements were prodigious. They did so much to enrich life in the altogether impoverished country. By talent and industry, they helped to transform their new homeland while remaining faithful to their customs and traditions. In Berlin remains palpable evidence of their presence: the world-famed French *Gymnasium* and the French Cathedral still exist. Two names should suffice to recall the prominence of their descendants: Theodor Fontane—of Huguenot extraction—was a great writer who depicted the life of his Brandenburg countrymen better than anyone else, who understood that the Huguenots had felt themselves as a group apart and yet in the service of the whole. In our own time Lothar de Mazière, East Germany's last head of government and the first to be elected democratically, helped his country's transition to freedom. Huguenots did remember their homeland and their ancestry; there are two lines by Fontane, lodged in my memory, that express this sentiment:

> Der ist in tiefster Seele treu
> Wer die Heimat liebt wie Du*

They refer to a banished Scotsman, but they suggest something more universal.

A brief mention of the historic contributions of Poles as patriotic exiles to new homelands must suffice. Two names may serve as exemplars: Marie Curie and Joseph Conrad. In America too there has been a long tradition, beginning in the eighteenth century with General Thaddeus Kosciusko and continuing down to John Shalikashvili today.

I have talked of the past: you—the panelists and audience of

* Loyal in the innermost soul / Who loves the homeland as you do

today—have lived this history: you lost your homeland, contributed decisively to the building of a new home, and sought
to promote reconciliation—often in opposition to the prevailing views of your fellow citizens. You stand for reconciliation
which deepens memory, while resentment dims it. You have
my deepest respect because your readiness to honor the past
by understanding it in all its complexity, by accepting while
regretting it, opens the way to something new, to a kind of
common house in Europe, which for future generations might
become a homeland.

I am leaving tomorrow for Breslau, my native city. I visited
there once before, in 1979: I discovered that in the much-
destroyed city the house we lived in no longer existed, but
went to my grandmother's old villa. The family living in the
villa—in socialist shabbiness—was that of a Polish cavalry officer, Czeslaw Ostakowicz; we could communicate only in
French. He took me to my grandmother's parlor, which was
now filled with drawings of children—many, many children—
drawings from Auschwitz. He showed me his camp number,
tattooed on his chest and told me of the years he had been a
prisoner in Auschwitz, Birkenau, and Buchenwald. On the
table was a tiny wooden bust of Father Kolbe—who in August
1941 in Auschwitz had sacrificed himself in order to save a
prisoner who had a family. Weeks earlier, on his visit to
Auschwitz, Pope John Paul II had praised the already beatified
Kolbe, whom he was to canonize a few years later.

I was awed by the coincidence: this man living in my grandmother's house suffered the fate most of my family had escaped. We shook hands and at that moment I had the rare
feeling: There *is* something just in the world; contingency *is*
meaningful.

Ambassador Reiter is taking me tomorrow to Wroclaw and
I will meet there with colleagues from the university—all this
thanks to Polish friends. Friendship is a kind of elective home,
a gift for all of us and an indispensable solace for those who
have lost their homeland.

◆◆◆◆◆◆◆◆◆◆◆ NOTES ◆◆◆◆◆◆◆◆◆◆◆◆

CHAPTER 1

1. Willstätter to Ehrlich, October 7, 1903, Paul Ehrlich Collection in the Rockefeller Archive Center. In publishing this lecture I have limited myself to providing references to quotations from the Ehrlich Archive. The scientific literature about Ehrlich is vast; the biographical studies are scant and rather unsatisfactory. I found especially valuable Timothy Lenoir, "A Magic Bullet: Research for Profit and the Growth of Knowledge in Germany around 1900," *Minerva* 26, 1 (spring 1988), pp. 66–88.

2. Ehrlich to Friedrich Althoff, November 1, 1906, Paul Ehrlich Collection.

3. Althoff to Ehrlich, April 14, 1907, ibid.

4. Althoff to Ehrlich, February 25, 1900, ibid.

5. Ehrlich to Althoff, November 1, 1906, ibid.

6. Althoff to Ehrlich, August 31, 1902, ibid.

7. Ehrlich to Althoff, July 27, 1907, ibid.

8. Ehrlich to Albert Neisser, April 15, 1904, ibid.

9. Hedwig Ehrlich, diary entry, November 10, 1910, ibid.

10. Ibid., December 9, 1910.

11. Ehrlich to Chaim Weizmann, February 13, 1914, and Weizmann to Ehrlich, February 16, 1914, ibid.

12. Shulamit Volkov, *Jüdisches Leben und Antisemitismus im 19. und 20. Jahrhundert* (Munich, 1990), pp. 146–180. Also see her reconsiderations "Juden als wissenschaftliche 'Mandarine' im Kaiserreich und in der Weimarer Republik," *Archiv für Sozialgeschichte* 37 (1997), pp. 1–18.

CHAPTER 2

1. Jacob Burckhardt, *Weltgeschichtliche Betrachtungen* (Tübingen, 1949), p. 323.

2. Jost Lemmerich, *100 Jahre Röntgenstrahlen 1895 to 1995* (Würzburg, 1995), p. 57.

3. Armin Hermann, "Die Deutsche Physikalische Gesellschaft 1899 to 1945," in *150 Jahre Deutsche Physikalische Gesellschaft*, ed. Theo Mayer-Kuckuk (Weinheim, 1995), p. F-64.

4. Max Planck to Arnold Sommerfeld, September 11, 1899, Sommerfeld Nachlass, Deutsches Museum, Munich.

5. Max Planck, *Physikalische Abhandlungen und Vorträge,* vol. 3 (Braunschweig, 1958), p. 382.

6. Ibid., p. 240.

7. Res Jost, *Das Märchen vom Elfenbeinernen Turm. Reden und Aufsätze* (Heidelberg, 1995), p. 269.

8. Cited in Hermann, "Die Deutsche Physikalische Gesellschaft," p. F-87.

9. Planck, *Physikalische Abhandlungen und Vorträge,* vol. 3, p. 75.

10. Ibid., p. 89.

11. Ibid., p. 74.

12. Ibid., p. 181.

13. Ibid., p. 398.

14. Albert Einstein, *Mein Weltbild* (Amsterdam, 1934), p. 144.

15. Max Planck, "Kausalgesetz und Willensfreiheit," (1923), reprinted in *Quantenmechanik und Weimarer Republik,* ed. Karl von Meyenn (Braunschweig, 1994), p. 127.

16. "Propaganda for Relativity," in Hermann, "Die Deutsche Physikalische Gesellschaft," p. F-69. Adolf Harnack, *Aus Wissenschaft und Leben* (Giessen, 1911), p. 19.

17. Thomas Nipperdey, *Deutsche Geschichte 1866 to 1918,* vol. 1, *Arbeitswelt und Bürgergeist* (Munich, 1990), p. 597.

18. Planck, *Physikalische Abhandlungen und Vorträge,* vol. 3, p. 77.

19. The most recent work on the Manifesto of the 93 is Jürgen von Ungern-Sternberg and Wolfgang von Ungern-Sternberg, *Der Aufruf 'An die Kulturwelt!'* (Stuttgart, 1996), esp. pp. 72 to 73.

20. *The Collected Papers of Albert Einstein,* vol. 8B (Princeton, 1998), p. 956.

21. "Gesamtsitzung der Königlich Preussischen Akademie . . . 14 November 1918," in the appendix of John L. Heilbron, *Max Planck. Ein Leben für die Wissenschaft, 1858–1947* (Stuttgart, 1988), p. 993. This is the German translation of Heilbron's *Dilemmas of an Upright Man: Max Planck as Spokesman for German Science* (Berkeley, 1986). The original American edition of this valuable biography does not contain the selection of Planck's speeches that the German edition carries.

22. Max Planck to Arnold Sommerfeld, December 15, 1919, Sommerfeld Nachlass, Deutsches Museum, Munich.

23. Albert Einstein to Max Planck, October 23, 1919, Einstein Archives, Hebrew University, Jerusalem.

24. Planck, *Physikalische Abhandlungen und Vorträge,* vol. 3, pp. 338, 336.

25. Max Planck to Max von Laue, July 7, 1922, Laue Nachlass, Deutsches Museum, Munich.

26. Max Planck to Max von Laue, July 9, 1922, ibid.

27. Letter to Albert Einstein, November 10, 1923, cited in Armin Hermann, *Max Planck in Selbstzeugnissen und Bilddokumenten* (Hamburg: Rowohlt, 1973), p. 67.

28. Adolf von Harnack, *Erforschtes und Erlebtes* (Giessen, 1923), p. 344.

29. Heilbron, *Max Planck: Ein Leben*, p. 279.

30. Rudolf Vierhaus, "Adolf von Harnack," in *Forschung im Spannungsfeld von Politik und Gesellschaft. Geschichte und Struktur der Kaiser-Wilhelm-Max-Planck-Gesellschaft*, ed. Rudolf Vierhaus and Bernhard vom Brocke (Stuttgart, 1990), p. 479.

31. Lise Meitner, "Max Planck als Mensch," *Die Naturwissenschaften* 45, no. 17 (1958), p. 407.

32. Adolf Grimme, *Briefe*, ed. Dieter Sauberzweig (Heidelberg, 1967), p. 237.

33. *Albert Einstein in Berlin 1913 to 1933*, vol. 1, ed. Christa Kirsten and Hans-Jürgen Treder (East Berlin, 1979), p. 245. See also Klaus Hentschel, ed., *Physics and National Socialism: An Anthology of Primary Sources* (Basel, Boston, and Berlin, 1996).

34. Max Planck to Fritz Haber, August 1, 1933, Haber Nachlass, Archiv zur Geschichte der Max-Planck-Gesellschaft, Berlin.

35. Otto Hahn, *Mein Leben* (Munich, 1968), p. 145.

36. Helmuth Albrecht, " 'Max Planck: Mein Besuch bei Adolf Hitler'—Anmerkungen zum Wert einer historischen Quelle," in *Naturwissenschaft und Technik in der Geschichte*, ed. Helmuth Albrecht (Stuttgart, 1993), pp. 41–63. I owe this reference to the kindness of Professor Erwin Hiebert, Harvard University.

37. Max Planck to Reichsminister B. Rust, January 18, 1934, Siemens Archive, courtesy of Gerald D. Feldman, University of California, Berkeley.

38. Meitner, "Max Planck," p. 407.

39. Max von Laue to Dr. W. F. Berg, August 21, 1934; Laue entrusted his letter written to Berg, a refugee scientist in England, to Berg's sister, who was traveling from Germany to England. Berg forwarded the letter to Einstein. Laue Nachlass, Deutsches Museum, Munich. Max von Laue to Albert Einstein, June 26, 1933, Einstein Archives, Hebrew University, Jerusalem. See also Alan D. Beyerchen, *Scientists under Hitler: Politics and the Physics Community in the Third Reich* (New Haven, 1977), pp. 118–119.

40. Ernst-Wolfgang Böckenförde, "Die Verfolgung der deutschen Juden als Bürgerverrat," *Merkur* 51, no. 575 (1997), pp. 165–170.

41. Max Planck to Arnold Sommerfeld, October 2, 1940, Sommerfeld Nachlass, Deutsches Museum, Munich.

42. Lise Meitner to Elisabeth Schiemann, November 3, 1946, Churchill College Archive, courtesy of Jost Lemmerich.

43. Max von Laue to Lise Meitner, November 1958, Churchill College Archive, courtesy of Ruth Lewin Sime; emphasis added.

44. Max Planck to Arnold Sommerfeld, February 4, 1945, Sommerfeld Nachlass, Deutsches Museum, Munich.

CHAPTER 3

1. Fritz Haber to Albert Einstein, March 14, 1929, Einstein Archives, Institute for Advanced Study, Princeton. I began working in the Einstein Archives in 1978 when they were still at the Institute for Advanced Study in Princeton and under the care of the sharp, all-knowing Helen Dukas, Einstein's aide and secretary for twenty-seven years. All the material I read in Princeton is cited as from the Institute for Advanced Study. The Einstein Archives were subsequently transferred to the Hebrew University of Jerusalem, and the material I consulted there—or in Boston at the office of the Einstein project—I cite as from the Hebrew University.

2. K. F. Bonhoeffer, "Nachruf: Fritz Haber," in *Chemiker-Zeitung* 58, no. 20 (1934), p. 205.

3. *The Collected Papers of Albert Einstein*, vol. 5, ed. M. J. Klein, A. J. Kox, and Robert Schulmann (Princeton, 1993), p. 511 (hereafter cited as CPAE).

4. As one felicitous example, see Martin J. Klein, "Great Connections Come Alive: Bohr, Ehrenfest and Einstein," in *The Lesson of Quantum Theory*, ed. Jorrit de Boer, Erik Dal, and Ole Ulfbeck (Amsterdam, 1986), pp. 325–342. See also the works of Gerald Holton, such as *Einstein, History, and Other Passions: The Rebellion against Science at the End of the Twentieth Century* (Reading, Mass., 1996). For a critical survey of works on German science, see Arleen Marcia Tuchman, "Institutions and Disciplines: Recent Work in the History of German Science," *Journal of Modern History* 69 (June 1997), pp. 298–319. My inquiry is deliberately biographical, with particular attention to unpublished sources.

5. Haber to Willstätter, ca. 1930, in the Fritz Haber Collection of the Archiv zur Geschichte der Max-Planck-Gesellschaft, Berlin (hereafter cited as HC). I read the correspondence with Willstätter in the mid-1980s; since then an annotated edition has appeared: *Fritz Haber. Briefe an Richard Willstätter 1910–1934*, ed. Petra Werner and Angelika Irmscher (Berlin, 1995), p. 118.

6. CPAE, vol. 5, p. 574.

7. CPAE, vol. 8A (Princeton, 1998), Einstein to Mileva Einstein-Marić, July 18, 1914, p. 47.

8. CPAE, vol. 8A, p. 51ff.

9. Ibid., p. 56.

10. Ibid., p. 54.

11. CPAE, vol. 8B (Princeton, 1998), pp. 789–791.

12. Erik H. Erikson, "Psychoanalytic Reflections on Einstein's Centenary," in *Albert Einstein: Historical and Cultural Perspectives*, ed. Gerald Holton and Yehuda Elkana (Princeton, 1982), pp. 153–160.

13. CPAE, vol. 8A, p. 135.

14. Sigmund Freud, *On Creativity and the Unconscious* (New York, 1958), p. 163.

15. CPAE, vol. 5, p. 586.

16. Albert Einstein, *Mein Weltbild*, ed. Carl Seelig (Zurich, 1953), pp. 141–144.

17. The literature on German Jewry and on German anti-Semitism is vast. A recent survey of nuanced interpretation with an impressive account of the scholarly literature is Shulamit Volkov, *Die Juden in Deutschland 1780–1918* (Munich, 1994). See also the fine study *German-Jewish History in Modern Times*, vol. 3, *Integration in Dispute: 1871–1918*, ed. Michael A. Meyer (New York, 1997). I have written about the world of German anti-Semitism in *The Politics of Cultural Despair* (Berkeley, 1961), in *Gold and Iron: Bismarck, Bleichröder, and the Building of the German Empire* (New York, 1977), and in *Dreams and Delusions: The Drama of German History* (New York, 1987; reprint, New Haven, 1999).

18. See Gangolf Hübinger, *Kulturprotestantismus und Politik. Zum Verhältnis von Liberalismus und Protestantismus im wilhelminischen Deutschland* (Tübingen, 1994).

19. See Felix Gilbert, ed., *Bankiers, Künstler und Gelehrte. Unveröffentliche Briefe der Familie Mendelssohn aus dem 19. Jahrhundert* (Tübingen, 1975), introduction.

20. A revised version of my lecture on the seventy-fifth anniversary of Haber's institute was published as "Fritz Haber: The Scientist in Power and Exile," in *Dreams and Delusions: The Drama of German History* (New York, 1987), pp. 51–76. Recently two biographies have appeared: Dietrich Stoltzenberg, *Fritz-Haber. Chemiker, Nobelpreisträger, Deutscher, Jude* (Weinheim, 1994), by a chemist, and a more balanced work by a historian, Margit Szöllösi-Janze, *Fritz Haber 1868–1934. Eine Biographie* (Munich 1998). I based my work primarily on my own earlier archival researches and earlier accounts.

21. Max Weber, "Science as Vocation," in *From Max Weber: Essays*

in Sociology, ed. H. H. Gerth and C. Wright Mills (New York, 1946), p. 134. See also the classic study by Joseph Ben-David, *The Scientist's Role in Society: A Comparative Study* (Englewood Cliffs, N.J., 1971), chapter 7.

22. See Reinhold Rürup, *Emanzipation und Antisemitismus. Studien zur 'Judenfrage' der bürgerlichen Gesellschaft* (Göttingen, 1975).

23. Richard Willstätter, *Aus meinem Leben. Von Arbeit, Musse und Freunden* (Weinheim, 1949), p. 396.

24. Charlotte Haber, *Mein Leben mit Fritz Haber. Spiegelungen der Vergangenheit* (Düsseldorf, 1970), p. 84.

25. Willstätter, *Aus meinem Leben*, p. 260.

26. Johannes Jaenicke, "Fritz Haber (1868–1934)," in *Fridericiana. Zeitschrift der Universität Karlsruhe*, no. 35 (1984), pp. 3–30.

27. Clara Haber to Richard Abegg, April 25, 1909, HC.

28. F. Haber to R. Abegg, February 7 and 12, 1901, HC.

29. *Karlsruher Zeitung*, January 31, 1927. Dr. Klaus-Peter Hoepke of Karlsruhe University was kind enough to send me this clipping.

30. F. Haber, "Über Hochschulunterricht und elektrochemische Technik in den Vereinigten Staaten," *Zeitschrift für Elektrochemie* 9, no. 16 (April 16, 1903), pp. 291–303, and 9, no. 18 (April 30, 1903), pp. 347–370; 9, no. 45 (November 5, 1903), pp. 893–898.

31. Haber to colleague, June 11, 1905, HC (emphasis in original).

32. Zeiss to Haber, July 20, 1904, HC.

33. The reports on this appointment are contained in Universitatsarchiv Karlsruhe, Berufungsakte 0-1-52. Dr. Klaus-Peter Hoepke made these available to me.

34. Sir William Crookes, "Address," *Report of the British Association for the Advancement of Science* 68 (1898), pp. 6, 17–18; for the price of saltpeter, see Lothar Suhling, "Fritz Haber und die Entwicklung der Ammoniaksynthese aus den Elementen," in *Fridericiana*, no. 35, p. 33. For an early, excellent account of Haber's work, by an English collaborator of his, see J. E. Coates, "The Haber Memorial Lecture," delivered before the Chemical Society on April 29, 1937, reprinted in *Journal of the Chemical Society*, November 1939, pp. 1642–1672.

35. L. F. Haber, *The Chemical Industry during the Nineteenth Century: A Study of the Economic Aspects of Applied Chemistry in Europe and North America* (Oxford, 1958), pp. 128, 176–179. The author, a historian-scientist, is Haber's son.

36. Ibid., p. 170.

37. Peter Borscheid, *Naturwissenschaft, Staat und Industrie in Baden (1848–1914)* (Stuttgart, 1976), p. 201.

38. Ibid., p. 207.

39. Kurt Mendelssohn, *The World of Walther Nernst: The Rise and Fall of German Science, 1864–1941* (Pittsburgh, 1973), p. 45.

40. Coates, "Haber Memorial Lecture," p. 1643.

41. Carl Engler to BASF Direktion, February 16, 1908, HC (emphasis in original).

42. See Ernst Wandersleb, "Fritz Haber: seine Beziehungen zu Jena und zum Zeiss-Werk," *Jenaer Rundschau* 5 (1960), pp. 109–113.

43. Haber to BASF Direktion, February 27, 1908, HC.

44. Agreement between Haber and BASF, March 6 and 7, 1908, HC.

45. Werner E. Mosse, *Jews in the German Economy: The German-Jewish Economic Elite 1820–1935* (Oxford, 1987), pp. 182–183. Also letter from the archive of Degussa to Frau Sandow of Archiv der Max-Planck-Gesellschaft, Berlin, March 31, 1980, given to me by Diana Barkan. Also Akten betreffend Koppel-Stiftung, 1905–1911, Archiv zur Geschichte der Max-Planck-Gesellschaft.

46. Carl Engler to BASF, October 24, 1909; Haber to BASF, October 21, 1909; BASF to Engler, November 3, 1909, HC.

47. Contract between BASF and Haber, November 15, 1909, HC.

48. Coates, "Haber Memorial Lecture," p. 1653.

49. As mere examples, see Haber to Arnold Sommerfeld, October 4 and December 29, 1911, Sommerfeld Nachlass, Deutsches Museum, Munich.

50. Willstätter, *Aus meinem Leben*, p. 246.

51. The literature on Einstein has grown enormously in the last two decades as interest in the man supplemented the older concern with his science. Volume 1 of *The Collected Papers of Albert Einstein* (CPAE) appeared in 1987, and volumes 8A and 8B, covering the years from 1914 to 1918, appeared in 1998; with their copious and ingenious notes, these volumes are indispensable. Two recent works are Abraham Pais, '*Subtle is the Lord . . .*': *The Science and the Life of Albert Einstein* (New York, 1982), and Albrecht Fölsing, *Albert Einstein: A Biography*, trans. Ewald Osers (New York, 1997).

52. Paul Arthur Schilpp, *Albert Einstein: Philosopher-Scientist*, vol. 1 (La Salle, Ill., 1969), p. 9.

53. Philipp Frank, *Einstein. Sein Leben und seine Zeit* (Braunschweig, 1979), pp. 24–25.

54. Felix Gilbert, "Einstein und das Europa seiner Zeit," *Historische Zeitschrift*, 233 (1981), pp. 11–12.

55. Schilpp, *Einstein*, p. 5.

56. CPAE, vol. 1, p. 310.

57. Ibid., p. 371.

58. Ibid., p. liii.

59. Ibid., p. 12.

60. Einstein to Pauline Winteler, May(?) 1897, ibid., pp. 55–56.

61. Ibid., p. 28.

62. Einstein to Maja Einstein, 1898, ibid., p. 211.

63. Einstein to Alfred Stern, May 3, 1901; Mileva Marić to Helene Savić, November-December 1901, ibid., pp. 296, 320.

64. *Albert Einstein–Mileva Marić: The Love Letters*, ed. Jürgen Renn and Robert Schulmann, trans. Shawn Smith (Princeton, 1992), p. 9. An invaluable correspondence, with an excellent introduction by the editors. In all other instances I have myself translated from the German in CPAE.

65. Einstein to Mileva Marić, August 6, 1900, CPAE, vol. 1, p. 251.

66. Einstein to Mileva, March 27, 1901 and August-September 1900, ibid., pp. 282, 257.

67. Einstein to Wilhelm Ostwald, March 19, 1901, ibid., p. 278.

68. Einstein to Mileva, March 27, 1901, ibid., p. 282.

69. Einstein to Marcel Grossmann, April 14, 1901, ibid., pp. 290–291. For Mommsen, see Fritz Stern, ed., *The Varieties of History* (2nd ed., New York, 1972), p. 193.

70. Einstein to Mileva, May 1901, CPAE, vol. 1, p. 304.

71. Einstein to Marcel Grossmann, April 14, 1901, ibid., p. 290.

72. Einstein to Mileva, December 17, 1901, ibid., p. 326, and April 4, 1901, ibid., p. 285.

73. Pais, *'Subtle is the Lord,'* p. 46.

74. Einstein to Mileva, July 1901, CPAE, vol. 1, p. 308.

75. Einstein to Mileva, September 1903, CPAE, vol. 5, p. 22.

76. Pais, *'Subtle is the Lord,'* p. 47.

77. Schilpp, *Einstein*, p. 4.

78. Frank, *Einstein*, p. 132; Einstein to Mileva, December 12, 1901, CPAE, vol. 1, p. 323.

79. Einstein to Michele Besso, January 1903, CPAE, vol. 5, p. 10.

80. *Albert Einstein–Mileva Marić*, p. xii.

81. Thomas Nipperdey, *Deutsche Geschichte 1866–1918. I: Arbeitswelt und Bürgergeist* (Munich, 1990), p. 667.

82. Planck to Einstein, July 6, 1907, CPAE, vol. 5, p. 50.

83. Einstein to Maurice Solovine, April 27, 1906, ibid., p. 40.

84. Pais, *'Subtle is the Lord,'* pp. 186–189.

85. Einstein to Jakob Laub, May 19, 1909, CPAE, vol. 5, p. 188; Einstein to Anna Meyer-Schmid, May 12, 1909, ibid., p. 181.

86. Robert Schulmann, "From Periphery to Center: Einstein's Path from Bern to Berlin (1902–1914)," in *No Truth Except in the Details*, ed. A. J. Kox and D. M. Siegel (Boston, 1995), p. 265.

87. Emil Fischer to Einstein, November 11, 1910, CPAE, vol. 5, p. 259.

88. Einstein to Heinrich Zangger, August 24, 1911, ibid., pp. 313–315.

89. Einstein to Heinrich Zangger, November 20, 1911, and December 25, 1911, ibid., pp. 352, 379.

90. Einstein to Michele Besso, May 13, 1911, ibid., p. 295. On Prague, see Gary B. Cohen, *The Politics of Ethnic Survival: Germans in Prague, 1861–1914* (Princeton, 1981).

91. Recorded interview of Res Jost with Otto Stern, 1961, part of the ETH Collection on Einstein; Einstein to Michele Besso, February 4, 1912, CPAE, vol. 5, p. 404.

92. Einstein to Michele Besso, November 17, 1909, ibid., p. 218; Einstein to Elsa Löwenthal, April 30, 1912, ibid., vol. 5, pp. 456–457.

93. Res Jost, interview with Otto Stern, 1961.

94. Einstein to Elsa Löwenthal, March 23, 1913, CPAE, vol. 5, p. 517.

95. Charles E. McClelland, "'To Live for Science': Ideals and Realities at the University of Berlin," in *The University and the City*, ed. Thomas Bender (New York, 1988), p. 194.

96. The literature on the Kaiser Wilhelm Society is vast. The leading work is *Forschung im Spannungsfeld von Politik und Gesellschaft. Geschichte und Struktur der Kaiser-Wilhelm-Max-Planck Gesellschaft*, eds. Rudolf Vierhaus and Bernhard vom Brocke (Stuttgart, 1990), in which appeared my much shorter essay, "Freunde im Widerspruch: Haber und Einstein." See also Szöllösi-Janze, *Fritz Haber*, pp. 196–255. For the context in which the Kaiser-Wilhelm-Society was founded, see Alan Beyerchen, "On the Stimulation of Excellence in Wilhelmian Science," in *Another Germany: A Reconsideration of the Imperial Era*, ed. Jack R. Dukes and Joachim Remark (Boulder, 1988), pp. 139–168. For a brilliantly candid and searching analysis of the first fifty years of the Max-Planck-Society, see the present president's speech on the fiftieth anniversary of the society: Hubert Markl, "Blick Zurück, Blick Voraus," Göttingen, February 26, 1998.

97. See the fine study by David Cahan, *An Institute for an Empire: The Physikalisch-Technische Reichsanstalt, 1871–1918* (New York, 1989). Also see Jeffrey A. Johnson, *The Kaiser's Chemists: Science and Modernization in Imperial Germany* (Chapel Hill, 1990).

98. For Althoff and for the German scientific milieu of prewar years, see the brilliantly imaginative work by Russell McCormmach, *Night Thoughts of a Classical Physicist* (Cambridge, Mass., 1982). Bernhard vom Brocke has written extensively on Althoff and German science policy.

99. Lothar Burchardt, *Wissenschaftspolitik im wilhelminischen Deutschland. Vorgeschichte, Gründung und Aufbau der Kaiser-Wilhelm-Gesellschaft zur Förderung der Wissenschaften* (Göttingen, 1975), p. 33.

100. Bernhard vom Brocke, "Die Kaiser-Wilhelm-Gesellschaft im Kaiserreich. Vorgeschichte, Gründung und Entwicklung bis zum Ausbruch des Erstern Weltkriegs," in *Forschung im Spannungsfeld*, p. 140.

101. Burchardt, *Wissenschaftspolitik*, p. 54.

102. vom Brocke, "Die Kaiser-Wilhelm-Gesellschaft im Kaiserreich," in *Forschung im Spannungsfeld*, pp. 45–46.

103. Letter from the archive of Degussa to Frau Sandow at MPA, March 31, 1980, courtesy of Diana Barkin. Also Szöllösi-Janze, *Fritz Haber*, pp. 215–219.

104. Haber to Krüss, January 4, 1913, CPAE, vol. 5, pp. 510–514; Res Jost, interview with Otto Stern, 1961.

105. Einstein to Michele Besso, January 1914, CPAE, vol. 5, pp. 588–589.

106. Einstein to Elsa Löwenthal, Oct. 16, 1913, ibid., p. 561.

107. See Chapter 2, note 19.

108. Einstein to Paul Ehrenfest, August 19, 1914, CPAE, vol. 8A (Princeton, 1988), p. 56.

109. Einstein to Romain Rolland, August 22, 1917, in ibid., pp. 504–507.

110. CPAE, vol. 6 (Princeton, 1996), pp. 69–71; Bernhard vom Brocke, "Wissenschaft versus Militarismus. Nicolai, Einstein und die 'Biologie des Krieges,'" in *Annali dell Istituto storico italo-germanico*, Trento X (Bologna, 1985), p. 409; Wolf Zuelzer, *The Nicolai Case* (Detroit, 1982), pp. 24–25; Einstein to Georg Nicolai, February 20, 1915, CPAE, vol. 8A, p. 92.

111. Einstein to Romain Rolland, September 15, 1915, ibid., p. 170; Einstein to H. A. Lorentz, August 2, 1915, ibid., pp. 155–157.

112. CPAE, vol. 6, pp. 211–213. The final version is in Berliner Goethebund, *Das Land Goethes. 1914–1916. Ein vaterländisches Gedenkbuch* (Stuttgart, 1916), p. 30. Einstein to Berliner Goethebund, November 11, 1915, CPAE, vol. 8A, pp. 193–194.

113. Einstein to Michele Besso, November 30, 1915, ibid., p. 210.

114. Einstein to Michele Besso, March 9, 1917, ibid., pp. 404–406.

115. Einstein to Heinrich Zangger, December 6, 1917, ibid., pp. 561–562.

116. L. F. Haber, *The Poisonous Cloud: Chemical Warfare in the First World War* (Oxford, 1986), p. 27.

117. Haber to Chaim Weizmann, January 1934, Yad Chaim Weizmann, Rehovot.

118. See Haber's memorandum to Krupp, September 18, 1917. I am grateful to the Krupp Archive (Essen) for providing me with this document. Haber to Rudolf von Valentini, January 2, 1916, HC.

119. Haber to Rudolf von Valentini, ibid.

120. For Haber's view on science in wartime, see his "Die Chemische Industrie und der Krieg," in *Die Chemische Industrie*, no. 31–32, 1920, HC. See also the masterly study by Haber's youngest son, *The Poisonous Cloud*.

121. Haber's letter was written on his wife's letterhead, Klara Haber, Dr. phil. The main part of the letter concerns the search for a successor to Adolf von Baeyer, preeminent chemist of his time. Haber analyzes the names Sommerfeld suggested; Willstätter was not mentioned, but received the appointment and thus ceased being Haber's neighbor in Dahlem. Haber to Arnold Sommerfeld, January 19, 1915, Archive of the Leo Baeck Institute, New York.

122. Gerit von Leitner, *Der Fall Clara Immerwahr. Leben für eine humane Wissenschaft* (Munich, 1993) gives an inadequately grounded account of her life and suicide. For a balanced view, see Szöllösi-Janze, *Fritz Haber*, pp. 393–399.

123. Wichard von Moellendorff to Haber, September 5, 1916, Nachlass Moellendorff, Bundesarchiv, Koblenz. See also Gerald D. Feldman, *Army, Industry and Labor in Germany, 1914–1918* (Princeton, 1966), chapter 3. Haber to Rudolf von Valentini, January 2, 1916, HC; Haber to Rudolf Stern, 1917, in my possession.

124. Haber to Carl Duisberg, February 11, 1918, HC. On moderates, see for example Bernd Sösemann, "Das 'erneuerte Deutschland.' Ernst Troeltschs politisches Engagement im Ersten Weltkrieg," *Troeltsch-Studien* 3 (1984), pp. 120–144.

125. Rudolf A. Stern, "Fritz Haber: Personal Recollections," *Leo Baeck Year Book* 8 (1963), p. 75.

126. Heinrich Scheüch to Haber, November 27, 1918, HC.

127. Haber to Wichard von Moellendorff, December 9, 1918, Nachlass Moellendorff, Bundesarchiv, Koblenz. See also David E. Barclay, *Rudolf Wissell als Sozialpolitiker 1890–1933* (Berlin, 1984), pp. 75–142.

128. Haber, "Die deutsche Chemie in den letzten 10 Jahren," in *Aus Leben und Beruf*, p. 20.

129. Einstein to Michele Besso, December 4, 1918, CPAE, vol. 8B (Princeton, 1998), pp. 958–960.

130. Einstein to Arnold Sommerfeld, December 6, 1918, ibid., pp. 962–963.

131. Einstein to Guste Hochberger, July 30, 1919, Einstein Archives, Hebrew University.

132. There are minutely different accounts of what J. J. Thomson said; see Marshall Missner, "Why Einstein Became Famous in America," *Social Studies of Science* 15 (1985), p. 269.

314 NOTES TO CHAPTER 3

133. *Albert Einstein–Hedwig und Max Born, Briefwechsel 1916–1955* (Munich, 1969), p. 39.

134. Friedrich Herneck, *Albert Einstein. Ein Leben fur Wahrheit, Menschlichkeit und Frieden* (East Berlin, 1963), pp. 156–184; Herneck's popular versions in the 1970s suffer from crude Marxist simplicities. See also catalogue to "Gedächtnisausstellung zum 100. Geburtstag von Albert Einstein, Otto Hahn, Max von Laue, Lise Meitner, Staatsbibliothek (Berlin 1979), pp. 90–93; and C. Kirsten and H.-J. Treder, *Einstein in Berlin, 1913–1933* (East Berlin, 1979), vol. 1, pp. 206f.

135. Alan D. Beyerchen, *Scientists under Hitler: Politics and the Physics Community in the Third Reich* (New Haven, 1977), p. 93.

136. Haber to Richard Willstätter, from Bad Nauheim, undated, (probably September 1920); also December 1920, HC.

137. Haber to Einstein, Einstein Archives, Institute for Advanced Study, Princeton, marked "probably 1919."

138. *Wissenschaft und Buchhandel. Der Verlag von Julius Springer und seine Autoren*, ed. Michael Davidis, Exhibition Catalogue, Deutsches Museum (Munich, 1985), p. 55.

139. Haber to Einstein, August 30, 1920, Einstein Archives, Institute for Advanced Study, Princeton.

140. Einstein to Michele Besso, September 8, 1918, CPAE, vol. 8B, p. 870. Einstein to Max Laue, September 29, 1928, Einstein Archives, Institute for Advanced Study, Princeton.

141. See Felix Gilbert, "Einstein und das Europa seiner Zeit," *Historische Zeitschrift*, no. 233 (1981), pp. 2–4.

142. On the Emergency Committee, see Gerald D. Feldman, "The Politics of *Wissenschaftspolitik* in Weimar Germany: A Prelude to the Dilemmas of Twentieth-Century Science Policy," in *Changing Boundaries of the Political: Essays on the Evolving Balance Between the State and Society, Public and Private in Europe*, ed. C. S. Maier (Cambridge, 1987), pp. 255–285. Richard Willstätter to Arthur Stoll, February 11, 1920. I am grateful to Professor W. A. Stoll of Meilen, Switzerland, who allowed me to read the letters exchanged between Willstätter and Stoll's father.

143. Haber, "Die Notgemeinschaft der deutschen Wissenschaft," Memorandum 1920, HC.

144. On Haber's postwar involvement with plans for new forms of chemical warfare as well as his work on insecticide, see Szöllösi-Janze, *Fritz Haber*, pp. 447–480.

145. Kirsten and Treder, *Albert Einstein*, vol. 1, p. 228.

146. Ibid., pp. 206f.

147. Einstein to Pëtr P. Lazarev, May 16, 1914, CPAE, vol. 8A, p. 18.

148. Einstein to Felix Bernstein, August 5, 1952, Einstein to Paul Epstein, October 5, 1919, Einstein Archives, Institute for Advanced Study, Princeton; Einstein to Central-Verein, April 5, 1920. Einstein Archives, Hebrew University, Jerusalem.

149. Haber to Einstein, March 9, 1921; Einstein to Haber, March 9, 1921, Einstein Archives, Institute for Advanced Study, Princeton.

150. Nicholas Murray Butler to Einstein, February 26, 1923, Columbia University Archives.

151. Einstein to Leo Arons, Nov. 12, 1918, CPAE, vol. 8B, p. 945.

152. Neue Rundschau 33, no. 2 (1922), pp. 815f.

153. Willstätter, Aus Meinem Leben, pp. 340–346; Haber to Richard Willstätter, June 1924, HC.

154. Rudolf A. Stern, "Fritz Haber," pp. 90–96; correspondence from Haber to Rudolf and Käthe Stern, in my possession.

155. Haber (from Luxor, Egypt) to Einstein, December 29, 1928, Einstein Archives, Institute for Advanced Study, Princeton.

156. On these multiple struggles within the scientific community, see Daniel J. Kevles, "'Into Hostile Political Camps': The Reorganization of International Science in World War I," Isis 62 (1971), pp. 47–60, and G. A. Cock, "Chauvinism and International Science: The International Research Council, 1919–1926," Royal Society of London: Notes and Records 37:2 (March 1983), pp. 249–289. Also see Paul Forman, "Scientific Internationalism and the Weimar Physicists: The Ideology and Its Manipulation in Germany after World War I," Isis 64 (1973), pp. 151–180.

157. On Einstein and the League's commission, see Albert Einstein, Über den Frieden. Weltordnung oder Weltuntergang, ed. Otto Nathan and Heinz Norden (Zurich, 1976), pp. 77–108, esp. pp. 81, 91, and 93. The original English version, Einstein on Peace (New York, 1960), is less reliable and poorly translated. See also Felix Gilbert, "Einstein und das Europa," pp. 22–23.

158. Haber to Chancellor Luther, December 8 and 31, 1925, Bundesarchiv, Koblenz, Akten Reichskanzlei, R43 I-814. For a comprehensive account of Haber's efforts in the promotion of German science abroad, see Brigitte Schroeder-Gudehus, "Internationale Wissenschaftsbeziehungen und auswärtige Kulturpolitik 1919–1933. Vom Boykott und Gegen-Boykott zu ihrer Wiederaufnahme," in Forschung im Spannungsfeld, pp. 858–885, esp. pp. 869–876, and Szöllösi-Janze, Haber, pp. 528–598.

159. Haber to Richard Willstätter, December 1924, HC. Also see Charlotte Haber, Mein Leben mit Fritz Haber (Düsseldorf, 1970), pp. 182–218.

160. I owe copies of the Haber-Solf correspondence to the kindness of Professor Brigitte Schroeder-Gudehus. See also Eberhard Friese, "Kontinuität und Wandel. Deutsch-japanische Kultur- und Wissenschaftsbeziehungen nach dem Ersten Weltkrieg," *Forschung im Spannungsfeld*, pp. 802–834. Einstein to Haber, July 25, 1931, Einstein Archives, Institute for Advanced Study, Princeton.

161. Haber to Willstätter, January 7, 1926, HC; Haber to Einstein, October 18, 1926, Einstein Archives, Institute for Advanced Study, Princeton.

162. K. F. Bonhoeffer, "Fritz Habers wissenschaftliches Werk," *Zeitschrift für Elektrochemie* 57 (1953), p. 6; Erwin Chargaff, *Heraclitean Fire: Sketches from a Life Before Nature* (New York, 1978), pp. 50–51.

163. Rudolf A. Stern, "Fritz Haber," pp. 96f.

164. Einstein to Haber, July 25, 1931, Einstein Archives, Institute for Advanced Study, Princeton.

165. *New York Times*, "Dr. Einstein urges Hitler Protests," March 1933, HC. See also Stefan L. Wolff, "Vertreibung und Emigration in der Physik," *Physik in unserer Zeit* 24, no. 6 (1993), pp. 267–273.

166. Julie Braun-Vogelstein, *Was niemals stirbt. Gestalten und Erinnerungen* (Stuttgart, 1964), p. 353; Kirsten-Treder, *Einstein in Berlin*, vol. 1, pp. 250, 265f.; Einstein to Max von Laue, June 7, 1933, Einstein Archives, Institute for Advanced Study, Princeton.

167. Elsa Einstein to Abraham Yahuda, July 27, 1933, Yahuda files, Jewish National and University Library, Hebrew University, Jerusalem.

168. James Franck to Haber, April 15, 1933, HC.

169. First published in Willstätter, *Aus Meinem Leben*, 273.

170. Haber to Max Planck, May 7, 1933, HC.

171. Haber to Hermann Haber, May 2, 1933, HC.

172. Georg Bredig to Haber, Haber to Bredig, June 23, 1933, and June 27, 1933. HC.

173. Haber to Richard Willstätter, undated, but clearly in May 1933, HC.

174. K. F. Bonhoeffer to Haber, May 5, 1933, HC.

175. Haber to Rudolf and Käthe Stern, June 9, 1933.

176. Haber to Chaim Weizmann, October 5, 1933, Yad Chaim Weizmann, Rehovot.

177. Richard Willstätter to Chaim Weizmann, October 23, 1933, Yad Chaim Weizmann, Rehovot.

178. Einstein to Haber, May 19, 1933, Einstein Archives, Institute for Advanced Study, Princeton.

179. Haber to Einstein, August 7 or 8, 1933; Einstein to Haber,

August 10, 1933, Einstein Archives, Institute for Advanced Study, Princeton.

180. Chaim Weizmann, *Trial and Error* (New York, 1949), pp. 350–354; Haber to Weizmann, October 1 and 5, 1933, Yad Chaim Weizmann, Rehovot.

181. "Publisher's Foreword," CPAE, vol. 5 (Princeton, 1987), p. xi. The foreword details the complicated relationship among the original trustees, Princeton University Press, and Hebrew University.

182. Haber to Richard Willstätter, January 16, 1934; Willstätter to Haber, January 21, 1934, HC.

183. Haber to Rudolf Stern, January 1934, HC.

184. James Franck to Rudolf Stern, February 24, 1934, and to Hermann and Marga Haber, February 6, 1934; Chaim Weizmann to Hermann Haber, February 4, 1934, HC.

185. Hermann Haber to Einstein, Easter 1934, Einstein Archives, Institute for Advanced Study, Princeton; Einstein to Rudolf Stern, July 20, December 3 and 10, 1940. These letters are on deposit at the Rare Book and Manuscript Library, Columbia University.

186. Einstein to Marga Haber, February 10, 1947, in possession of Mrs. Agnes Lévy, St. Sulpice, Switzerland.

187. April 1954, Einstein Archives, Institute for Advanced Study, Princeton.

CHAPTER 4

1. Walther Rathenau, *Schriften und Reden. Auswahl und Nachwort*, ed. Hans Werner Richter (Frankfurt am Main, 1964), p. 379. Hereafter cited as Richter, *Schriften*.

2. Walther Rathenau, *An Deutschlands Jugend* (Berlin, 1918), p. 9.

3. Count Harry Kessler, *Walther Rathenau: His Life and Work* (New York, 1930), p. 11.

4. Walther Rathenau, *Gesammelte Schriften*, vol. 1 (Berlin, 1918), pp. 188–189.

5. James Joll, *Intellectuals in Politics: Three Biographical Essays* (London, 1960), p. 87.

6. Richter, *Schriften*, p. 249.

7. H. M. Ledig-Rowohlt, "Ein Verleger in Berlin," in *Berliner Lektionen*, ed. Manfred von Ardenne (Berlin, 1988), p. 123.

8. Kessler, *Rathenau: His Life*, p. 151.

9. Ibid., p. 44.

10. Harry Graf Kessler, *Walther Rathenau. Sein Leben und Werk* (Berlin-

Grunewaid, 1928), p. 51. There are minor differences between the German and the English editions; I have used both.

11. Walther Rathenau, *Gesammelte Reden* (Berlin, 1924), p. 264.

12. *Walther Rathenau-Gesamtausgabe*, ed. Hans-Dieter Hellige and Ernst Schulin, vol. 6 (Munich, 1983), p. 308.

13. Kessler, *Rathenau. Sein Leben*, p. 137.

14. Kessler, *Rathenau: His Life*, p. 122.

15. *Walther Rathenau-Gesamtausgabe*, vol. 2, ed. Ernst Schulin (Munich, 1977), p. 651.

16. Kessler, *Rathenau: His Life*, p. 176.

17. Ernst Schulin and Wolfgang Michalka, "Walther Rathenau im Spiegel seines Moskauer Nachlasses," *Schriften: Friedrich Ebert Gedenkstätte*, no. 14 (Heidelberg, 1993), p. 33; Rathenau, *Walther Rathenau Briefe*, vol. 1, 2nd ed. (Dresden, 1926), p. 212.

18. Kessler, *Rathenau: His Life*, p. 225.

19. *Walther Rathenau: Industrialist, Banker, Intellectual, and Politician. Notes and Diaries 1907–1922*, ed. Hartmut Pogge von Strandmann (Oxford, 1985), p. 229; Rathenau, *Briefe*, vol. 1, p. 303.

20. Gerhard Hecker, *Walther Rathenau und sein Verhältnis zu Militär und Krieg* (Boppard am Rhein, 1983), pp. 416–420.

21. Rathenau, *Briefe*, vol. 1, p. 274.

22. *Walther Rathenau-Gesamtausgabe*, vol. 2, pp. 301, 303.

23. Ibid., p. 448.

24. Ibid., p. 474.

25. Ibid., p. 352.

26. Ibid., p. 563.

27. See Ernst Schulin's excellent essay, "Max Weber und Walther Rathenau," in *Max Weber und seine Zeitgenossen*, ed. Wolfgang J. Mommsen and Wolfgang Schwentker (Göttingen, Zurich, 1988), pp. 434–447.

28. Rathenau, *An Deutschlands Jugend*, pp. 107, 110.

29. Kessler, *Rathenau. Sein Leben*, p. 265.

30. Rathenau, *Briefe*, vol. 2, 2nd ed. (Dresden, 1926), pp. 68–70.

31. Ibid., p. 72.

32. Ibid., pp. 94–95.

33. David E. Barclay, *Rudolf Wissell als Sozialpolitiker 1890–1933* (Berlin, 1984), chaps. 3 and 4.

34. Hecker, *Rathenau*, p. 474. On the controversy with Ludendorff, see pp. 473–476.

35. Ibid., pp. 474–484.

36. Richter, *Schriften*, pp. 360, 364.

37. Ibid., p. 333.

38. Ibid., p. 238.

39. Ibid., p. 370.

40. Ibid., p. 423.

41. For an excellent study of the intellectual background of Ehrhard's ideas, see A. J. Nicholls, *Freedom with Responsibility: The Social Market Economy in Germany, 1918–1963* (Oxford, 1994).

42. Kessler, *Rathenau: His Life*, p. 277.

43. Richter, *Schriften*, p. 427.

44. Gerald D. Feldman, "Der unschlüssige Staatsmann. Rathenaus letzter Tag und die Krise der Weimarer Republik," in *Ein Mann vieler Eigenschaften. Walther Rathenau und die Kultur der Moderne*, ed. Thomas P. Hughes (Berlin, 1990), pp. 84–96. See also Feldman's magisterial *The Great Disorder: Politics, Economics, and Society in the German Inflation 1914–1924* (Oxford, 1993), pp. 418–452.

45. *Die Kabinette Wirth I und II*, ed. Ingrid Schulze-Bidlingmaier, vol. 2 (Boppard am Rhein, 1973), pp. 636–637.

46. Heinrich Küppers, *Joseph Wirth. Parlamentarier, Minister und Kanzler der Weimarer Republik* (Stuttgart, 1997).

47. Ernst Schulin, "Noch Etwas zur Entstehung des Rapallo-Vertrages," in *Was die Wirklichkeit lehrt. Golo Mann zum 70. Geburtstag*, ed. Hartmut von Hentig and August Nitschke (Frankfurt am Main, 1979), pp. 177–202.

48. David Felix, *Walther Rathenau and the Weimar Republic: The Politics of Reparations* (Baltimore and London, 1971), p. 134.

49. Viscount D'Abernon, *Versailles to Rapallo 1920–1922: The Diary of an Ambassador* (Garden City, N.Y., 1929), p. 323.

50. A psycho-historical interpretation of Rathenau's end can be found in Peter Loewenberg, "The Murder and Mythification of Walther Rathenau," in his *Fantasy and Reality in History* (New York, 1995), pp. 108–118.

CHAPTER 5

1. C. V. Wedgwood, *Velvet Studies* (London, 1946), p. 154.

2. Fritz Stern, "German Historians and the War: Fischer and his Critics," in *The Failure of Illiberalism: Essays on the Political Culture of Modern Germany*, Morningside ed. (New York, 1992), pp. 147–158.

3. Bryce and Mary Lyon, eds., *The "Journal de guerre" of Henri Pirenne* (Amsterdam, New York, and Oxford, 1976), p. 19.

4. Sir Llewellyn Woodward, *Great Britain and the War of 1914–1918* (London, 1967), p. xii.

5. Quoted in John Higham with Leonard Krieger and Felix Gilbert, *History* (Englewood Cliffs, N.J., 1965), p. 535.

6. Modris Eksteins, *Rites of Spring: The Great War and the Birth of the Modern Age* (New York, 1990), p. 84.

7. Theodore Ziolkowski, ed., *Soul of the Age: Selected Letters of Hermann Hesse, 1891–1962*, trans. Mark Harman (New York, 1991), p. 74.

8. Marc Bloch, *Memoirs of War*, 1914–1918, trans. Carole Fink (Cambridge and New York, 1988), p. 78.

9. Woodward, *Great Britain*, p. xiv.

10. R. H. Tawney, "The Attack," in *The Attack and Other Papers* (London, 1953), pp. 15–16.

11. Ibid., p. 14.

12. Myrna Chase, *Élie Halévy: An Intellectual Biography* (New York, 1980), p. 39.

13. Halévy to Xavier Léon, September 23, 1914, as quoted in ibid., p. 169.

14. Halévy to Xavier Léon, December 15, 1914, in Alain (Emile Chartier), *Correspondance avec Élie Halévy et Florence Halévy* (Paris, 1958), p. 343.

15. Bloch, "Réflexions d'un Historien sur les Fausses Nouvelles de la Guerre," in *Mélanges Historiques*, with an introduction by Charles-Edmund Perrin (Paris, 1963), pp. 41–57.

16. Tawney, "Some Reflections of a Soldier," in *The Attack*, pp. 21–25.

17. Bloch, *Memoirs*, p. 159.

18. Bloch, *The Historian's Craft*, trans. Peter Putnam (New York, 1953), p. 194.

19. Quoted in Bronislaw Geremek, "Marc Bloch, Historien et Résistant," *Annales ESC* 5 (September-October 1986), p. 1095.

20. Woodward, *Great Britain*, pp. xviii–xix.

21. Winston Churchill, *The World Crisis 1911–1918*, abridged and revised version (London, 1931), p. 523.

22. Nicholas Murray Butler, *Across the Busy Years: Recollections and Reflections*, vol. 2 (New York and London, 1940), pp. 142–143.

23. Siegfried Steinberg, ed., "George Peabody Gooch," in *Die Geschichtswissenschaft der Gegenwart in Selbstdarstellungen* (Leipzig, 1926), p. 131.

24. Quoted in David Cannadine, *G. M. Trevelyan: A Life in History* (New York and London, 1993), pp. 86, 88.

25. Felix Gilbert, *A European Past: Memoirs, 1905–1945* (New York and London, 1988), pp. 26–27.

26. Wolfgang J. Mommsen, *Max Weber und die deutsche Politik 1890–1920* (Tubingen, 1959), pp. 208, 207, 226.

27. Klaus Schwabe and Rolf Reichardt, eds., *Gerhard Ritter: Ein politischer Historiker in seinen Briefen* (Boppard am Rhein, 1984), pp. 208–209.

28. Hans-Georg Drescher, *Ernst Troeltsch: Leben und Werk* (Göttingen, 1991), p. 453; F. Meinecke to L. Aschoff, October 21, 1918, quoted in Drescher, *Ernst Troeltsch*, n. 107. I developed this theme on German silence in my book *Das Feine Schweigen. Historische Essays* (Munich, 1999).

29. Henri Pirenne, *Souvenirs de Captivité en Allemagne (Mars 1916–Novembre 1918)* (Brussels, 1920), esp. pp. 47–50.

30. Bryce and Mary Lyon, eds., *The Birth of Annales History: The Letters of Lucien Febvre and Marc Bloch to Henri Pirenne (1921–1935)* (Brussels, 1991), pp. 4, 8.

31. Johan Huizinga, *The Waning of the Middle Ages: A Study of the Forms of Life, Thought and Art in France and the Netherlands in the Fourteenth and Fifteenth Centuries* (New York, 1954), p. 31.

32. Johan Huizinga, *In the Shadow of Tomorrow* (New York, 1936), p. 373.

33. Johan Huizinga, *Mein Weg Zur Geschichte. Letzte Reden und Skizzen* (Basel, 1947), title page. For Huizinga's uncompromising opposition to National Socialism in 1933 and later, see Gerhard Hirschfeld, "Die Universität Leiden unter dem Nationalsozialismus," *Geschichte und Gesellschaft* 23, no. 4 (1997), pp. 560–591. Also J. Huizinga, *Briefwisseling*, vol. 2, 1925–1933 (Utrecht, 1990), pp. 443–471. I am grateful to Lionel Gossman for our conversations about Huizinga.

34. Élie Halévy, "The World Crisis of 1914–1918: An Interpretation," in *The Era of Tyrannies: Essays on Socialism and War*, trans. R. K. Webb with a note by Fritz Stern (London, 1967), p. 162.

35. Quoted in Richard Hofstadter, *The Progressive Historians: Turner, Beard and Parrington* (New York, 1968), p. 287.

36. Charles A. Beard, *Crosscurrents in Europe Today* (Boston, 1922), p. 1.

37. Friedrich Meinecke, *Ausgewählter Briefwechsel*, eds. Ludwig Dehio and Peter Classen (Stuttgart, 1962), p. 346.

38. March Bloch, unpublished letter to Lucien Febvre, October 8, 1939, Archives Nationales, 381 Mi 1. I want to thank Peter Schöttler (CNRS) for this reference.

39. Bloch, *Historian's Craft*, p. xiv.

40. Geremek, "Marc Bloch, Historien et Résistant," p. 1105.

41. Fritz Stern, ed., *The Varieties of History: From Voltaire to the Present*, 2nd ed. (New York, 1973), p. 60.

CHAPTER 6

1. Isaiah Berlin, "Chaim Weizmann," in *Personal Impressions*, ed. Harry Hardy, with an introduction by Noel Annan (New York and London, 1980), p. 61.

2. Jehuda Reinharz, *Chaim Weizmann: The Making of a Zionist Leader* (Oxford, 1985), p. 14.

3. See Steven J. Zipperstein, *Elusive Prophet: Ahad Ha'am and the Origins of Zionism* (Berkeley and Los Angeles, 1993).

4. *The Letters and Papers of Chaim Weizmann*, vol. 2 (London, 1971), pp. 301–322 (hereafter cited as *Letters and Papers*).

5. Ibid., p. 253.

6. Judith Shklar, "The Liberalism of Fear," in *Liberalism and the Moral Life*, ed. Nancy Rosenblum (Cambridge, Mass., 1991), pp. 21, 29.

7. *Letters and Papers*, vol. 2, p. xi.

8. Reinharz, *Chaim Weizmann: The Making of a Zionist Leader*, pp. 191–192.

9. Isaiah Berlin, *The Crooked Timber of Humanity: Chapters in the History of Ideas*, ed. Harry Hardy (New York, 1991), p. 245.

10. Richard Hofstadter, ed., *The Progressive Movement, 1900–1915* (Englewood Cliffs, N.J., 1963), p. 15.

11. Isaiah Berlin, "Felix Frankfurter," in *Personal Impressions*, p. 89.

12. Algernon Cecil, "Arthur James Balfour," entry in *Dictionary of National Biography, 1922–1930*, ed. J.R.H. Weaver (Oxford, 1937), p. 42.

13. J. L. Talmon, "Israel among the Nations: Reflections on Jewish Statehood," *The City College Papers*, no. 9 (New York, 1968), p. 23; David Ben-Gurion, "Preface," in *Chaim Weizmann: A Biography by Several Hands*, ed. Meyer Weisgal and Joel Carmichael (New York, 1963), p. 2; Norman Angell, "Weizmann's Approach to the British Mind," in *Chaim Weizmann: Statesman, Scientist, Builder of the Jewish Commonwealth*, ed. Meyer Weisgal, with a foreword by Felix Frankfurter (New York, 1944), p. 79.

14. Leonard Stein, *The Balfour Declaration* (Jerusalem and London, 1983), p. 143.

15. *Letters and Papers*, vol. 7 (Jerusalem, 1975), pp. 23, 28; Stein, *The Balfour Declaration*, p. 126.

16. *Letters and Papers*, vol. 7, p. 38. "The phrase 'the Asiatic Belgium' . . . . sounds like an echo of a passage in Chapter 42 of George Eliot's *Daniel Deronda*, where Mordecai predicts that a Jewish Palestine will be 'a neutral ground for the East as Belgium is for the West.'" Ibid., p. 28.

17. Harry Sacher, "The Manchester Period," in Weisgal, *Chaim Weizmann*, p. 191.

18. Ibid., p. 126.

19. Richard H. S. Crossman, *A Nation Reborn: A Personal Report on the Roles Played by Weizmann, Bevin and Ben-Gurion in the Story of Israel* (New York, 1960), p. 43.

20. On acetone, see Jehuda Reinharz, *Chaim Weizmann: The Making of a Statesman* (New York, 1993), pp. 40–72.

21. Roman Szporluk, *The Political Thought of Thomas G. Masaryk* (New York, 1981), p. 81; Steven Beller, "The Hilsner Affair: Nationalism, Anti-Semitism and the Individual in the Habsburg Monarchy at the Turn of the Century," in *T. G. Masaryk (1850–1937)*, vol. 2, ed. Robert P. Pynsent (London, 1989), pp. 52–76; Michael A. Riff, "The Ambiguity of Masaryk's Attitudes on the 'Jewish Question,'" in *T. G. Masaryk (1850–1937)*, vol. 2, pp. 77–78; also Hillel J. Kieval, "Masaryk and the Czech Jewry: The Ambiguities of Friendship," in *T. G. Masaryk (1850–1937)*, vol. 1, ed. Stanley B. Winters (London, 1990), pp. 302–327.

22. Chaim Weizmann, *Trial and Error: The Autobiography of Chaim Weizmann* (New York, 1949), p. 407.

23. Michael E. Parrish, *Felix Frankfurter and His Times: The Reform Years* (New York, 1982), pp. 134–135.

24. Charles Webster, *The Art and Practice of Diplomacy* (London, 1961), p. 114.

25. Michael Howard, *The Lessons of History* (New Haven and London, 1991), p. 24.

26. Reinharz, *Chaim Weizmann: The Making of a Statesman*, p. 410.

27. Ibid., p. 218.

28. Weizmann, *Trial and Error*, p. 191.

29. Kenneth Ingham, *Jan Christian Smuts: The Conscience of a South African* (London, 1986), pp. 141–143. On his fervent support of Weizmann, see W. K. Hancock, *The Fields of Force, 1919–1950* (Cambridge, England, 1968), pp. 129–131, 278, 529–530.

30. See Ben Halpern, *A Clash of Heroes: Brandeis, Weizmann, and American Zionism* (New York and Oxford, 1987), esp. pp. 233–269, on the deeper causes of their break.

31. Arthur A. Goren, "The View from Scopus: Judah L. Magnes and the Early Years of the Hebrew University," in *Judaism* 45, no. 2 (spring 1996), pp. 203–224.

32. Weizmann, *Trial and Error*, p. 331. On the British favoring exotic Arabs over demanding, self-possessed Jews, see the vivid account in A. J. Sherman, *Mandate Days: British Lives in Palestine, 1918–1948* (New York, 1997).

33. On Jabotinsky, see Gideon Shimoni, *The Zionist Ideology* (Hanover, N.H., and London, 1995), esp. 236–266; Albert Einstein to Chaim

Weizmann, November 29, 1929, Weizmann Archives, Yad Chaim Weizmann, Rehovot.

34. *Letters and Papers*, vol. 15 (Jerusalem, 1978), p. 156.

35. Weizmann, *Trial and Error*, p. 32.

36. *Letters and Papers*, vol. 18 (Jerusalem, 1979), pp. 368–372.

37. Chaim Weizmann, *The Essential Chaim Weizmann: The Man, the Statesman, the Scientist*, ed. Barnet Litvinoff (London, 1982), p. 160.

38. Weizmann, *Trial and Error*, p. 384.

39. Anita Shapira, *Land and Power: The Zionist Resort to Force, 1881–1948* (New York and Oxford, 1992), p. 293.

40. *Letters and Papers*, vol. 22 (Jerusalem, 1979), pp. 169–173.

41. Weizmann, *Trial and Error*, p. 454.

42. Ibid., p. 476.

43. *Letters and Papers*, vol. 22, p. 309; Weizmann, *Trial and Error*, p. 454.

44. Meyer Weisgal, *So Far: An Autobiography* (London and Jerusalem, 1971), p. 278.

45. Thomas Carlyle, *On Heroes, Hero-Worship, and the Heroic in History* (London, 1940), pp. 239–240.

46. Berlin, "Chaim Weizmann," in *Personal Impressions*, p. 33.

❖❖❖❖❖❖ ACKNOWLEDGMENTS ❖❖❖❖❖❖

MY DEBTS—institutional and personal—are many and my gratitude is great. The Alfred P. Sloan Foundation supported my work on Haber and Einstein with two grants, one facilitating travel to archives and the other helping to free me from teaching for a semester; as a consequence I was able to spend the fall semester of 1989—a memorable moment in history!—as a visiting scholar at the Russell Sage Foundation. I returned there in the spring semester of 1993, benefiting once more from the stimulating atmosphere that Eric Wanner has created.

I thank the Trustees of the Tanner Lectures on Human Values, who invited me to give two lectures at Yale in 1993; for that occasion I wrote an early version of my essay on "Freedom and Its Discontents."

Most of my archival research concerned the subjects of the central essay of this book, "Together and Apart." I am grateful to Eckhart Henning and Marion Kazemi of the Archive of the History of the Max-Planck-Society in Berlin, with its rich holdings of Haber material and much else. I have been most kindly treated by the Einstein Archives, first in Princeton, then in Boston, and finally at their permanent home at the Hebrew University in Jerusalem, where in particular I thank Margaret Cohen and Hannah Katzenstein of the Jewish National and University Library there. I also wish to thank Ze'ev Rosenkranz, curator of the Albert Einstein Archives. The early help of John Stachel was invaluable, as has been the continuous help and advice of Robert Schulmann; my thanks also to Nehama Chalom of Yad Chaim Weizmann in Rehovot, Beat Glaus of the Archives of the Federal Technical University (ETH) in Zurich, Jürgen Real of the Bundesarchiv in Koblenz, and Darwin Stapleton of the Rockefeller Archive Center in Tarrytown, New

York. To these and other archivists mentioned in the notes, my appreciative thanks.

My conversations in the 1950s and 1960s with my uncle Otto Stern gave me a first and unforgettable glimpse into the German world of physicists in the age of Einstein. Family correspondence with Fritz Haber and Richard Willstätter was a further incentive, as was a memorable conversation with Albert Einstein himself in 1944.

In my essays, I try to suggest the value of collegial collaboration; I have myself benefited from such kindness, and it is to friends and colleagues that I owe special thanks. My earlier efforts to study Einstein's German world were greatly assisted by Marshall Claggett, Martin Klein, Reimar Lüst, Abraham Pais, and I. I. Rabi. Subsequently I had the opportunity to talk or correspond with Lutz Haber, Res Jost, Robert Merton, Max Perutz, Ruth Sime, Victor Weisskopf, and Eugene Wigner. Colleagues who have generously answered my many queries on various themes include Alan Brinkley, Diana Barkan, Ronald Breslow, Arthur Goren, Lionel Gossman, Albert Hirschman, Andreas Huyssen, Donald Kelley, Jürgen Kocka, Jost Lemmerich, Peter Loewenberg, Jerry Muller, Robert Pollack, Michael Stanislawski, Jay Winter, Harry Woolf, and Hans-Georg Zachau.

I have had splendid help from graduate students acting as library sleuths; most recently these included Mark Landsman, Eliza Johnson, and Max Voegler. Without Carleen Roeper's cheerful help, I would have drowned in unordered paper. Dorothea Phares of the Institute for Advanced Study in Princeton prepared countless drafts with astonishing care and patience.

I wish to thank Walter Lippincott and Brigitta van Rheinberg of Princeton University Press for their early interest in this book.

My friend Christoph Kimmich read several of these essays and I have gained much from his wise, incisive comments. The late Felix Gilbert and the late Martin Schwarzschild were invaluable mentors and critics, whom I still miss.

The book is dedicated to my wife Elisabeth Sifton—in love and gratitude. Her passion for clarity has immeasurably benefited the book; her life-enhancing presence has sustained me.

Convention dictates that I acknowledge sole responsibility for all errors. I do—and for all infelicities as well.

Fritz Stern
New York
January 1999

INDEX